Margery.

JIM PHELAN was born in 1895 into a poor family and grew up in Inchicore, at that time a small village outside Dublin. He had little formal education, leaving school at the age of eleven to run the streets of the Dublin Liberties. He held many jobs in a long, wandering career, and he started to publish in 1937, establishing a reputation for his tales of life among the Irish peasantry, travellers and convicts. But it was the open road that was Phelan's favourite theme, and he became well known as a radio broadcaster for his talks and stories of the vagabond world. He published over twenty books, and died in 1966.

AMONG JIM PHELAN'S PUBLISHED WORKS

Lifer (1938)

Jail Journey (1940)

Turf-Fire Tales (1947)

Bog Blossom Stories (1948)

The Underworld (1953)

D1374853

B GIBSON
JULY 93

THE NAME'S PHELAN

•

THE FIRST PART OF THE AUTOBIOGRAPHY OF

Jim Phelan

THE
BLACKSTAFF
PRESS

BELFAST

FOR MYSELF

First published in hardback in 1948 by
Sidgwick and Jackson Limited
This Blackstaff Press edition is a photolithographic facsimile
of the first edition printed by Hazell Watson and Viney Limited

This paperback edition published in 1993 by
The Blackstaff Press Limited
3 Galway Park, Dundonald, Belfast BT16 0AN, Northern Ireland
with the assistance of
The Arts Council of Northern Ireland

© Kathleen Phelan, 1948
All rights reserved

Printed by The Guernsey Press Company Limited

A catalogue record for this book
is available from the British Library

ISBN 0–85640–499–3

AUTHOR'S PREFACE

For a teller of tales, a fiction-spinner, such as I have been for most of my life, even before I was a writer, any attempt at a straightforward factual narrative is very difficult indeed. It is so easy, and the temptation is so great, to round off a passage or tidy up an episode, to make a neat story instead of the succession of inconsequentialities which a life-story usually is.

Add the fact that I have always rather tended to dramatise my own existence, as also that I would much rather forget a great many of the things which have happened to me, and it will be plain that the ordinary difficulties of autobiography are for me multiplied.

In desperation, I had almost decided to do a "documentary," to write nothing that could not be checked from the records of somebody else. It might have been good fun—my school-certificate as an infant of eighteen months could have gone cheek by jowl with my dossier as a convict; some eulogistic notice from the *Times Literary Supplement* might have stood beside a photo from the *Hue and Cry,* showing me as a wanted gun-runner; a theatre bill naming me as a character actor would balance an indenture proclaiming me a craftsman; an hotel bill from the Riviera would pair with a ticket from somewhere like Rowton House.

It might have been good fun. But it would not have been the story of my life. Wherefore, because I have had an interesting time and have glimpsed many unusual angles of existence, I have tried to compromise, to tell the story as it is known to me and only to me, but at the same time to safeguard myself from apologetics or evasions.

Accordingly, at the points where one is—quite inevitably—tempted to show oneself as a combination of martyr, hero, philosopher, and other things, I have cut the narrative to the bone, left in only things already on record elsewhere.

That way, the story may not be so thrilling. But it is more consistent, comes nearer to what I commenced to set down—the story of how one writer came so to be.

THAMES DITTON, 1948.   JIM PHELAN.

CHAPTER I

"Once," said the Mock Turtle, "I was a real turtle," and Alice felt inclined to say, during the lengthy pause that followed, "Thanks very much for your most interesting story."

When this writing of mine is finished, I think the result may perhaps resemble that quotation from *Alice in Wonderland*—but in reverse. Instead of being the life-story of a writer, it will probably turn out to be the tale of a mock turtle who became a real turtle without noticing it. Neither the praise nor blame will be mine, and the book may be none the worse. However . . .

I am a tramp.

That is almost all my story. Now I shall write a long and, I hope, an interesting book about the things I have done. But at the end I shall only have amplified the statement in that short line. It is strange that few of my friends, and none of my enemies, ever discovered the truth.

There is some excuse for the misunderstanding. One does not, as a rule, look for a tramp in the offices of New York or Dublin, in the West End of London, or down the newspaper-streets of the capitals! Besides, I have never looked like a tramp except on the few occasions when I was not one.

Yet anyone who had ever conversed in understanding with a vagrant, and who knew me, should have seen through the superficialities of culture, professional industry, and occasional wealth, to the drifter beneath. But almost always the externals misled. Only two people in my lifetime ignored appearances and took me for what I was.

Meeting me on terms of intimacy with peer or publisher, artist or editor, they still treated me as one who had just strayed in off the road, who was by no means certain where he slept on the morrow, or whether that morrow brought a meal. No one else did.

Nearly all the literary and business people with whom I forgathered knew I was not an ordinary writer, knew there was something unexplained in my background. Inevitably they sought it.

Some took me for a high-up detective, some for a high-up malefactor. I have been placed as an English secret-service man, and as an Irish Republican organiser, as a Socialist agitator and an *agent-provocateur*. Except for one man and one girl, nobody knew me for a tramp. I married the girl, and the man is my friend. Need I add that, in spite of appearances, they are both tramps too?

Very often I quarrel with my writer-friends about the general ideas—which *they* help to perpetuate—regarding vagrancy. Some few take the romantic view-point, about the wide white road and the wind on the heath and the longing to be free. With a hey-nonny-nonny and a hi-diddle-diddle is the only comment that occurs to me at the moment. Tramps are not like that.

The others, and they are the majority, tend to be practical, scientific, looking for economic causations, and seeing the vagrant as a by-product of the industrial system. When there is plenty of employment, there are few tramps; when there is no employment there are many vagrants. Q.E.D.

If they are right, then I found myself out of a job, and in the middle of an unemployment crisis, in the spring of the year 1899, at the age of four. Because in that year and at that age I left home, deliberately and, so far as I was concerned, finally. That it was no infant stray-away I have been proving, in spite of myself, from that day to this.

There is little doubt that, in 1899, I was already different from the youngsters around. We lived in Inchicore, then a little separate village some miles from Dublin, and I remember all my child-contemporaries very well indeed. Fortunately for their parents they were not at all like me, in any way.

For one thing, I was a kind of infant prodigy, although, I believe, not nauseatingly so. I had already been going to school nearly two and a half years. (I have a school-photo and certificate which place me as twenty-one months old.) In a little Irish community, and with parents of peasant origin, it can be imagined what *that* meant. Of course I had no chance of ever being a child—until I took it for myself, later. I am still taking it.

Long before I was three, I had discovered and exploited the fact that I differed from my playmates. It was not merely that I could read much better than my mother—I had taken all that for granted—but I found out that all the other children, and the grown-ups too, spent most of their time trying to tell lies. The funny part was that they could not tell lies. I could, and all the others believed them. That was how I knew.

I seem to have been big, good-looking, and of a most innocent demeanour. There is a huge photo of me, taken at two years old (with the school for background of course: trust a peasant mother not to miss a thing like that), which shows a fairly attractive youngster of positively angelic appearance. A little saint, in fact. I must have heard myself so described thousands of times by admiring people who could not even tell decent lies.

Already I had learnt to get my own way. The English I spoke, modelled on my father's conversation, must have been exceptionally good for that time and place. But in addition I had a quiet, good-humoured, coaxing manner—which paid me many a thousand pounds in dividends later, and got me out of many a scrape.

Nowadays it is my natural manner, as more than one publisher or film-producer can testify. But when I was a baby, as I recall very clearly, it was an act, deliberately put on in order to influence people. It was not mere placation; I studied. Nor did I fool myself; again and again I tried to be like the other children, but no one would let me. So I acted.

3

Bigger, then, than I should have been, a scholar, an incipient saint, I always had more of an audience than I wanted. A powerful child, able to run and fight, able to make up games, I had my following among the young of Inchicore. Also I knew words which most of the grown-ups of the place did not. Besides which I could tell the most convincing lies. Naturally everyone liked me.

Followers of Sigmund Freud may, if they like, find significance in the fact that I did not like my father at the time I first left home. Earlier, I remember, I had idolised him, as I suppose every little boy idolises his father. But we had been estranged—there is no other word for it!—for many months.

He was a big man, very grave and reserved, I imagine, to those around him, but of course a marvellous person in my eyes. A surviving picture of him shows an unmistakably Victorian gentleman, with side-whiskers, umbrella, watch-chain, and seals, looking very middle-class and respectable. He was not anything like that. But I believe he never knew.

Widely read and widely travelled, he had an Irish revolutionary background, to which he owed his knowledge of the world and his exceptional acquaintance with books. Imprisoned when young, during an upheaval some thirty years before I was born, he had "seen abroad" as the Inchicore people used to say. They treated him as a superior, although he was only a workman and had never been anything else except a peasant. Looking back, I think he must really have been far above workman-average.

He had been a marine engineer, in early tramp steamers, a store-keeper at Sierra Leone in its wild days, a gold-prospector in America. Further, he had been a foreman at Krupps of Essen, at about the time they were beginning to copy Woolwich Arsenal. Also he had been a watch-maker in Switzerland (he had scores of curious watches, with which he tinkered continually), and he had boxed.

He told me stories. May the gods of chance be thanked and praised, he told me many stories. One result was that long before I was seven, instead of *The Three Bears*, I could tell detailed lies about having been in Guatemala—and pronounce the place-names correctly. I think another result was that at four I cleared out, finished with my family and my father for good.

It is clear to me now, but of course I did not realise it then, that at the time I left home my father was a dissatisfied man. He had walked in the world and done things, was exceptionally well-educated, had proved himself something of a mechanical genius, had written and sold a few short stories. Now he was finished.

Nearing fifty, he found himself thrust into the groove of a workman in a railway shop—he was then a springmaker in the Southern Railway Works—with never a chance of getting out of it until he died. It happens to many.

A vagrant at heart, my father was trapped by a job and a home, a wife and a family, by his duty in life. Too moral to walk away and desert us, he stayed, earned a good deal of money, spent literally every penny of it on us, and of course went sour. Just about when I was four, he became a very grim, silent, distant man. I detested him, then.

My mother was a lovable peasant woman, uncultured, industrious, utterly incapable of understanding the hankerings of anyone like my father—or later myself. Existence, as far as she was concerned, was an opportunity to work, save money, rear a family, love them and give them a chance in life, then die and go to heaven.

It could never possibly dawn on her that a man might *want* to go to Sierra Leone, where he had nearly died of fever, or wish to starve again in the hills of California. A man had a job. He stayed in it. Then died and went to heaven.

I suppose she was right in her outlook, and I suppose my father was right. Looking back, I love them both for their simplicity and unselfishness. There are millions of lovable people like that in the world. It might have been a great deal easier for me if I had been made in that mould. Of course I cannot say. At any rate, I was not.

My mother also was a great story-teller, but of a type very

different from my father. His were personal narratives—with a good travel-background, as we would say to-day. Hers were all of the far-distant past, but with absolutely no sense of time.

In her tales, Irish giants and fairies were mixed up with the "good black man" who had buried my father alive in a jungle to sweat the malaria out of him. Saint Patrick was often indistinguishable from a legendary Irish magician called Gownseer.

She believed the lot. As far back as I can remember, I tried to sort them out for myself, making infant attempts to achieve credibility, but she believed the lot, timeless and place-vague as they were.

She simply did not credit that people could write stories, or tell them for their own satisfacton. With the evidence before her eyes of the existence of books, she did not believe in fiction, did not know of its existence.

Large numbers of her contemporaries shared her views. Vast numbers of people share them to-day, even people who go frequently to the cinema. There is nothing I can say in comment—I do not understand. But I know my mother believed that there were no stories except true stories.

When, at about three and a half, I sang a song about a tree I had seen felled across the road at Chapelizod, a nearby village, my mother soundly whipped the girl who had been in charge for "letting me fall on my head." Anything strange, any deviation, however small, from the simple, straightforward, factual outlook on life was explained, for my mother, by the assumption of a fall on the head.

What chance had she of understanding the big, powerful, sombre man who formerly told the lovely stories, but who now sat in broody silence, when he came from "the Works," ate, and went to bed? What chance had she of knowing that I wanted—until I was ready to scream I wanted—to know about people and places, not about silly lies that weren't lies at all, not half as good as my own?

How could the poor woman know the kind of thing that

6

was going on, even then, behind my little-saint face? I planned for three days before I left them.

My school was only a couple of hundred yards from our house. Each morning I was given a penny for sweets, which was quite a lot of money for a small child in those days. I would turn right for the sweet-shop, then come back because the school was to the left, and pass the bottom of the road, my mother waiting at our door to wave and see me past.

One morning, having gone through the ritual, I hid for a while. Then when I thought my mother would have gone indoors, I turned back and hurried away from Inchicore.

The road ran close to the railway, which, I knew from family conversation, went to Tipperary. Jim Maher, a kind of god or giant who had visited us once or twice, lived in Tipperary. (Long afterwards I discovered that Jim was my cousin.) I was going to Jim Maher, for ever and ever.

Two women who knew my mother came along the road, and I hid in a hedge until they had passed. Then I hurried on towards Tipperary. It was a hundred miles, but I did not know that, only that it was past Chapelizod Bridge, which was as far as I had ever been.

For some time I played on a grass-slope, and sang again and again the song about the woodmen felling the tree at Chapelizod. "Far away my many parties" was one line, I remember.

If I could explain what the tree-felling scene meant to me, or what it was I tried to sing, there would be no need for me to write this or any book. I cannot explain. But one thing is sure—I have never thought or done, written or felt, anything that pulled at my deep emotional life, without seeing the tree on the road or hearing the clock-ticking sound of the axes, through the eyes and ears of the three-and-a-half-year-old child.

I mean that once when I was near to being shot and once when I was near to being hanged I saw the bulk of a tree stretching from wall to bank, men swinging axes. I mean that once when I had to kill a man, and knew I had to kill him, I

7

heard myself singing, *was* myself singing, the song about the fallen tree, and did not kill him.

Many writers have tried to explain that strange continuity and persistence of an isolated thought-group down the years. Perhaps Hugh Walpole's fanciful explication of the wild-white-horse origin of the Herries name and family is the most satisfactory. I have no explanation, only a picture.

One is to see a high and endless white-stone wall, flanking one edge of a narrow road, the road's other side unfenced, steep slope of grass going up to steep slope of grass, and then to thorn bushes hiding the hill. From inside the white-stone wall a great tree has fallen, breaking the wall and stretching across the road, the crown and spread of it, with the birds' nests in, jammed crashing and crushed into the grass bank.

Horses with harnessed chains, dragging, come by men balancing near the grass bank swinging axes. More men by the white-stone wall wave axes too, while horses heave and blue smoke withers and dies, in the air, from a fire of the twigs from the tree. Then follows the calling of the men, and the clock-ticking sound, the loud and powerful clock-ticking sound, from the axes by the bank and the wall.

Up the grass bank, waving and excited, shouting the song of the tree over the wall, there will be a tall child in petticoats, counting the horses and men, watching the strokes of an axe, singing for each of the limbs as they come to the ground.

Petticoats were usual wear for boys up to five or six in Ireland when I was young. What the tree-scene conveyed I have no idea, but it is as clear to me now as it was when I was not yet four. All my life I have had the picture, and have remembered its importance.

The song, I think, was equally vital for me then. Perhaps picture and song only meant that I could not yet think properly. But I believe not. There are my school records, with a good deal of other evidence besides my own memories, to the contrary.

SKYFALL

Sky low. Sky low. Far a- way my ma-ny par-ties. Fall him

down and take his da twine. Fall him down and take his da twine.

Sky low. Sky low. Far a- way my many par-ties.

The few simple sounds bulked larger in my life than the birth of my sister, the anger of my father, or my school-time sweets. That will suffice. On the day of my walkaway, I sang the central line a score of times, until it almost became the song. Then I got out on the road again.

Deceit or innocence, I am not clear which, got me through Chapelizod without being stopped. An old, bearded man with a stick—a tramp, I imagine—walked along beside me for some distance. I talked to him, telling about sweets, and our chickens, and my father, but not mentioning Tipperary.

When he asked where I lived I answered, "Down there," pointing ahead. Presently I took his hand, and we walked along through the village of Chapelizod. On the outskirts I just let go his hand and walked away. Deceit rather than innocence, I am inclined to believe, because twice I have had exactly the same trick worked on me by small children, since!

A woman at a farm gave me a drink of milk, and said I was a good boy, and told me to hurry home. For a while I thought of living at that farm for ever, but swiftly decided for Tipperary. The road looked good.

In a field I saw daffodils growing wild, for the first time in my life, and hurried to pick some. I loved that field. Years later I revisited the place, and found my memory of the details almost perfect.

The broken gate, the rotting tree-trunk, the nettle-bed and the wild daffodils, the smell of the cowshed in the field—indeed, they have crept into a dozen stories, almost without my knowing it. But on that particular morning they were the cause of my downfall. The people on the farm knew me for a "stray" and kept me for the police.

Playing with two kittens, I was quite happy until the policeman arrived. Even then I was by no means frightened. He was a nice man.

He was exactly the kind of man to help a small boy whose name was Jim Phelan, whose father's name was Jim Phelan, and who came from Graigua, Gortnahoe, near Thurles, in Tipperary, the father having gone home on the train, not knowing that the small boy had got out to play.

That policeman never rose from the ranks, I am prepared to swear. Because that was the story I told him, in the lisping, sweetly-innocent singsong which even then one sister called my "fibbing voice," and he believed it all.

Whether there was telephonic communication between Irish rural police-stations in those days I am not certain. But I was kept for some hours, perfectly happy, while enquiries were made.

They must have got in touch with the district in Tipperary which I had described so precisely, and found that there were plenty of Jim Phelans, old and young, in the region. (Naturally; they were mostly my relatives, although I was unaware of their existence.) Presently I was put on a train, given some cakes and a bottle of milk, wakened from a long sleep, and handed out to a policeman at a lovely place which did not look in the least like home. I was in Tipperary.

The local policeman saw through me at once. "That's no Tipp'rary chiseller," he announced to his wife, who mothered me while I answered questions. "A Dublin jackeen. Or

English maybe." He pressed me with queries, but I stuck to my fibbing-voice story, and was presently left alone while he discussed the matter with his wife.

Jamesey Phelan, of Woodsgift, it appeared, had several children, but the youngest was nine. Jim Phelan from Ballingarry had only one son, a two-year-old. Mat Phelan—that was it. "Listen, son. Your father's name wouldn't be Mat, now, would it?" I repeated my story, but began to cry. This was not a nice policeman.

At last I was put on an outside car, and driven to Graigua, where I was, as it were, exhibited to the several sections of the Phelan family. At the third house came Nemesis.

A woman I had never seen before ejaculated, "Glory be to God—that's Jamesey Phelan's boy from Inchicore. And how did he get *here*?" The only bright spot, I remember, was that she blamed it all on the unfortunate policeman!

Next day I was sent home, and had a terrific beating. Naturally that decided me to go away again, as soon as possible. I have been doing it ever since.

CHAPTER II

THE pattern sketched in that first chapter, and in the first four years of my life, will fit every phase of my existence up to now. It is better to give it in the beginning, although it hurts a little, so that later things of which I shall write may not appear inexplicable or merely crazy. They follow the pattern.

Always, in any danger or difficulty, my immediate impulse is to turn round and head for the horizon. Bearing in mind that I have, and have sometimes (although not often) deserved, a reputation for being courageous, tenacious, imperturbable, this will sound strange. Especially this will sound strange to the people who have known, at first hand, any of my later story. It is true, though.

It may be that on occasion I drove so wildly away from a danger or an unpleasantness that I passed through other and greater dangers without noticing them. I have never been conscious of such things—and my field of consciousness is wide. But always, in any crisis, unless I made a very great effort, I simply went away.

That is the tramp outlook, which cannot be explained in terms of romantic urge or the latest spell of unemployment. Nor by simple dogmatism about lack of moral courage. Nor by psychiatric glibnesses about instability. I know all the theories well, some of them much better than the theorists, and in the end I call it simply the tramp outlook.

H. G. Wells (I think it was) once put forward an amusing but tenable explanation of modern vagrancy. Mediterranean civilisation, he showed, included two very large fractions from earlier and widely different societies.

One group was made up of people whose forefathers had been nomadic—wandering shepherds, only a few generations earlier. The other section came from the peoples of the cities and settlements, already old, on the fringe of the sea.

It would take a few thousand years to strike a balance. That balance had not been reached in the early days of Greece, for instance, and much trouble resulted, when some citizens just went away instead of getting on with their civic affairs. Restlessness, we call it to-day, without knowing quite what we mean.

A good deal of exploration, colonisation, foreign settlement, can be attributed to that same restlessness. But I think those things are secondary, come by accident. The first thing is to go away. To this day I am convinced that the Pilgrim Fathers neither knew nor cared much about the places to which they were going. They were just going away.

The Wells explanation has always been fairly convenient for me, needless to say. When anyone complains that Jim Phelan is riding a lorry up the Great North Road, instead of finishing a promised story, it is consoling to think that he must blame the Greeks or the Eastern nomads, not me!

Weakness or strength, courage or cowardice, heredity or personal choice—it may be any of these things. Certainly, as far as I am concerned, every place is a starting-point, still. But I stayed peacefully at home, for over three years, after my beating for the Tipperary excursion. Not because of the beating, but because I did not want to go.

My father had now a better job, with another railway company. We moved a long way, to a larger and nicer house, and he himself was more friendly and talkative, for a time at least.

Feeling back, reaching out in sympathy to the poor devil, thwarted and stultified and nearly crazy with loneliness, because he had no one, literally no one except myself, with whom he could talk, I can see now that this was his last, almost desperate attempt at a come-back. He was trying to be Jim Phelan, and he nearly made it.

The watches, a whole boxful of them, strange, beautiful little things which played a big part in shaping my ideas of metal-form, came out again after a long sojourn in the dust. My father worked, and whistled, and was happy.

He talked, to my mother, about places in Germany, until I (not she) could almost have made a plan of Hamburg city docks. Also he wrote, and sold, a story called *The Bog of Blossoms,* or something of the kind.

There is no doubt whatever that I, and I only, was his public, in the home circle. Certainly my mother just took the bog story as a wonderful narration of fact. So did Ann Gaynor, a familiar of the family. So did Jim Maher. This in spite of their having seen it written, with an ordinary pen in an ordinary notebook, and of knowing that he was in Dublin, at home, when the events of which he wrote took place in Tipperary.

Poor devil! I have often thought of Robert Burns, to whom nearly the same thing was done, in nearly the same way, and of François Villon, to whom worse things were done in the same way. But they escaped.

Partially, belatedly, with the twists and scars of the environment on them, they escaped. Jim never did. He remained a good workman, a good husband and father, to the end, doing his duty. Perhaps—but only perhaps—that is why I have never done mine.

My reaction to the bog-blossom tale must have thrilled my father. I thought he was the loveliest liar I had ever known! I read the story half a dozen times, can feel the lilt of the phrases now, hear the lifting and lull of the breeze that came over the bogs. That last line, I think, may well be in a story of my own, somewhere. Or it may have been in a chapter of the bog-blossoms. Thus hard it hit me.

Of course I was happy again. I was not going away from *that*. Nor from the wonders of our garden, where there was a tortoise and four white rabbits. Nor from the fascination of a sawmill nearby, with its adorable humming noises and every-

14

day evidence of the miraculous things that could be done to and made from trees. Nor from the giant tree, mysterious, whispering, bird-filled, beckoning, which overshadowed the little group of houses where we lived, and whose story I wrote only last year.

I was not going away from all that. Besides, I had discovered Marjorie, aged four, and the thrilling, never-palling miracle of the difference between boys and girls. It is a great wonder I did not turn into a *voyeur* in later life, I spent so much time in the investigation of feminine anatomy. But I was never caught or punished; perhaps that was my insurance. Maybe not. There were other restraints.

It is incredibly difficult to explain nowadays, and the world is a happier and cleaner place because it *is* difficult to explain. But it is a fact that, for a little boy of five to see a little girl of four, naked, was at that time roughly equivalent to arson, mayhem, or the wrecking of a crowded train. It was so, and the year was 1900, not 1300.

For most people who read English it will be almost impossible to grasp the meaning of such a convention. It still survives, in some out-of-the-way places, but they are getting fewer.

We had it in full blast. In contemporary Ireland I have seen the children of a friend tumbling around his big garden with their nursemaid in their birthday suits. In England and the United States I have seen whole troops of youngsters, in nursery schools, whose only reaction to nakedness was that it was jolly convenient for playing. In Ireland, in 1900, we did not have anything like that.

The thing did not and does not belong only to Ireland. I recall that, in a remote English village, only seven or eight years ago, I was walking on a road with my small son Seumas, then about two. During the summer Seumas ran in the woods, wore nothing, unless he wanted to go up the village, when he put on a pair of shoes. Walking on the road with him one day we met a filthy old woman.

She nearly fainted at the sight of the naked child. Shrinking away, with a squeal of horror, she stayed by the side of the road until we had passed, covering her eyes with her hands exactly as if Seumas had been a seven-foot husky with hair on his chest. Peeped through her fingers, too, probably to observe the enormity of his crime! Ireland was like that when I was a child.

The teaching of the Catholic Church, or any church, had nothing to do with it. (Personally I think Queen Victoria was much more responsible, poor old dear.) I think the Catholic law fixes the age of a child's development of consciousness at seven. But inevitably, for ignorant people, every restraint of their own poor twisted minds is wished on the nearest religion —which is then blamed.

I need say no more except that all my major activities, of my five-year-old days, were very furtive and secret. Both my parents were not only deeply religious: they were very moral as well.

The morality, without words either written or spoken as guide, forbade practically everything, including discussion of the morality. People did not talk about such things—that in itself was frowned on. War, pestilence, and famine, combined, can never have approached, even remotely, that morality's list of victims.

My mother would have died, I think, or turned me out of the house for a devil incarnate (at five!) if she had known that most days I stripped a small girl naked in the shed at the foot of the garden, and examined her with interest and care. But of course she did not know.

Religion and morality were beginning to loom up as seriously threatening things in my life, even before I was five and long before I knew more than the sound of the words. Because, of course—and will the reader please know it for tragedy, not a joke—I was a little saint.

At that time, as still in many parts of Ireland, people said the Rosary every night in their own homes. One person read the prayers from a book, and recited the Litany. The others responded. I was the reader, naturally.

Already, at five, I could read much better than anyone of

16

our family except my father. I could control my voice, to make the reading sound properly devout. (My English-holiness talk I called it—only to myself—because of the accent I used!) The trouble was that the reader of the prayers was, *ex officio* as it were, regarded as a very religious person indeed.

For every moment of the prayer-time I was on the edge of screaming. Nightly, seven times a week, I went through tortures of fear. Because I knew I was not religious, but a very wicked boy indeed.

Not for me the silly half-lies—I knew about Marjorie. Further, I knew that God was much cleverer than my mother, not to be dismissed with a few carefully-worded lies, or fine phrases of my English-holiness talk. At night, in the dark, I stayed awake worrying about God. But in the morning I forgot, because I was five years old.

At that time or shortly afterwards two terrible things happened to me. It must have been late 1900 or early 1901, because I remember a song, "The Queen is dead, the Queen is dead; afar the message flew," which puts it near the end of the South African War. Probably a psychiatrist would set them both down as small ordinary things, but between them they largely determined my character, such as it is. Both concerned my father.

He had been much more cheerful and friendly for a long time, told stories again, took me walks, showed me a real ship. We were great friends once more and, with an ally of such importance, I did not worry so much about God. One Sunday morning my father took me for a walk in a park which is now the garden of the Dublin Parliament House.

Some boys, near a fountain, wanted me to play. My father —I suppose not liking to see me so strange and aloof—told me I should. I refused, sheepishly and in a half-whine. The boys insisted. After coaxing me, so did he. I refused. He ordered me. I whined outright. Then he got angry.

What he did not know was that they were much older boys, all about nine or ten, with all the ordinary cruelty of young things. Each time we had passed to the hidden side of the fountain they had attacked me, the biggest lad with the slogan of "I'll dash your brains out," which he very nearly did, against the stone basin of the fountain.

Then on my father's side they would be just innocent children again, playing merrily with their new-found friend. All children do things like that, at some time or other. But I was being ordered to stay there, instead of running for cover, which is the ordinary rule of the game. Also the very grim and sombre father was back. I blubbered.

Then my father beat me—great open-handed smacks on the face, from the powerful craftsman hands, each of which made me feel as if my head was bursting. He *ordered* me to play! While I was gulping down sobs and trying not to vomit!

When he bent down to tell me more quietly, in a hard whisper, I spat in his face and jabbed one hand, open, in his eye. Then I knew the end of the world had come, and that God was angry, and that very wicked boys were being punished in hell, even while he smacked me again, and knocked me down, before he dragged me home.

I know he never forgave himself for the outburst, spent long years of slaving devotion to make up for it. But I never forgave him either until the night when, sixteen years old and weighing nearly two hundred pounds, I beat him to a pulp in a fair fight. He *should* have known.

The other incident was worse. My mother was away in a nursing-home—having a baby, I think. I slept with my father instead of in a cot. I remember thinking, on the first night, that now I would get a super long story. But I did not.

At that time my eldest sister, a big, powerful, handsome girl, about fourteen, but fully grown and looking much older, was fighting back hard against parental authority. This meant that she declined to go to bed at eight o'clock, after the Rosary —probably wanted to run around with boys or something of the kind.

Plainly, a state of war existed between her and my father. On a certain night he decreed that if she was not home at eight o'clock she should "stay out on the streets where streetwalkers belonged!" She did not come home. He locked the door and we went to bed.

It will be obvious that the thing went much deeper than an ordinary child-parent quarrel, was in fact what is sometimes called an Œdipus situation. My sister was, from her contemporary photos, much more attractive than the average adult chorus-girl. My mother was away from home.

It is a familiar situation in Ireland, Wales, many other countries. The locking-out, on any flimsy pretext, is really an insurance by the parent against the breach of taboos. But of course they do not know.

That night I was sleeping with my father. That night I dreamt of my girl-friend, Marjorie, and went in for some of the manual investigation which preoccupied me. Except that it was not Marjorie but my father.

I had to piece it all together, years afterwards, in a hundred half-conversations and dropped hints from my parents. Even now it will be very difficult for a modern English or American reader to understand. Yet I have to explain.

Many Irish people never mention sex—indeed, they know no words with which to do so. Definitely, when I was a child, the use of words like penis, vagina, genitals, was roughly equivalent to open blasphemy in a crowded cathedral.

There are sections of every community, from Tokyo to Tuscaloosa, in which this is so. In the Ireland of my childhood I think the section was large. If my small son pawed me about while he was asleep I should turn him over and let him sleep on the other side, might and might not think it worth while mentioning to his mother or nurse. In those days and in that place my father and his contemporaries knew only the old, hard, murderously-stupid conventions.

I woke, afraid, in the dark, to hear a terrible menacing whisper, "Do you want to go where your sister is?" I froze, and never uttered a sound. But I stayed awake until morning.

Thereafter, for years, I had nightmares, about bulls and black dogs and a strange headless, legless creature which glared murder from terrible eyes in its breast.

Damn it, I was only six.

The next day I commenced preparations for a second walk-away. But it was nearly a year before I went. Because almost at once things improved, from my point of view.

A whole series of delightful experiences, for me and for the other children, commenced at about that time. Delectable pictures of lovely places and marvellous people crowded on me. We had many new houses, found hosts of new friends. I was riotously happy, my days filled by strange facts and faces, my nights too crammed with pleasurable memories to leave much time for fear.

Only long afterwards I learnt that my father had lost his job, lost the greater part of his diminutive savings, was nearly penniless. Our many changes of residence and environment reflected his attempts to rehabilitate himself.

Resourceful and courageous to a degree I have never even remotely approached, he fought a losing battle, stage by stage. A dozen shifts and turns and counterstrokes were tried, vainly, until at last he was forced down to defeat and the verge of pauperism.

Of course I knew nothing of that. All we children knew was that our lives changed constantly, were always filled with new pleasures, lovely dirt and smells, curious talk from many and widely-different child-friends, strange houses, new sights and sounds.

We had a small house—I climbed on the roof of it the first day, causing panic—where an old woman lived upstairs. She had white hair, continually made the funniest chewing motions, and talked always. Once she said it was her house, but my sister and I stopped all such folly by a magic formula we had learnt from some children in the street.

Hand in hand we stood together in front of her bed, watching her fixedly, while we repeated with great intentness the words, "Bloody hell, bloody hell, bloody hell," waiting for her to collapse. (My sister's theory was that the old woman would drop dead.) It must have worked, because she did not say it was her house any more.

There was dirt at the back, and a pile of ashes that smelt, in which one could not play without being smacked. But just outside was a real canal, with canal-boats going up and down, drawn by horses.

The canal widened out into a huge water called The Basin, and enormous ships made rattle and song, with shouting, while big hills of coal grew and grew, on the bank. Sometimes a boy, if he was a good boy with English-holiness talk, would be allowed to go up a gangway, and once a fat man on a ship gave me a rice pudding in a little dish.

It was a wrench to hear that we were leaving such a lovely place, but the excitement of packing and making ready for the move compensated for much. An incident on the last night made my sister and I glad that we were moving after all.

Almost from the first day in our "new house" we had been thrilled, frightened, horrified by the thought of a wicked man who kept a large terrifying house and yard near where we lived. Everything we had heard about Bluebeard, about monsters and ogres and cruel people, went into the stories we made about that yard.

It was full of cats, caged up all round the walls, waiting their turn to be—— Our infant imaginations ran riot at that stage, and the horrors of torture for which the cats waited, helplessly, varied from day to day. But every version agreed that the owner was a very terrible person indeed.

On the last night before we moved, my sister and I were both in bed, ill. It must have been fairly serious, I think, because one symptom was that we both lost our voices. Neither could speak above a very thin and strangled whisper. We were supposed to stay in bed continuously.

When all was quiet, we got out of bed and over a wall. Then by a back wall we managed to reach the terrible place. We stood in the dark yard, with the black bulks of the cages all around us, only an occasional cat-mew breaking the silence. Hastily my sister opened the first cage.

An orgy of liberation followed. We opened cage after cage, until the yard was full of newly-freed cats, hissing at one another, growling, arching their backs, squalling in a dozen different notes and rhythms.

I hurried with my work of mercy. Then, from one cage, a small dog plunged out, snapping and yelping, to terrify me. At the same time I heard a frantic sibilance from the other side of the yard, as my sister tried to tell me we were discovered.

We scrambled over the wall and scurried home, exchanging whispers, with difficulty, about the few poor cats we had had to leave locked up. In three minutes we were in bed and asleep. Not for several years did we know, *to admit it,* that the place was a Cats' Home.

Our next house proved swiftly more marvellous even than the place we had left. It was more than a house. My myriad infantile visions of heaven, a kind of super-beautiful lumber room, and my hundred hankerings for secret receptacles and possibly magical hiding-places, acquired from *Grimm's Fairy Tales,* all came true. We had a shop, a general store, a place of delight in which anything might and constantly did happen.

Naturally I did not know it was a huckster-store in a slum street. But I did know I was allowed to get up at five in the morning, to go with my mother to the fruit and vegetable market.

This place was so big that I never saw its end, the noise was lovelier than the rattle and song of the ships, everyone laughed and was happy, fat, red-faced, friendly, smiling men gave pennies to good boys, almost any woman handed over plums or pears.

Without a scrap of difficulty to-day, I can glimpse and smell the big flickering oil-flares of the early morning, see the plunging horses, drawing high-piled loads of cabbage or carrots, hear the hundred voices, loud, clamorous, good-humoured, insistent, and inhale again the ever-changing but always delightful scents of the thousand corners. That was how the market came to me, forty-odd years ago.

Our "shop" was a huge success, for me at any rate. I do not

know what torments of poverty and insecurity my parents knew there, but presently there was no more shop, and we moved again. The next life was even better.

Horses! Carts and a big yard, the smell of stables and the clank of harness. Shouting of men, with lovely magic words like "bloody hell," at vast loads of hay or straw under which the horse and cart could hardly be seen.

There was the delight of being allowed to brush a horse, of learning to walk under his belly—back and forward, again and again, for the delectation of my sister—and acquiring new names like dandy-brush, curry-comb, collar and bridle and trace. Horses, in a big yard.

This was a brief and desperate attempt to found a carrier-business—always the basic peasant emerged in my father—but it must have gone down into ruin without respite. I remember leading out "Brassar," a big grey horse, our last, on the morning my father took him to be sold. We all cried bitterly.

Another fairyland opened almost at once, however. This time even I knew there was something wrong about our house. Many other people, some of them dirty and smelly, lived in the place and would not go out, even when I told them. They went up and down the stairs, in and out of rooms, and would not let me enter. If it had not been for the caves I should not have liked that house.

The caves were next door. A huge open space had many lovely hills, went humping up and down, far better than any flat street or yard, and had a hundred little paths. Enormous square sticks, a lot thicker than my body, crossed and criss-crossed among the piles of bricks, helped to hold up the little humpings of the surface, made the caves.

All day my father sawed and sawed at the huge timbers, cutting off tiny short bits and still cutting them off. At night I could hear him sawing, when I was in bed next door, and in the morning before I had my breakfast he was sawing too. But in between I played in the caves.

We lived in a single room, in a huge tumble-down slum

tenement. Next door, a similar vast slum house had long since fallen down.

The great timbers, oaks a foot square and thirty or forty feet long, still lay about, green with moss, here and there buried under the piles of brick-rubble, making the caves where we played and where I made a thousand stories. All this was ours—mine!

My father had spotted the mighty timbers, had bought the rubbish of the ruin for little or nothing. Now, with a small handsaw and a chopper, he was reducing the prodigiously long, foot-square oaks to firewood, for sale.

Relatively speaking, I suppose it was a gold-mine. No one had ever thought the wreckage could be turned to any use. My father must have multiplied his investment money twenty or thirty times over.

But the work! The sixteen or eighteen hours a day, with flimsy tools, single-handed! I only know one character in fiction who at all resembles my father—Gilliatt, in Victor Hugo's *Toilers of the Sea*. That was his type.

The firewood venture must have petered out like the others, because presently we moved again. This time I knew better than to order the other people out of our house. I knew about tenements. We lived at the very top of a six-storied tenement, again in a slum district.

I had been going to various day-schools all this time, moving from one to another as our address changed, finding nothing to interest me. At one school, I remember, I was given a book in which the first lesson commenced, "An ox. My ox. Is it an ox?" I was only six. The book would have bored me at two.

From our one-room residence in the top of the big slum house I went to another school, for young children. The teachers were women, of course, and I was always terribly ashamed when my father spoke to me about the school, since he continually referred to "he" when speaking of my teacher.

I was so ashamed that I used to say, ". . . and she told me

so-and-so," slurring over the initial "s" in the pronoun! The pretence was important, I remember.

I stayed at that school for several months, even after I had practically taken over the place. My status can be summed up in a few words. The head-mistress and I used to borrow books from one another—while I was learning how to read "Can you tell how poor Nell fell in the well? Up she ran, with her can. In she fell. Toll the bell, for poor Nell in the well."

The day I was promoted to the "Poor Nell" class, the head-mistress lent me a book on Arctic exploration, dealing with the voyages of the *Erebus* and *Terror*. In return I lent her Pope's *Homer,* which I had smuggled out from among my father's books. Meanwhile I got on with the adventures of Nell. Now it will not be wondered at that I went away again, at the first unpleasantness.

At the back of the house where we lived there was a truly marvellous view of the Dublin mountains. The house was on a hilltop in the highest part of the city, and was itself of a great height. In the early evening it often seemed that the mountains were leaning forward, coming closer to the window, pressing towards the house-top.

There is no question of a poetical imagination or anything of the kind having been at work in me, or in me only. All the family shared my views about the hills, all said at one time or another the things at the end of the last paragraph. In the early evening we often put out the light, and my parents would sit, with us around, watching the hills come close and hearing them whisper.

"You can see them coming in, and hear them whispering." That is not my line, but a quote from my mother. She was almost illiterate, peasant-stolid in demeanour, knew nothing of fiction, or of poetry except ancient ballads. But that is her line.

My father amplified it in a hundred ways. We must have been a strange family after all, and I cannot have been the imaginative boy they and everyone said I was. Because all the other people in our slum could see the hills too, and they never mentioned anything like that.

The mountains were the cause of my downfall, however. Almost literally so!

Living in a tenement, and having no land or garden, nor even a yard, naturally the drying of clothes and so on was difficult. To my father, with his sea-faring and gold-camp experience, that problem was easy of solution. He built two strong spars from the two big windows of our place, to carry clothes-lines. Projecting ten or twelve feet, each carried a cross-piece at the end, with a pulley at either extremity, by which a clothes-line could be manœuvred in and out.

Sixty or seventy feet above ground-level, and on the top of a hill, this made a marvellous drying-ground for clothes. My mother was the envy of the slum. But no one copied. Perhaps they were wise. Or perhaps their children were not like us, and they were terrified of the temptation.

By and large, they must have been right. Because the extremity of the longest cross-jack soon became my favourite seat. Occasionally my young sister claimed the other, when opportunity offered. But she went to school, and her opportunities were few.

My mother worked, then. The other children were out at school. Only gradually it dawned on me that our "house" was empty all day. I left my school, without a word of explanation—I hated the place already for its dullness—and spent the middle part of each day at the end of one of the long poles, reading a book or watching the mountains.

Twice, terrified slum women stopped my mother in the street and attempted to tell her of the "danger." But they had no chance; adults and experts in their own foolish brands of deception as they were, they had no chance. Contemptuously I twisted and perverted and ridiculed each story, until my mother believed them all to be crude, vulgar exaggerations. Then one day my eldest sister came home unexpectedly and found me out on the cross-jack.

Very cleverly, as I see it now, she enticed me back into

the room, avoiding any sudden remark that might have startled me and sent me hurtling down. Afterwards I suppose the long strain of suppressing her anger and fear got the better of her, for she tricked me into looking out, then closed the heavy window on my neck, leaving me trapped.

She might have strangled me, or even cut my head off, guillotine fashion! But apart from that, I already had and have now one funny twist of character. I did not and do not permit anyone to lay hands on me roughly.

Some day I shall be killed in a vulgar, empty, trivial brawl because of that twist. Many people, down through history and at the present time, had and have it—I wish I had not. But it was already strong, even when I was seven.

Struggling madly, I managed to heave up the window, I do not know how. Laughing helplessly at first, my sister must have known what was coming, and fled. The first thing that came to hand, a clothes-brush, I sent after her, and she fell senseless. Then, grabbing a bottle of milk and part of a loaf, I hurried away.

I had not liked the old school anyway, and I had read all the books in our house except those in my father's big trunk, which was locked. Besides, the old head-mistress was getting very dull, took a week to read a book, and talked silly things about it even then. So I would have to go away in any case.

Only that morning there had been trouble about two apples. I had not taken them, but my father was going to smack me for it just the same. So I would have to go away in any case.

Also I would be beaten for what I had done to my sister, and they would not know how terrible it was for her or anyone to handle me like that. So I would have to go away in any case.

I crossed the city, made for the place where The Basin was, where the canal began. I was seven.

CHAPTER III

The Basin was a deepwater dock, connecting with the River Liffey and the open sea. Out of it, on the landward side, the Grand Canal of Ireland started, modestly enough, with a cutting that led into the docks. Then it headed away to— it might have been to Guatemala for all I knew. But that was the way I was going.

Even now, with much experience of pier-head jumps, passage-working, surreptitious trafficking by wharves and railways and docks, I still think I must have been fairly resourceful in that seven-year-old summer. "Stowing away" on a canal boat was difficult—probably it would have been impossible for a man.

Most of the afternoon went in watching the boats pass, and making stories about this "sailor," or this one, walking up to me and asking if I would like to work on his boat. A boat would stop—for some reason—below the bridge where I loitered. Then a very kind, red-faced sailor would come up on the bridge and say hello. Then presently he would ask me—as a favour—if I could possibly steer the boat for him, his own boy being sick. Of course he would.

No reader, I hope, will be feeling either sentimental or superior concerning the small child on the canal bridge. Because enormous numbers of us think in some such fashion to-day, only getting down to the hard facts of existence when the butcher and baker, the landlord and the candle-stick maker, are about to call. For myself there is little need for adjustment—I still think that way. Sometimes the fantasies work out, too.

But most of us learn, from bitter experience, not to bank on fantasies, not to go in for silly wish-thinking, and not to expect too much. I think perhaps a tramp is a person who never learns. Certainly no possible alternative to the day-dreams even momentarily occurred to me, that day on the bridge.

Although later I sneaked through a fence, and pretended to be playing on a waste patch, near a loaded boat, I was still quite sure that the men would be delighted to have me. Watching until the two men were engaged, and skipping aboard to hide under a tarpaulin, I felt neither guilt nor fear. They were bound to be nice men.

The boats, at that time, carried a hold full of cargo, the remainder piled to a height of several feet above the deck, with a tarpaulin over all. I snuggled myself in, at the rear end of the long, roof-like, tarpaulin-covered pile, and waited, tensely, for a long time without moving a muscle. Then I heard a man shouting to a horse, a few thumps and clump-ings, and the boat moved.

There was very little to be seen, in the slit between the two ends of the tarpaulin, except a large man at the tiller and bits of the canal-bank as we passed. Presently it was dark, and I could see only the dim form of the steersman. I did not stir.

I must have sat there, immobile and wide-awake, for hours. Quite clearly I remember thinking about God and my wickedness, wondering if my mother would cry when I did not come home, almost getting off the boat when I recalled that one of my father's books was on loan to the head-mistress and now he would lose it. But I forgot about those things very soon.

My immediate problem was more urgent. It is nearly forty-five years ago, but I have not worked over any problem whatever with the same intensity since. Yet I only wanted to make water.

Several times I have had to take a chance on being killed, I have been sentenced to death and sentenced to life, have cracked the most intricate chess problems, and written a couple of middling-good detective novels. I thought strenuously at such times. But for sheer intense brainwork I have never approached that night.

What I had to decide was whether (*a*) I should be a dirty, careless slum-boy, and earn the contempt of the boatmen when they found out, by urinating on the cargo—boxes of margarine, I think. Or (*b*) whether I should discover myself, make friends with the men, and have a pee-pee afterwards. Or (*c*) whether I should attempt the almost impossible feat of sneaking out—within a few feet of the steersman, be it noted. In the end I decided to sneak out.

Twice the boatman almost touched me, as he moved the tiller, and I could not have been more than a yard from him, at the utmost. But I got to the edge at last and urinated into the canal. I was not a dirty boy, and the canal men would not despise me.

It is amusing to recall, now. But, remembering, I have never once made the mistake of dismissing a child's problems and attempts at solution as unimportant. Kiddies go through hell in the modern world. There does not seem to be anything we can do about it. I try, with Jim Phelan junior, but . . .

When I got back into my cranny I tried to sleep, sitting on a box, but could not. It did not matter. The boat was still going, and I was going with it. Presently—perhaps to-morrow—I would go out and speak to the men.

They would make me welcome, take me down into the cabin, perhaps pay me to steer the boat. Then they would not have to stay awake all night, as the man at the tiller was doing. While I—I liked staying awake all night.

Music came, lovely soft music like flowing water—no, like flowing milk, because it was softer and smoother. Jerking up, I found I had been dozing, and that the music had come in a dream. But now I was awake and the music was still

30

there. I widened the slit between the tarpaulins and peeped out.

The dim figure was still at the helm. But he was straddling it now, steering the boat with his legs, while he held a flute with both hands and played my music.

The whispering mountains near our house, beckoning branches of the giant tree I had known, laughter and loud-calling happiness of the scented market, my toys, the feel of my mother's arm, and my tree-felling song—"Far away my many parties"—they were all with me, in that moment, in the music of the flute as the boat went along in the dark. I had not known that my canal could be so lovely.

Little things like that stay with us. Generally, I think, they cluster, too, like attracting like, so that even one small memory of happiness will present itself to the later recollection as if set in a frame composed of a dozen resembling it.

Plotting and planning, civics and sociology, even the most informed, can do nothing more for human happiness than to provide a few opportunities for the clustering. Here is the centre of one of my clusters:

BOATMAN WITH FLUTE

The music was interrupted by a shout from somewhere ahead, a single word, a monosyllable. The steersman immediately repeated the word, loudly, took the tiller in his hands and pulled slightly to one side. Our speed decreased, and soon we were nearly at a standstill. Then a horse could be heard passing, and a hoarse voice called, "Hello there, Bill-ee." A boat passed in the opposite direction, only a few inches away, ghost-like in the darkness.

Every word of the hurried conversation carried on by the two steersmen, in the few seconds while the boats passed one another, was of course seized upon and treasured by me. It was all very interesting. But I was sorry there was no more music.

However, I busied myself working out the rule of the road for canals, trying to discover how the men avoided having one boat run plunk into another, head on, in the darkness. Checking it later, I found I had got it nearly enough right.

The man leading "our" horse, far away ahead in the darkness, met another horse, drawing a boat, coming towards him. He immediately shouted the single word "Horse." That was what I had heard—just "horse," and no nonsense. Each steersman then keeps to the right, the man who has called stops his horse, allowing his tow-rope to sink, the second boat passes over it.

But how if a steersman did not recognise his own horseman's voice? How if——? Then I went forward with a jerk, wakened, and it was morning.

The boat was still moving, but a different man was at the helm. The sun was shining and there were birds. Gasping with delight, I peeped out through the slit and watched the marvellously beautiful places we passed.

I know the district well, now, a cutting between tall hawthorns, in a dull, flat, pasture country. But that morning it was the whole of the Grimm and Andersen countries to me, with a little of *Coral Island* and a hint of the wilds investigated by the *Erebus* and *Terror*.

The smell of a turf fire, and of bacon frying, wakened me

completely; I reached for my hunk of bread and the remains of my milk. The tramp, the stowaway sailor, was going to have his breakfast.

Right through that day and well on into the afternoon I sat tight, motionless except for an occasional peep through the slit at the beauties of the canal bank. No idea of the distance we might have covered occurred to me. Indeed, I had little notion of distance, have not much more to-day. We had come a long way; that was enough for me. Even though I was getting hungry, I sat still.

Finally, my problem of the previous night recurred, urgently, except that now the sun was shining and the man would be sure to see me the minute I moved. I pulled the tarpaulins apart and stepped out, almost into the arms of the steersman.

The huge rustic must have had a life-size shock, for he started back and let go the tiller. Then, quite unnecessarily since we were still on the boat, he grabbed me by the shoulder, shouted, and glared.

Another man came running from the front of the boat, to stop open-mouthed when he saw me. Dimly I began to feel that they might not be nice sailors.

"Examine all the possibles," is a basic thought-rule with me nowadays, especially since I play chess seriously and sometimes work on a film-script. I must have examined at least a hundred possibles that day before I showed myself. But I had never dreamt of the thing that actually occurred.

A shout to the horseman slowed the boat. A pull at the tiller sent it to the edge of the canal. Two vast hands lifted me, not roughly or angrily, and without a word I was dumped on the grass at canal-brink. The horse moved on, the boat gathered way, and I was left on the bank, crying bitterly.

Trying to remember back, I think the men must have been scared stiff. As a rule, country people in Ireland are extremely generous and thoughtful, placid, easy-going, totally unlike the city-dwellers, who have to be harder. I think the boatmen acted in pure panic. But they had acted, and had gone away, and a sad, lonely boy wept on the grassy bank.

Not until it was nearly dark did I come to any houses, and then it was only a group of cottages near a lock of the canal. Before I had a chance to ask for food or turn on my fibbing-voice, I was sitting down to a meal of bread-and-milk at a cottage, being treated sympathetically as a "stray." The boatmen, passing through, had told of having seen me along the canal, if nothing else.

My meal finished, a man took me by the hand and we walked for some distance. Then we met a priest, and the man seemed to think his problems were solved, for he handed me over with the fewest possible words. I went to the priest's house.

This was rather unfortunate, for me. A priest, as far as I knew, was God. No skill with my fibbing-voice, no bits of my English-holiness talk, would serve. I told him the whole story.

He must have been a marvellous old chap. Only one priest in literature comes near him—Monsieur Bienvenu in *Les Misèrables* is nowhere. The old man was like the priest in Frank O'Connor's *First Confession*. I have often thought I should like to have written that story.

That night I slept at the priest's house, after a long talk about books, and Brassar the grey horse, and a bird called a snow bunting, which bird I had discovered from the deck of my ship *Erebus* in the Arctic. Also there was talk about my school, and how dull it was to pretend to read "Poor Nell fell in the well." I liked that priest.

Later, in bed, I cried because now I was found out and I would have to be a little saint again, maybe have to be a priest. And I did not want to. The old man lit an oil-lamp, and brought a funny toy in which two men hammered on a block with wooden hammers. He seemed to know about people not wanting to be priests or saints, too, because I felt better and went to sleep.

Next day I was sent home, in the train, with a letter from the priest. My father, instead of beating me, only looked at me coldly and said nothing. My mother flogged me, naked, with a leather strap, until I broke from the room, rushed down six flights of stairs, and dashed through the streets, screaming and streaming blood, pursued and finally captured by a crowd of raucous, gloating slum-children.

They dragged me, jeering, through the streets, and even now I can recall, clearly, the surprise and amusement of the passers-by, in the broad, well-lighted highways, at seeing a perfectly naked boy being dragged by a group of others.

By any standard it was a terrible experience, and it bit deeply into my brain, marked me for long. Even to-night I can feel the mud of the street, know embarrassment worse than my pain and fear, because the mud is spattered and smudged on unaccustomed parts of my naked body.

Very plainly I can see the faces of the people, gazing at the mud and blood on my nakedness, and I know again the horror of helplessness, that came from being clutched by a dozen hands. It would have been a terrible experience for any sensitive child. For me, with the additional strange twist of mind which made me hate physical restraint, it was torture ultimate.

The biggest boy, about twelve or so, was drooling with delight while he grinned and twisted my arms. Even then, gripped on all sides as I was, I managed to strain upwards and bit into his throat. But he laughed and slapped me down, nearly strangled me. Then they dragged me home to my mother.

Shamed and horrified, and I think badly frightened by what she had done, she said nothing, but gave me my clothes to dress. I dressed, and walked out.

My mother and my sisters commenced to cry as I left, but I was not going far, was not running away at all. It may be old-fashioned and sentimental, grossly egotistical, and based on a wholly wrong philosophy of life, but I am still pleased to remember that I went in search of the twelve-year-old.

When I could not find him I cried much more bitterly

than I had done on the canal bank, or in the park when my
father had beaten me down, or when I was being flogged
and dragged through the streets. A dozen times that night I
woke, screaming, not from the pain of my wounds, but from
rage and hatred, especially for that large, grinning boy.

Next day I was taken to a school run by the Christian
Brothers, a semi-monastic order who concentrate on teaching.
This particular school had been my Mecca for some time, but
I could not be transferred from my school-mistress, because
I was too young. Now the letter I had brought back from
my "voyage" had apparently eased things.

Probably the priest, or a relative, paid such fees as were
necessary, because at that time my family must have been
very hard-up indeed. From the first minute I knew I was
going to like this school—I heard a class of bigger boys
learning some subject of which I did not even know the
name! A real school!

Being seven, I was put in the lowest class. Swelling with
pride, deciding not to run away from home any more, revel-
ling in the discovery that there really were schools where
people knew about boys who found little books dull, I was
moved up after an hour. In my happiness I almost forgot the
terrible weals on my back and legs, from the flogging with
the strap.

In the second room to which I went, the results of the
flogging were discovered. My clothes were stuck to my
wounds, and I could not sit down, nearly fainted with pain
when I tried. A big man, wearing a biretta and a black gown,
came to question me, hissed his breath in surprise when I
stripped.

A note from the Head accompanied me when I was sent
home. Most bitterly I cried, and protested that the weals did
not really hurt, that I could sit down now—I thought I was
being ejected from the new school. But I went home, with a
boy for company.

The note was really a scare for my mother, the Head
thinking she was a brutal slum-woman, which of course she

was not. He terrified her, at any rate, and I heard the note discussed, many times, in the following days.

What my mother got out of it was that she was risking her immortal soul, and would be punished, not by the law, but by God, for ill-treating a gifted child obviously destined for a bishopric. The Head, I think, did not put in anything like that, but my mother's version satisfied *me*. I settled down at the school, and after a few days set about beating the twelve-year-old.

This was no easy job, apart entirely from the fact that I was only seven. Powerful and loutish, the boy was even bigger for his age than I was for mine.

Anyone who has read a story of mine, *Matter of Balance,* knows what I did. I laid him a booby-trap. Except that in the story the man who laid the trap was killed. I was not killed.

He and all the slum people thought I was a murderous little savage, thought I wanted to kill him, but I did not want anything like that, just to hurt him, before everyone, and make him a fool, and have him laughed at and give him welts to swell so that he could not sit down.

That was what I did. Knowing my own history, I think he was lucky the settlement was not postponed.

Years of peace, of great and unbroken happiness followed for me. I have never wanted anything except to be given a few books and a typewriter, to be let walk along the roads when and where I like. In those years after seven I did not want anything at all except to be left alone, at school.

Unfortunately, the Head's first letter confirmed my parents in some of their previous ideas, to wit, that I was gifted from God, a great genius, and was going to do big things. In a peasant country that means—money.

So I was to be a priest, perhaps a bishop, or a famous surgeon, or a judge, to the greater glory of God and the lasting profit of the clan O'Phelan. Every Irish intellectual—and many of the Scots—have suffered in the same way.

It all sounds very mercenary, but is not really so. Peasants are like that—practical, accustomed to planting things, and then reaping a harvest. Peasant people are clannish, loyal; blood is thicker than water, for most. The boy who becomes a doctor, a high Civil Servant, or wealthy in business, re-members and rewards the often poverty-stricken parents who have slaved to pay for his education.

Continually I wished people would stop making silly plans and leave me alone. Brother Redmond and I had a million things to do. Redmond—a marvellous teacher—was the Head.

It was a good school, by any comparison. The brothers, not priests but living monastically, only emerging to teach (I think), had a great pride of learning, in the real tradition of the Schoolmen, but with an eye to modern exams and prac-tical results.

The school was Catholic, but there was little insistence on the purely religious aspect of education. The brothers prided themselves, justly, on their ability to teach geography, maths, logic, English, Irish, French, and history.

Other things looked after themselves, well enough. I never dropped back for even a moment, from the first day, and had got as far as I *could* get before I was ten.

It is easy to remember by age, because one day the Head came and, in a jolly informal talk, went over the list of can-didates for the next Intermediate exams. I was in the Sixth, from which group the candidates would normally be taken.

The lowest entering age was thirteen. The Head ran off the first names, and checked the ages of the boys who were old enough to enter. Then came some of the brighter boys, and the Head's surprise and pleasure showed more and more in his face as they gave their ages. Twelve. Twelve. Twelve.

"What! Are you fellows *all* twelve?" He beamed around the group.

"No, sir." Eleven. Eleven. Eleven.

When it came to my turn, I was almost ashamed to say my age, because it made me feel an awful prig. Ten. I should stay three years in the same form before the rules, or the law, would let me go any farther.

Thereafter the teachers, every one, concentrated on giving me the greatest possible chance, without forcing me. A big chap named Mulhall, then about fifteen, a most brilliant scholar, had a kind of roving commission, since there was really nothing in the curriculum to fit him. After a while I found myself drifting into that stage too.

I was allowed to take languages and geometry with boys several years older, allowed to teach, although it was against the rules, could come and go almost as I liked. The teachers were shrewd and capable men. Brother Redmond, the Head, was a pedagogic genius. They all decided that I was going to make history.

Well, well; so I did, I suppose, but not in the way they or I expected. But I remember that twice the venerated list of past pupils was taken out for me, artists and priests and poets and politicians. There were many.

In my home, the reaction to such things was direct. I was a genius. That meant I was a kind of slot-machine—my family placed some books and some money in the slot; presently the machine would yield quantities of gold. They meant no harm. One does not live among peasants for nothing.

My father was to blame indirectly. Regarding himself as a failure (which he was not, *if he had but known*—I wish I now had half his erudition and experience), he wanted *me* to fulfil all the ambitions he had not himself realised. My mother was more direct. I would be a priest and/or a doctor and/or a judge. (She was blissfully vague.) Then I would be good to my mother.

I did not want anything like that.

Almost it looked as if they were trying to *make* me run away. Plotting your studies and planning your future and fixing everything up, years ahead—if only they would let a fellow alone, and give him a few books. Planning futures!

(Years afterwards, a young fellow-writer and I took a room together, to save our money. The first evening we were busy for a few hours, fixing our scrawny library and so on. Then he drew up two chairs to the table and put the tips of his fingers together. "We must plan our future——," he commenced. I knocked him cold, where he sat, and slept in a tramp's lodging-house that night. I had *had* my planning, when I was ten.)

Any plotting I did, in my ten-year-old days, was purely negative! What I wanted was to read books. That was all. It did not matter whether it was *De Belli Gallico,* the *Odyssey,* or *Kit Carson*—any book would do. All the schoolbooks were interesting. Very well, then.

Most certainly I was not having the responsibility for a proud and ancient if impoverished family laid neatly on my shoulders, at ten. *If they weren't very careful, I wouldn't be a genius at all, and then what?*

There was another aspect of the matter. Perhaps it was just as well, for me, that it was forced into prominence in time. But I do not know. Much torment came my way because of it. There is a temptation here to advance many glibnesses, but—I do not know.

My father always talked a lot of rubbish about "The Family." (The family estates at that time consisted of a patch of farm-cum-bog, from which an unbroken stream of Phelans crowded off into Australia, the United States, Sierra Leone, or the South American republics.) We were the main line, the head of the crowd, so to speak. I was the eldest son. Ergo . . .

Ergo another load of responsibility for the ten-year-old, such as getting married and having a son and so on, for the honour of the family. This hit me very hard indeed. Because at that time I knew I was impotent, eunuch, a bullock, wrong, different, knew that *I* could never, never have a son.

I had half a dozen completely perfect memories to account for my supposed condition. Sometimes it was a bearded man in a forest who had "cut" me. (I knew no forests, but of course that made no difference.) Sometimes it was an accident, in a push-cart, when a baby. More often it was my father who had gelded me. I took it for granted that fathers did things like that.

Castration-complex plus guilt-feeling, in Freudese. My four-year-old girl-friend Marjorie versus that murderous morality. I knew savage, tempestuous torment.

Blindly, so it seemed to me, my parents maintained the unceasing flow of comment about gifted scholars, heads of proud families, and plans for the future. It passed bearing-point, but I said nothing to anyone.

With many regrets, but coldly sure of myself, I decided that I was going to leave my school, that I was going to be a "ragamuffin boy," i.e. dull and ignorant and not a genius any more. The genius business could go to hell.

The school-leaving scheme came to fruition, too, although I was nearly defeated at least once.

My father had long since got over his basic difficulties, had money, friends, contacts, a job, and good health. At his first opportunity we moved to a decent house.

A six-roomed cottage with a vast stable-yard attached, this was about a mile from my school. It was a lovely little place, after the tall slum tenements, but I remember being very much ashamed of the address.

Since it was a thousand times superior to our previous residence, the snobbery was peculiar. I think it must have arisen because our house was near the Coombe, a Dublin highway with roughly the same associations as Petticoat Lane in London or the Bowery in New York.

I dealt with the situation by copying the address of someone's country house and giving *that* to the school people. No one was going to say I lived in the Liberty, which was the name of the ramshackle and demi-mondaine district through which the Coombe ran.

Almost immediately I began to impress on my mother the danger and difficulty of going "all that way" to school. There was no bus or tram. Would it not be better if I went to a big school which was quite near our house?

41

The place I had in mind was what at that time was called a National School—a dreadful hole. If one imagines a very bad elementary school in a poorer-class district of an English city, that will do. Of course, it was completely worthless to anyone like me—even at ten I should say I was mentally much better equipped than their average teacher. Which was just what I wanted.

Naturally my mother did not know anything about that. To her, poor woman, all schools were alike, places where gifted boys got education and became judges or doctors and were good to their mothers.

I knew—I was always top at logic—that boys from elementary schools went to work in factories, or were telegram boys, or played around street corners, with no jobs and no genius and no responsibility and no family. I wanted that, too.

My mother came with me to my old school, to discuss the suggested change. The Head was outraged. He read my mother a severe lecture on her short-sighted selfishness in depriving me of my chances. Then he showed her some comparative figures—about telegram boys, coal-heavers, and dockers as against poets, statesmen, and doctors—and explained that boys came miles to his school. So that was that and it was left to me to agree.

Stolidly, and in a nasal whine, sounding and feeling very stupid, I pointed out that it was too far. Finally, I had my way.

Then I ran loose, barefoot, in the streets, for several months. When I was roped in and sent to school, I went to the National place.

I was eleven, and I went in the top form. The reader may believe or not believe, at pleasure, that the form contained boys of thirteen–fourteen, and that I could have been top of it, easily, at nine.

On the first day I spotted two teachers using loose English, and rejoiced in secret. On the same day I solved all the set problems in "Jommethry" in ten minutes—I had done them all, long before, at my own school, had a good memory, knew that text-book backwards.

That afternoon I was given a "Composition" on Agriculture, brazenly reproduced verbatim a lesson from one of my seven-year-old reading books, and got top marks. This new school was fine!

In close on two years at it I learnt nothing, except a few swear-words, the smell of dirty children, the technique of "lining" a girl as explained by the fourteen-year-olds, and the archaic polyglot jargon of the Dublin slums, then and later beloved by James Joyce, and sold to an unsuspecting Britain as literature. I was very happy.

My father knew little of what was passing. Utterly incapable of deception, he was easy to deceive; I fooled him along with glib answers whenever he asked about my studies. I even made a show of borrowing some advanced books of his, but that was mainly for the purpose of getting his treasured book-trunk unlocked. As an advanced and gifted scholar, almost an equal, I got it.

Now I could read as much as I liked, on the quiet, and no one would talk about the fine things I should do. Slum-school finished at three in the afternoon. For me, Life commenced a few minutes later.

I read books about physiology, with plates, and shorthand, with subsidiary works, translations of old Greek writers, metallurgy and watch-making and Shakespeare and select Irish poetry and select English poetry and select French poetry and magnetism and Bret Harte and Jules Verne and practical welding and the *Reporter's Companion*.

Now I would read, and no one could stop me. Bloody hell, bloody hell, bloody hell.

This was a lovely time. My father had a fine selection of books. Also I joined a Public Library. (I remember taking out my first book, being shocked three hours later when I found I could not change it on the same day.) Then I was thirteen and I was going to work.

My mother was nearly crazy when I announced my intentions. But I talked her round—nowadays we would describe my method by saying I appealed to her peasant instincts! If I had a job, I pointed out, then I would have money; I could study at night and give her the money just the same.

The law did not allow boys to work before they were fourteen years old. Except in one job—I never discovered why the exception was made. Wherefore my first ambition was realised. I was going to be a telegram boy. That was the only job for thirteens.

CHAPTER IV

WHILE I was waiting to be "called up" for my telegram job, I went to Tipperary for a few weeks. Actually I wanted to let my mother talk my father out of the opposition I knew he would raise. All in all, I enjoyed myself. Basically, I suppose, the trip meant unhappiness—but basic unhappiness was normal with me by that time.

In the wide bog country, I drifted around, met many Phelans, was made a great fuss of by all, as the great genius and scholar who was going to ——. If they had only known I was going to be a telegraph messenger!

The seemingly illimitable bogs, the calling of curlews, and the sight of a flight of wild geese, the smell of turf fires, the soft broad speech whose sound I had nearly forgotten, the general unthinking hospitality and friendliness, almost incredible after the cold hardness of the city, these captured me at once.

Had my friends but known, there was no need to talk of genius. *They* were the genius, they and their background. I was not anything like that. Between them, they wrote more than one of my books, many of my stories, then and there.

But all I thought of during those first days was that I loved the place and the people. Presently I would go away, to be a telegram boy, and they would be disappointed like my mother and the others. None of that mattered. Tipperary was lovely.

Elect as I was, I could ask a lift from anywhere to anywhere, be certain of a welcome wherever I arrived, could sleep in any one of a dozen widely scattered houses. Being thirteen, a big, powerful boy, inevitably I found a girl for myself.

Even the mean, dirty little mind that was then mine came near to being loosed and healed by the clean bigness of the bogs and the natural freshness and innocence of their people. But the inner load, I suppose, was too heavy, the wasting, sterilising force of the guilt-feelings too powerful.

"Lining" a girl, as explained by the slum-children in my National School, was a furtive and filthy business of sniggerings and shame and whispered meanness. At the end of my affair, I took my girl in a quiet heather-banked part of a bog, and proceeded as indicated by my slum-scholars.

It was Ireland, rural Ireland nearly forty years ago. The girl and I both knew we were about to damn ourselves! My healthy, big-bodied, smiling partner had nothing to say about such things. I, of course, was a failure. The poor girl had committed a deadly sin, risked sending herself to hell, without even attaining a few minutes' happiness.

Seemingly I did not mind much. I had known beforehand that I was different, wrong, helpless, that I could not line girls. So I did not mind much. Then I went back to Dublin.

My mother's way of breaking the news to my father had been to tell him nothing whatever. Wherefore, one night, I told him I was going to work next week. He responded enthusiastically. Good. Going to work on biology? Wasn't it a bit early? Perhaps he could help? Anyway, there were a few good text-books of his own and . . . I said I was going to be a telegraph messenger.

Then the explosion came. But I had my way, although I was on the edge of a dangerous thrashing.

In the end he nearly cried, realising that I had defeated him, that I was not going to provide him with any vicarious triumphs, nor be any kind of genius, nor carry any families on my back, nor get married and try to line girls when I knew I could not. He was beaten and knew it.

The interview with my old Head was nearly as bad. It was necessary to have a reference from him, to get the job—and he refused point-blank to consider anything of the kind.

"A hewer of wood and a drawer of water," he commenced. "James Phelan, the greatest intellect it has been my privilege to train, in forty years of training famous men—a hewer of wood and a drawer of water, carrying wretched telegrams to grubby bookmakers and filthy people in sordid shops. Rubbish. Good-bye. Tell your mother to come and see me."

Almost in desperation, I stuck to my point. Suddenly he asked if I was "doing this for money." I said yes, that we were very poor, which was a lie. How much would I earn, was his next question. I said ten shillings a week, which was also untrue.

"Very well," he summed up. "I'll give you ten shillings a week. Stay at that school until you are tired of it. Then come to me. Will that do?"

Meanly, scared to the marrow, I hedged. A lecture followed, in which he showed he knew everything that was in my mind, about responsibility and all the rest. But I remained unshakable, terrified because I was on the point of being sent back to be "gifted" again.

When he discovered that without his recommendation I would not get the job, he gladly refused to give me even one line. But I knew the answer to that one. Truculently I told him he would have to call me a liar to the Post Office authorities, because I would tell them I had been his best pupil and ask them to write him. I had my way.

Poor Brother Redmond, one of the ten finest teachers in the world, I think, in this century up to now. He knew the possibilities of me, but not the handicaps, knew the power, but not the down-gearing of that power.

That was the end of the attempts to make me a scholar; the end of Brother Redmond's mounting hopes. A lion of learning I was to be made, his way. But I was no lion, nor did I wish to be. Indeed, I went near to becoming a wolf instead, but came in time to be just a masterless dog, road-wandering. With ready fang-slash for threatening hand, but readier tail-wag for every new face—a masterless dog, roaming the roads.

CHAPTER V

My first few weeks at Dublin Central Post Office were very busy and happy. Getting to know the newspaper offices, the Stock Exchange, the Law Courts, the surface life of the big hotels, kept me interested, fed the curiosity which was still the biggest part of me.

At some of the large hotels, a telegram boy who was particularly anxious to please would take the wires upstairs, saving time. Most of my mates dumped the telegrams on the nearest uniformed servant. I was always *very* helpful—my chief interest at the time was to know What Went On In Hotels.

Similarly at the newspaper offices. At a couple of places, late in the evening, one would be called Good Man or given a pat on the shoulder for taking a wire through instead of leaving it with the porter.

Commonsense indicated the porter for the majority. Curiosity always took me upstairs—the newsroom was a paradise. But I never managed to get as far as the machines, although the smell of them fascinated me as it does to-day.

The curiosity got me into trouble once, and almost into Heaven once. The first case was overwhelmingly amusing, except to one unfortunate bureaucrat.

For all minor jobs in the big central offices of the postal department, a boy was temporarily "taken off the streets." Most of us liked these casual assignments—one saw new things and new people. I loved them.

One day I was sent to work in a suite of offices upstairs.

This was the Returned Letter department, and a certain lot of old files were being destroyed. Copies of letters dating back some fifty years were being got rid of, among other things. My job was to sort through the myriad batches of letters, take out the brass fasteners and pins, leave everything else for destruction.

That was all. I was to remove the pins and fasteners, then put the letters in sacks to be burnt. By this time, no reader will be surprised to know that I read every word of every letter—thousands on thousands of them.

Some of the girls, and a few of the clerks, spotted what I was doing and were amused. But one fat old man, who appeared to be in charge, was horrified. I was reading "Government Documents," without being so ordered. He puffed and blew in indignation, threatened to send me back on the streets. All the others were laughing.

The threat was effective—I was exactly the type of boy to be terrified by such things and people. But—I had reached the turning-point in one beautiful series of letters, as interesting in its own way as one of the "Crime-File" type of detection stories. Street or no street, I wanted to know how that battle of epistles had ended.

The war had opened quietly enough, several decades earlier. Someone in Limerick had written asking that the postal authorities should refund him the sum of sixpence, plus his expenses in writing them, sevenpence in all. Because he had been overcharged for the delivery of a letter.

After a further exchange of a few letters he had hit out, with a curt demand for his money, now one shilling and one penny. The Post Office had riposted smartly. A severe communication indicated that his letter had lacked threepence in stamps, for registration. It pointed out that all such omissions were charged double. Hence the sixpence.

Next blow, a few weeks later in date, was from the Limerick man again. His letter, he pointed out, had not been registered, had not needed registration. Therefore, etc. And his expenses were now one shilling and twopence.

That looked like victory. But the Post Office of last century had had a concealed blackjack. Triumphantly the bureaucrat of those days—I imagined him as my fat man's father—had replied with a blast of quoted regulations. Section Z, para. 944: any letter suspected of containing valuables might be registered compulsorily. Under this rule—and so on.

This heavy blow sent three letters in each direction before it had exhausted its force. Then Limerick sent a short communication. His letter had contained no valuables. His expenses were now one shilling and sixpence.

Thereafter the postal people had really hit out. Would Mr. Limerick please find enclosed a copy of the official form (BG 22822), filled in by the official who had compulsorily registered the letter. Would Mr. Limerick please note the reason given, to wit, "Contains a ring"?

No detection-fan ever awaited a *dénouement* as tensely as I waited to grab for the next letter on the file. At which stage my bureaucrat rebuked me for reading the Government's secrets, and ordered me to go on picking pins.

Like a Phillips Oppenheim conspirator, I hid the file, and watched my opportunity. When one came, I dived for the last letter of the correspondence.

It was well worth while. Mr. Limerick had enclosed the envelope of his letter, with a nice plain circular mark on it, where some postman had obviously fumbled round with a thumb. A ring!

He had also enclosed the circular cardboard top of a pill-box. Also a doctor's note saying, "This pill to be taken only in the case of a severe attack." Also a statement that his expenses were now one shilling and eightpence.

The fat man caught me at that moment and had me back on the streets inside half an hour. It was worth while.

The other incident was almost the same, except that it showed a dividend. Also, I think it must have been a turning-point in my life—I made the staggering discovery that an interesting story need not necessarily be a tangle of lies.

In the Instrument Room, where the telegraphists dealt with

the incoming and outgoing wires, there were office boys and messengers in the ordinary way. Telegram boys were not allowed. But again, in an emergency, a couple of boys would be taken off the streets. Wistfully, from the beginning, I had hoped I might get in there one day.

When at last I was sent, in an emergency, my job was even duller than picking out brass fasteners. As a telegraphist scribbled a message from the rap-tapping instrument, I had to pick it up and carry it a few yards to a table for sorting. Outgoing telegrams I distributed along the line of telegraphists. That was all.

Of course I read every word of everything.

Mentally I collected a thousand scraps and fragments, totally unrelated and mostly ambiguous. Like an O. Henry character, who was snow-bound for a whole winter with only one book, an *Enquire Within About Everything,* I was not interested in knowledge—information was different. Again the clerks were amused.

Well on into the third day, in the middle of the pot-pourri, I found that three separate bits of three telegrams going to different people added up to a story. It was very interesting. Then I spied over a fourth telegram, and found another bit that fitted.

Divorce was uncommon in Ireland, then as now. I found myself on the inside of a divorce story. It is difficult to put a name on my dominant emotion, but I can recall my feelings with the greatest ease—I knew something no one else knew yet.

Only as an afterthought, on my way home in the early evening, it occurred to me that everyone would know about this in a few days, when they read the papers. While I. . . . Although I carried no telegram, I hurried to a newspaper office, past the porter, and upstairs.

Years afterwards I worked with the young fellow to whom I gabbled out that night's story. He recalled the incident as clearly as I did, still named it a good job of work.

During the whole of my first recital, and part of the

second, he held out his hand, impatiently, for the telegram I was supposed to carry. Then his manner changed suddenly and he began to ask questions.

At the end he gave me a shilling, and said That Was The Boy. But while I turned away, glowing, he added, "Come in to-morrow. If it's right you get ten shillings. If you're spoofing—I'll have you in Glencree."

Glencree was the big reformatory place, where juvenile offenders went, away on the top of the Dublin mountains!

Nowadays it is easy to see that he had a juicy story, but was taking a chance on a dozen libel suits. If I had misread the many telegrams, or lied about them . . .

But I did not go to Glencree. From that day to this I have never missed even a fragment of a story. *They always add up, somewhere, some time.*

From a thousand small pictures and memories I have chosen only those two, as indicating my reactions to the business life of Dublin. Of all the other myriad things, there was nothing that struck at me, bit into me, or lifted me up. With my companions I was always odd man out, unable to mix, partly because of my "ejjicated" way of talking, partly because I was shy and frightened, considered myself their inferior.

From the earlier chapters, it might appear on the surface that I should have been toughish, quick-witted, a fighter. The direct opposite was nearer the truth. Life at the Post Office did nothing to alter any of my basic thoughts about myself, or about life.

A rather awkward, very reserved boy, probably appearing impassive but generally frightened underneath, I came and went in Dublin Central as on a stage. There were no friends, I had no acquaintances even among the telegram boys, and of course I never spoke to a girl. When an opportunity arose to have myself transferred to a distant sub-station, with only four boys, far down the river, I took it at once.

The sub-station, then called Sir John Rogerson's Quay, was very unpopular with the boys in general. It was a long way from the city, in a muddy, coal-dusty district, with much walking and wandering around docks. I jumped at the chance. The office was right on the riverside, by the ships.

There were three other boys, continually seeking transfers back to the city, continually changing. I stayed. The old lady in charge, a very sweet person, did not take me for a great scholar, nor for a little saint. In the beginning she must have taken me for a half-wit!

Our office was far from busy, which left me with much time for prowling. Most of the telegrams were for shipping offices, for ships in the river, or for the few dockside factories. For a certified postmistress, of however amiable a disposition, the continual search for a telegram boy, among cranes and warehouses and in the galleys of steamers, can only have been a strain. In the end we came to a working agreement, without any words.

If any of the business or shipping executives of the period survive, and chance to read this, they will forgive me, and maybe understand this apology for some of the telegraphic delays of the time. The postmistress and I compromised.

When she had a telegram for me to deliver, she stuck it up in a quayside window. Then, poking my head out occasionally from fo'c'sle or galley or crane-house, I would spot the little orange envelope and hurry back. A very *Dublin* kind of compromise, lovely for me, of course.

For several months I was almost blank, in a dream-state. Books no longer bothered me, nor was I concerned about finding any meaning for the million impressions I soaked in on the riverside. Simply I looked and listened. From the gossip of other boys I knew about "wanting to go to sea," but the idea never occurred to me. Up the docks and down the river, I simply drifted blissfully, receptive, questioning always.

Some of the things I considered important come back to me. The *Cambrian Queen* had five masts, all square rigged. The cook on the *Adela* would give coffee when one brought a telegram. Somebody played the bagpipes, in the fo'c'sle of the *Zillah* from Troon. Going up on the bridge of the *Coquet,* if you weren't careful, you would burn your hand with a steam-pipe, taking it for a handrail.

Hanahash was what the stevedores shouted, when it was dinner-time. "All clear aft," then two long whistles, then a splash as the hawser went into the river, then the rumble-chunk-a-rumble of the donkey engine taking in the loose rope, that was a steamer outward bound. The very farthest bit of Dublin was an iron bollard. You could sit there and look at things. The farthest bit. After that there was no more Dublin, only the sea.

Ventura de Larrinaga should be a Spanish ship, by her name, but the steamer had Liverpool on her stern. Kjobenhavn was the real name of the place geography books call Copenhagen. Grain was a better cargo than coal. *Beryl* and *Cornelian* must be precious stones, because the other ships of the same line were called *Pearl, Diamond, Agate,* and so on.

Suwanee—oh, miracle—was an oil-tanker from Texas, named after the place silly people called, in songs, the Swanny River. The wife of the cook of the *Bessie Barr* had had a baby in Bristol, where the Severn came down to the sea. The cranes, the big cranes, the magic of the giant cranes—and there was a telegram in the window.

Some of the things I considered important come back to me!

I only lasted about six months at Sir John Rogerson's Quay, and it was a miracle I survived so long. One day, in a very foolish brawling fashion as I can now see, I simply refused to carry a telegram, manœuvred the three others into similar refusal. We were all reported for insubordination, I as the ringleader, and I was dismissed on the spot. Stupefied with horror, I went home, not feeling like a ringleader of anything, a very frightened boy whose world had come to an end.

Next day I was to hand in my uniform and equipment, draw my few shillings in wages, and so on. But naturally my mother did not know anything of the immutability of dismissal from a Government job—she made me write a series of apologies to everyone concerned. (The personal factor bulked very large in the Ireland of those days.) I wrote the letters and took them along with my uniform.

Near the office on Sir John Rogerson's Quay, before delivering the long written apology to the postmistress, I faltered and hung around the quayside for a long time. My thoughts consisted mainly of daydreams in which everything turned out all right. But I loitered along the quays nevertheless. Then I had a cup of coffee in the galley of the *Braeside,* to cheer me up a little.

Dicker Graham, the cook, passed some joking remark about my being in "civvies," otherwise nobody noticed. The *Braeside* often came to Dublin with coal, and I knew every corner of her. Blank, preoccupied, and entirely without plan or purpose, I loitered in a corner of the steerage.

Then I heard sounds I had only known, previously, from the quayside. "Let go aft" was followed by the splashing, the whistles, the chug-a-rum-arum of the donkey engine, and a few minutes later the steerage of the *Braeside* began to go up and down.

If I had any thoughts that night, they have left few memories. All I recollect is a quiet, stupid satisfaction, wakeful dreaminess, as I swayed to the heavings of the steerage. Except that I went over, several times, a story I had heard on Dublin riverside.

This was about two men who stowed away on a big steamer. They concealed themselves in the chain-locker—the place where the anchor-chain is coiled below, when the anchor is up. The narrators, in the cafés of dockside Dublin, would pass over that part casually, merely describing how the men got a couple of coats and settled down for the night when the ship had sailed.

Then—there would be a pause here—hours later out at sea a war-vessel signalled the steamer to stop. She dropped her anchor. So the two men came up through the hawse-hole, in bits the size of your hand. Out in the Irish sea, that night on the *Braeside,* I remember shivering because I was not *too* sure where the chain-locker was.

Dicker Graham swore, but only in astonishment and amusement, when I strayed into the galley next morning. Neither he nor the mate bothered about me. As far as they were concerned, it was a joke—I had stayed a little too long aboard, had been fetched out to sea by accident. Long before I had finished breakfast I believed it myself.

Decent fellows that they were, Graham and the others at once set about working out some means of getting me home. There were many chances—the *Braeside* was bound to Glasgow, and there were always steamers loading coal for Ireland there. But in the end they whipped round the few shillings to pay my fare back. Chief embarrassment was that the mate wanted to send a wire to my mother.

Of course I was never going home any more, but I took the money for my fare, and wrote down the instructions for finding the passenger steamer. When the *Braeside* tied up in Glasgow, I waited for Dicker Graham to take me ashore and, having listened carefully to all his instructions, turned blindly up the first side-street as soon as we parted.

To me Glasgow looked, smelt, and sounded like a dream-town. Now this was a real foreign city at last. I could not understand one word of the speech. Heaven!

After the first couple of hours' wandering, I drifted away from the city centre and the shops. Something like the Coombe district in Dublin, I judged the place where I found myself. (Later I learnt to call it the Gallowgate.) From some ragged boys I learnt about lodgings—share of a slum room cost fourpence, and two of the boys lived there. Carefully, almost religiously, I set myself to imitate their speech.

Years later I knew a wealthy and cultured young Frenchman who, having had the misfortune to slay someone during his first few hours in England, found himself in prison for years. Promptly and of necessity he learnt English—in Dartmoor and similar places.

It was vastly funny to hear him break from the French

equivalent of an Oxford accent into, "I ups an' ses to 'im, I ses, 'Look 'ere,' I ses, 'wotcha tike me for?' I ses." He told me, often, that the English language sounded marvellous to him. That was the way I learnt to speak Scotch, in the Gallowgate.

The *Braeside* money, and my few shillings wages, lasted for nearly a month. Towards the end, after walking about all one winter's night, I learnt to "keep my stall," to retain the fourpence for my lodging-money at all costs. This fourpence, with a penny for breakfast of tea and bread, made up the bulk of my day's expense. I was very happy.

Sometimes, with other slum boys, I went to beg from the workmen who came from Park Head Forge. One caught glimpses of great flashing fires, heard the thumping of mighty hammers somewhere. Then the crowds of men came out, on their way home.

The begging was very simple. Many of the men would be carrying home part of their midday meal, uneaten. We stood, in a little crowd, and repeated continually, "Any bread? Any bread?" The men gave us much more than we could eat.

(Almost I had forgotten! Our chorus was "Onny br-raid? Onny br-raid?" My own accent was the thickest and most raucous of the group.)

Most of my days were spent in prowling, in the neighbourhood of the docks for preference. But the riverside was not at all like Dublin's. Big warehouses, dead walls, locked gates, hostile men with notebooks, came between the prowler and— and whatever it was I looked at. All I remember is a meaningless list of ships and ports.

My companions were far too practical for any such occupation, and again I began to feel over-shy and reserved, something from which I had known blessed freedom for a few weeks. Gradually I came to dislike the boys, discovering them as clumsy, foolish liars *who could not even tell lies*. The end came one evening at the "pickshers."

A sailor had given me a shilling, and although penniless except for the solitary coin, I had spent eightpence on taking a boy to the cinema, retaining only the vital fourpence "stall."

The pictures cannot have been very enthralling (it was 1908), for the other boy and I talked most of the time. A slum-boy, with one leg, a drifter like myself, he lived at my lodgings, had no family as far as I knew. That evening he told about having escaped from a reformatory.

I had read about Glencree near Dublin, knew of reformatories by hearsay only. But after the first few minutes I picked a hundred holes in the story. These were the silliest lies I had ever heard—far worse than even Ann Gaynor used to tell herself, when I was two, in Inchicore. And this one-legged boy, fourteen or so, was the leader, the bravest and most experienced of all. The Gallowgate was beginning to let me down!

The most thrilling part of the escape story ended with the loss of my boy-friend's leg. How, I enquired. Shot off, he explained. He carried a pair of crutches, got about with ease, had no wound or bandage. Yet his leg had been "shot off" some seven weeks earlier. My Gallowgate dream-world began to fall apart.

Outside the cinema I simply walked away. Although it was evening and I still clutched the fourpence in my trouser pocket, I did not go near the lodging-house, went prowling aimlessly along the river. To-morrow I would find another stall; I was never going back with that crowd any more. Shot off!

Wandering, I had come to an unfamiliar part of the river without noticing. Men were at work, although it was late, and there was much crashing and dirt. Coal was pouring down, by the million tons it seemed, from a high framework where railway wagons continually tipped. I had never seen coal loaded before—in Dublin it always came *out* of the ships.

Then I jumped, as if my mother had spoken to me, and knew a pleasure I have known a thousand times since. Yet it was only a name on the stern of a ship, the *Zillah* of Troon. I jumped again when a man shouted, "Hello there, Ninety." Ninety was what the crew of the *Zillah* called me for preference, instead of my name. (It was the number I wore on the collar of my post-office uniform.)

Everyone on the steamer knew me, and I was having a man-sized supper in the galley within ten minutes. The man who had hailed me, the donkey-man, was a great reader—we had talked books by the hour when the steamer was in Dublin, with special reference to the writings of one Robert Burns, whose works I had stolen from my father's trunk.

Almost without words it was decided that I was going to Ireland with them—they were taking a cargo of coal to Dublin Gas-works. Next morning I skulked past Sir John Rogerson's Quay post office, and headed for home.

There was no beating, with leather strap or otherwise, at that home-coming. (My parents had thought I was drowned in the Liffey: the relief cancelled the anger.) In the following days no one mentioned school. Nor did anyone suggest that I should go to work again!

For several months thereafter I ran around with boys from the slum streets, something which had been frowned on before. Apparently my mother knew little of what I was doing. My father knew nothing.

Again I was thoroughly happy. Raucous and brawling, untidily dressed, telling a thousand lies about my seafaring, I roamed the streets.

Almost without cessation I swore and blasphemed, as befitted a hard-bitten sailor, the whole in a very thick and powerful Scots accent. Books I never thought of, nor any nonsense about being a genius. I was a ragamuffin boy at last, and life was very good.

CHAPTER VI

It would be foolishly unfair to the reader, to myself, to my parents, and the Irish people in general, if I left the story of my early years to stand without a word of comment. Of necessity, I have touched only on the high-spots of my childhood. The result may be to leave a false impression of my parents.

Although I did not know at the time, I am well aware now that certain events were important in shaping my life. Calculated to mould a statesman or judge, they produced instead a tramp who writes middling-readable stories. Intended to evoke something equivalent to the orations of Demosthenes, in time they fetched forth the terse pragmatical slogan, "Onny br-raid?"

Perforce I have stressed those events, and as an inevitable consequence, my parents may be seen as the villains of the piece. Through no fault of mine or of theirs, there may be a conception of them as cruel or even brutal people, alternately bullying a small sensitive child into premature and unhealthy erudition, or inflicting the most savage and inhuman floggings for very minor offences. They were not thus.

My mother was a very lovable person indeed, the kind of woman who would literally have died for her children. Her maternal affection I can only describe by calling it fierce, unreasoning, animal. Mothers nurtured in cities, living in the busy places of the world, seldom attain such intensity of feeling. It may be just as well.

As for me, I was always her favourite, quite apart from her apparently mercenary hopes. That lasted. Long after she knew

I was never going to be any of the things she had planned, it lasted. Often, later, when I drifted in from nowhere, she gave me her last few pounds.

In my childhood she only really beat me twice, on the occasions of which I have told. Only in falsehood or folly should I leave the two incidents to stand as representative.

The lashing with the leather strap—I can see and feel it now; it was a long, dark-brown leather band from my schoolbooks—certainly was a terrible beating. But, one must remember that we lived in a predominantly peasant country.

In an industrial city, in the towns of mechanical civilisation, if a capstan lathe or a drilling machine goes amiss, one uses oilcan or wrench. Where mule, horse, and donkey are the machines, other habits become natural. That explains nearly all.

But I think a major factor, each time my mother beat me, was definitely and unmistakably a growth from the fierce, powerful mother-love. She was crazily afraid, always, that after one of my runaways a mangled, smashed little body would be carried home, from railway siding or cliff bottom. The apparent cruelty followed.

My father only beat me once, to speak of, by the fountain in the Dublin park. There was another occasion, when at fifteen I spoke roughly to my mother, and he just knocked me cold with one punch on the chin, but I was a man then and deserved it. He, too, was devoted to all of us. His life went in struggling, with an intensity which I *could not* at that time comprehend, to make things easy and to give us some minor advantages in the world whose harshness he knew so well.

But there was never any real contact between us. Grave, logical, intensely religious, he was quite incapable of making friends with me or with any boy. Chief barrier was the fact that he always spoke in a dignified, stilted speech, totally unlike that of the people around him, which did not facilitate confidences.

They called him "Gentleman Whalen" in the places where he worked and the districts where we lived—maybe that will sum him up. From England or America I can think of only one person who might perhaps have been able to converse confidentially with my father—W. H. Davies, author of *The Autobiography of a Super Tramp*.

("Hold," said the marshal. "Did not I myself observe you loitering listlessly by the water-tank, even while the east-bound train departed?" A town marshal in the United States once said that, or something like it, to Davies, according to the diary. Any marshals I ever met would have shortened the oration to "C'mon, you." But if Gentleman Whalen had been the marshal, he would have addressed Davies in just such a speech.)

Of course there was not the slightest chance of my father and I ever understanding one another—in time for it to make any difference. To-day no one will call me a Pharisee for being glad it was so. Although or because I am a tramp.

Many writers on vagabondage have set out to make the position clear. They show the choice between misery and hunger, but with freedom, on the one hand, and comfortable security, but with galling restraint, on the other. Readers will be familiar with the problem, and with a tramp's solution of it, as told by various gifted writers on the subject.

> *"In belly-need I will pay the price,*
> *But—God—let me be free,*
> *For once I know, in the long ago,*
> *They made a slave of me."*

That poem sets forth the dilemma, and the choice, as Robert Service saw them. Any tramp in the world will agree with me that no greater balderdash was ever penned. But it gained currency, because it was at one time a *sine qua non* that people who wrote about tramps should never have been tramps.

Until Jack London and Bart Kennedy, W. H. Davies, Jim Tully, and the rest set up real vagrant-literature against the other effusions, like nugget by goldbrick, only spurious writings on vagabondage were considered acceptable. I think the author of the vagrant verse was, of all things in the wide round world, a bank-clerk.

Tramps do not become tramps in order to pay prices nor to know belly-need nor to be let go free. While I am glad my father and I never ran in harness together, I am only pleased with what I think a sensibly-selfish pleasure, because in my own way I got to know a host of likeable people, did a thousand lovely things, walked along the roads because I liked it, learnt to write of the walking that other more practical people might like it too.

No belly-need. No price. Freedom? Any man can have that, anywhere—in a ship-chandler's office, or Park Head Forge, or in a jail-cell twelve by seven—if he knows what he wants.

Sometimes, in the road wanderings, I have not eaten, true. But no one must expect me to sing about belly-need, or to name the hunger as the price I pay for freedom. A doctor friend of mine gets fifty guineas a week from many patients for starving them on orange juice and water. But it cannot have been this kind of belly-need R. W. S. had in mind.

A wealthy friend once invited my wife and myself to lunch, to discuss some business. Actually, the business consisted of working out the best method for him to give me quite a large sum of money. In brief, he liked my work, and was prepared to back his liking with several hundred pounds. He had done as much for many other writers—the list would be longish. A genuine modern Mæcenas!

During lunch, his daughter and he spoke of many subjects allied to Yogi. Both had gone deeply into such matters. From there we went on to the subject of fasting, religious, medical, and other varieties.

All of us knew a little about hunger-strikes and starvation-cures, about the astonishing feats of some Eastern mystics in abstention from food. But the choice of subject seemed rather bizarre, since my wife and I taxed the resources of the fashionable restaurant to the utmost, eating enough for six hungry labourers.

The incongruity must have amused our hosts, because a little later, with twinkling eyes, my friend made some dry comment about our voracity. Everyone laughed.

"Oh! Forgot to tell you," explained my wife. "We haven't had a meal for close on two weeks."

It was true, too. Nor was it the first time. *But it was the writers who were starving, not the tramps.*

A tramp, as distinct from an itinerant work-seeker, is a man or woman whose outlook on the purpose of life differs from that of the majority. That is all one can say and be certain. Having talked, argued with, and studied the top-rank tramps of Britain and France, Ireland and Italy and the United States, that is as far as I can go, even now.

At the very beginning of this book, in the story of my four-year-old days, we have seen what happens to the theory that tramps are produced by unemployment crises. The immediate alternative will not suffice either. It is not the slightest use saying that a tramp is a person too lazy to work.

No wage-worker ever laboured as hard as a tramp will, on occasion. Personally I have often worked sixteen, eighteen, twenty hours a day. Once I wrote a sixty-thousand-word book in a week, because I would have to pawn my typewriter and get out on the road at the end of that time. Harvesting farmers, in the Middle West of America, know the almost incredible exertions which may be expected from a tramp if he likes harvest-work. The glib explanation of laziness will not serve.

The equally glib dictum about lack of tenacity is of even less value. Compare the degree of tenacity required to keep a job, by going to the office each morning at nine without fail, beside that called for by a walk from Calais to Vladivostok or from New York to San Francisco. Yet people have walked those distances. With no purpose known to anyone on earth, not for pleasure or profit or pride, people have walked them. Tenacity!

By this time anyone will know me for a quite sufficiently dogmatic person. Neither I nor anyone else can dogmatise

here. But the dissipation of spurious dogmas, from romantic
or uninformed writers, helps a little. It helps to take the reader
with me, in understanding how I was to be shaped in early
Dublin, and how the shaping went wrong, and why I am glad
my father and I never properly communed.

In the nature of things it was simply impossible for us to get
together. Therefore, since he was a man and I was a boy, I
avoided him as much as possible after my return from Glasgow.
Meanwhile I ran wild.

Thus, in South Earl Street, near the Coombe of Dublin, any
evening in the summer of 1909, a yell might be heard from
some ragamuffin boy of "Jim Phelan, here's your father."
Then a large, sunburnt, particularly ragged and generally barefoot boy, with a strong Scots accent mainly used for swearing,
would duck into a doorway.

Presently a tall, erect, springily-stepping man who looked
straight in front of him would pass. Whereupon the boy would
emerge.

Often he passed within a foot of me without noticing. (He
never came to know even one person in the whole district,
during many years. In my rags and dirt, I believe I could have
confronted him face to face; he would have glanced, unseeing,
past the slum boy.)

When my father had passed, I would wait until he had had
his supper and gone to bed before I went home. In the morning he would have gone out before I was up. So that he simply
had no idea what I *was,* at that time. Work-weariness, general
apathy, and frightened evasions by my mother helped to post-
pone, again and again, any real enquiry as to what I was
doing.

I was, in fact, enjoying life very much indeed. About nine
in the morning I slipped out, after my breakfast, to run with
eight or ten slum boys in a nearby street. Here again I was
without any real friend or acquaintance, and I was always
"one odd," but I managed to conceal it successfully.

The uncouth speech and thought-habits remained always
beyond my comprehension. Nor could I make the myriad little

self-deceptions which seemed to be such an important part of life for my companions. (God! How I wanted to do just that! How I wanted to be careless and happy and without any inner biting, like Monkey Miles, Jewman Timmins, Dogger Dale, and the rest.)

My being "ejjicatified" was always a serious barrier. But I took care that it was offset by the fact that I had been a sailor, spoke Scotch, and could swear much more loudly than anyone else.

We swam many times a day, climbed trees, caught pigeons and sold them, wandered far afield after mushrooms, gathered bundles of hay on market-days and sold them for sweet-money. Later we picked blackberries, and gave them away so that we could boast of having been "down the country." (Dubliners seldom go far from the city, even nowadays. In 1909, a walk of five miles after blackberries was an Odyssey—for adult or juvenile.)

For the rest of our time we fought and scrambled and ran yelling through the streets. No one ever stole anything, I remember, nor did we smoke, and we never tried to "line" girls, so that we were, in fact, fairly harmless. Just slum boys, in a slum.

Looking back, quite coolly, I thank my great good fortune for having had the experience. Because, with my tautly drawn inner strings, if it had not been for the brutal and primitive healthiness of those few months, almost anything could have happened to me.

There might have been somewhere, now, a kinky, unhappy neurotic snarling his vicious fantasies at the world. Or a queer warped unpleasantness leering at boys in a city centre. Or a wretched *voyeur* earning an occasional month's imprisonment as a Peeping Tom in some public park. All the possibilities were there. The crude, healthy animalism of my slum-running saved me.

After the first week or two in the Liberty, as the ancient, ramshackle district was called, I discovered, with something of a shock, that the language there was every bit as interesting, in its own way, as that of the Gallowgate in Glasgow. Previously, before my Post Office days, I had made two or three attempts to mix with the slum boys, but had never completely succeeded. Now I was one of them, and I was learning.

The curious, twisted, old-world, lumpy speech of slum-Dublin comes back to me as I write—a strange mosaic of word-fragments from half a dozen countries. Although I tried hard, I could never use it with ease. (Probably the gulf between my father's pedantic English and what was later to be called "Joycean prose" was too great.) I knew the language, though, almost as well as Dogger Dale and better than the author of *Ulysses*.

Jack bung your eye had a fol-the-diddle-eye-doh hanging down to his knee, and if you were a Moxer, with a sign on your body, you could give a wigger a flah up the long entry or even polka lowri up a motts geesh, if she was a hair-baiter, smood.

James Joyce? A passage from *Finnegan's Wake*? Well, no. That is Jewman Timmins, from Mulluckses Coort in the Liberty of Dublin, talking of the things adolescents discuss, in the ordinary slum-talk of the district, *circa* 1909.

For many years I have had an almost passionate interest in philology. It dates from those days, by the Coombe. Why "flah," I wanted to know, very early indeed, since I knew already from nudge and snigger that the word meant the pro-creative act. But no one in the Liberty could help. My companions knew little of any other words than their own.

For long I have been proud because I discovered for myself the philological principle that "embarrassment" words, about sex and excretion and the like, also swear-words and blasphemy, are very often borrowed from the previous language of the country in which they are used. The discovery was forced on me in 1909. I simply had to find out about words like flah!

Naturally I carried my "researches" too far, as did, later, the many students of Joyce who found esoteric and ultra-Freudian significance in phrases like "up the long entry." As a slum boy, knowing the words at first hand, I did not fall into that particular error.

Unlike some savants—especially one industrious but unfortunate German—I knew about Long Entry. It was an alley in Joyce's time, is now a brick-rubbled ruin, but the official place-name still survives. However, there is a sufficiency of genuine Liberty language in Joyce!

Nibbling in the dictionaries, for some clue to the words we used daily, I found that many of my companion's words were the Gaelic equivalents of what one may, for politeness, call the strong "Anglo-Saxon monosyllables." But my companions did not know that. Nor did their parents. Hardly any adults, even in Dublin knew. I found out. Once again I knew something no one else knew yet!

Joyce found out too. My belief is that he never discovered much besides, about those words, never got beyond the secretive-exultant stage.

I can write the word "flah" here without offence. To print the English translation-word would be illegal. Flah, flah, flah —one can easily imagine it sounding wonderful to a certain type of mind.

Now I am taking the reader along with me at last! I came very near to having that type of mind too. But my barefoot-running, my knowledge of the facts as well as the words of slumdom, saved me. Besides, I had had my magic words, in full measure, and the maximum thrill from them, at six. Of course I had—bloody hell, bloody hell, bloody hell!

Adapting myself to the use of the Liberty words was by no means as easy as it may sound. I was never very happy about it, was acting all the time, would have been on surer ground with Latin or French or even the intricacies of the Gallowgate dialect.

Quite clearly I remember being alternately jeered at and praised for my "ejjification." Until one night I talked a policeman round, after he had caught a gang of us plundering a strawberry garden. After that I was not jeered any more.

Probably the incident could not have occurred anywhere else

but in Ireland. We had raided the same garden on the previous night, and very foolishly repeated our visit. A policeman was hidden in the bushes, waiting.

He collared two of us—I was one—and shepherded the others into a corner by moral force. While he hesitated, probably cogitating over the best way to arrest nine healthy fourteen-year-olds, I began to argue. My fibbing-voice was back, instead of the harsh imitation-Glasgow accent I then habitually used, and after a few seconds the policeman pricked up his ears.

Deliberately and of malice aforethought I used the phrase *in flagrante delicto* twice. An Irish policeman, in my reckoning, would know the phrase, would be proud of his Latin, would talk back to someone who also understood such learned and weighty discourse.

He did. We talked, and I flattered that policeman's conceit of learning shamelessly. We talked, and in the end he completely dismissed the purpose for which he had been sent there, praised me, recalled that he had himself learnt Latin from serving at Mass.

We talked, and he quoted a long poem called "Mesgedra," while we walked along by the canal towards Dublin, my companions trailing warily behind. At the edge of the city he said good-night, with all the grave punctilio due from one scholar to another, told me, almost *en passant,* not to raid gardens any more.

Thereafter I was famous by the Coombe. Alas for my poor mother's hopes—here was the first-fruit of the gifts and the learning; it tasted very sweet indeed to me.

In that summer I learnt to catch pigeons by hand, learnt the ways of fish in a canal and the method of milking a cow, furtively, at night in a field. But the home-life of the slums, to which I came only occasionally, was always the most thrilling.

Casting round for some picture or incident which may serve to limn the Liberty, three things come back to me. The marriage of Mary Ellen leaves me uncertain, even to-night, whether to growl with rage, choke down a half-sob of pity, or laugh.

Mary Ellen was just barely below the norm of slumdom, which is to say she was on the edge of being weak-minded. About five feet high, twentyish, with the gangling gait of such people, she had a little innocent face which every now and then, in the strangest way, aged suddenly. One was never quite certain whether Mary Ellen was fifteen or eighty-nine.

She had fantasies, naturally. Two of them were common property around the Liberty. In one, she would have wealth and be happy when her father came down from the pillar. (The pillar was the Nelson Monument in Dublin. Lord Nelson was Mary Ellen's father in the story, and was to be "turned back from stone," when she would live happily ever afterwards.)

Her second story was about a soldier lover who had gone to the wars. (There was no war at that time.) He would fetch home a ring, a frock, and a wrist-watch soon. Then he and Mary Ellen would be married.

Completely crazy, that much of Mary Ellen seemed, but she was sufficiently slum-practical in most other ways. Her stories were of course a joke in the district. A hundred people in a day might enquire when her soldier was coming home.

Oilcan Odlum, about twenty-five, was rather less than five feet high, thin and chinless. His physique may be deduced from his nickname—a Dublin oilcan had shoulders which sloped at the rate of one in two. He also was feeble-minded. He also had fantasies. But no tramp or beggar in the world was ever so moderate in his wish-thinking as Oilcan.

"I might get a job for the Christmas." That was what Oilcan said, when drunk or feeling boastful or in particularly cheerful humour. Just that—he might get a job for the Christmas. The fantasy sufficed for several years. Then one day Mary Ellen claimed that Oilcan was her soldier returned from the wars.

Oilcan's mother, a beggar-woman who did something else for a living at night, up the long entry way—I never found out what—threw a kettle of water over Mary Ellen the first time she called. But Mary Ellen called again. Oilcan liked it. In time he almost remembered having *been* to the wars.

Beggars, slum women, racecourse drifters, tramps, ballad-singers, rag-pickers, apple-women, and all the colourful, raucous, roaring, drunken denizens of the Liberty took the pair to their bosoms at once. Everyone encouraged them. Oil-can was given countless pints. Mary Ellen started a collection, from door to door, for her dowry. Then they went to the priest and announced that they wanted to get married!

The priest, like a sensible man, in effect told the two poor imbeciles to run away and play. That concluded the business, and Mary Ellen decided that, after all, Oilcan was not her returned soldier.

But the beggars-opera populace around Mulluckses Coort (the name on the street wall was Molyneux Lane) would not be denied. Mary Ellen and Oilcan had a wedding.

Drunken parties, in a big way, were common in the Liberty. A prostitute would "have luck"—with some sailor-man's well-filled wallet. The racecourse drifters might get on the right side of some drunken farmer who had won heavily at the races. Scutchy Callaghan the ragman occasionally got several pounds for a load of old clothes bought from "country mugs" for a few shillings. Some gay-girl's tip for a race, picked up from a client, might result in temporary wealth for a dozen people. The sequel was always a "hooley."

Open house, in one of the crazy, foul-smelling rookeries of rooms, quantities of liquor for all-comers, was a "hooley." But there had never been any "hooley" to compare with Mary Ellen's marriage.

It started in a spirit of half-drunken, half-mercenary mischief. Some of the slum women induced Mary Ellen herself to provide the funds, close on thirty pounds. They sent her around the whole Liberty district to beg at every door, "For her wedding." It was a district-wide joke, and the money flowed in.

Instead of stealing the dowry, Mulluckses Coort held a wedding for Mary Ellen and Oilcan. Reeling and rolling, squabbling drunkenly or laughing like clowns out of some nightmare pantomime, bawling the crudely-obscene but always interesting ballads of the Liberty, they married Mary Ellen.

Scutchy Callaghan's rag-bag furnished a clergyman's clothes, worn by a loafer called the Bishop, who was alleged to be, and may possibly have been, an unfrocked priest. Some two dozen drunken rag-pickers and beggars fought for the privilege of being best man.

The rest needs no writing. Hogarth never came even remotely near the picture of Mary Ellen's marriage. I can still see an ancient, witch-like, hunchbacked creature, with red eyes and white hair, pressing Mary Ellen to choose a lover from between the ragmen, all returned soldiers.

Throat-growl or strangled sob or . . . Well, it is wrong of me, I suppose, very wrong; I can only laugh at the memory. But on that particular night I considered throwing a big can of paraffin on the floor—there was no gas or electric light in the Liberty—and sending up the lot in flames. It would have been a perfect finish to the saturnalia!

The second picture places itself not far away from Mulluckses Coort, in an alley called Screaming Gap, I never discovered why. (The place had no postal name, I believe.) One evening I strayed into a small house with some of my boy-friends. Only after several minutes, after a bottle of lemonade and some cakes, I discovered that there was a dead girl in a bed.

The Liberty people sat and drank and quarrelled all night around her, spending the money they had got from the insurance company. Then, in the dark hours of the morning, they carried her a few miles out into the country, dug a hole in a little village graveyard, slipped her in and hurried away.

No funeral expenses. No cemetery fees. No fuss and nonsense, and a saving of all the money for liquor. While at the same time—a very important matter in Ireland—the corpse was buried in consecrated ground! Again, a very *Dublin* solution. Hundreds of people have called *The Slip* my best story. It came from there.

Dogger Dale and Jewman Timmins took me to "fadge" one summer evening. In a wide thoroughfare, cutting through the heart of the Liberty district, a little crowd of men and women gossiped outside a pub. Occasionally a few went inside, a few others emerged, and the group was in fairly constant motion. A ballad-singer bawled a song about "A twang-shop on the banks of Pim-lee-co," and much money went into his ragged hat. From the pub came the sound of a banjo.

Many of the Liberty residents were, in one way or another, camp-followers of the big race-meetings. After each there was a celebration. Beggars and bookmakers, touts and tramps and tricksters, gay-girls and adjuncts, everyone celebrated. Jewman and Dogger picked the most drunken and begged. That was fadging.

It would have been easy to feel superior, because I did not want to fadge. But I had the good sense to remember that I had my "stall" and the others had not! Presently I was fadging sixpences from a drunken, red-faced man and his brilliantly scarved partner, from a girl who wore silk stockings and high-heeled shoes but had a dirty shawl for the rest of her clothes, from the negro with the banjo.

The last was a gross blunder, since the banjoist was in effect fadging himself. He had been brought from the races, on an outside car, by some of the half-drunken Liberty people. Angry and nearly drunk, he pushed me away roughly, threw me down on the pavement. A burly ponce from the Mulluckses Coort district promptly felled him. Someone else hit the ponce with a bottle.

In three minutes the wide street was filled with staggering, swearing, flailing people. Screams and oaths rang around the Liberty, and as I hurried away towards home, the crash of breaking bottles sounded behind.

Those three pictures will serve to paint the place where I learnt not to be "ejjicatified," but where I was happy as a ragamuffin boy. Living less than three hundred yards distant, my father had no knowledge of any such life, my mother only knew of it from frightened and half-heard whisperings.

In my few months around the Liberty I grew very fast. There is a photo, taken one day when I had been cleaned up for some forgotten purpose—a bulky, brown-faced youth, about five feet eight, with broad shoulders, deep dark-brown eyes, a weak chin.

That last item will sound amusing to those who know me. For many years I have had a kind of battering-ram chin—a very determined appearance, as old-fashioned people would say. There was no hint of it in 1909.

G. B. Shaw asserts, in effect, that if a person wants to live for three hundred years, he need only so decide—and mean it. Somewhere in the Christian Scriptures it is apparently stated that a man cannot, by taking thought, add a cubit to his stature. Only apparently—because the passage is really a question. Before ever I had read Shaw, my answer to that question would have been, "Certainly."

No money of mine is available to wager that a man could swim the Atlantic if he so desired. At least . . . Well, I am not certain! *But I think Oilcan Odlum wanted to be Oilcan Odlum, down at bottom.* I think if a man really meant it, he could most certainly add a cubit to his stature.

As soon as I learnt about strong men with determined chins, about 1909, I wanted myself changed. Most clearly I remember that it used to hurt my jaw like hell, "wishing a big chin on myself." Amusing sequel is that nowadays I would rather not have the long jaw—but I am too lazy to start wishing it back.

I was growing to be a big powerful boy at the end of my Liberty running. My arms were very strong, and I could lift a boy nearly my own size in my teeth, with a belt around his middle. My showing-off of this accomplishment brought my slum-life to a close.

Gradually, as always, I had come to feel awkward and uncomfortable with my companions, to dislike them, to feel contempt for their crude habits of thought and speech, even while I envied and hankered to imitate them. Slowly I drifted again into the isolation which had been my torment, always, everywhere. There were no words for it in my life, but I knew, clearly, that I was coming to be a failure as a ragamuffin boy.

Inevitably, I suppose, I came to depend on the trump cards of my size and strength. The other boys did things I was afraid to know, talked of things I feared, deep inside me, to understand. Odd man out, again, I ran less with the gang, found my only triumphs in heaving a big stone, or in lifting a big boy between my teeth.

One evening, on a side-street pavement, I had lifted a boy in this way for the delectation of various slum women, when the evening shout of "Here's your father" sounded with unusual urgency. I could not drop the boy—such an attempt may rip out one's teeth—and before he had reached the pavement my father was standing over me, white with passion, his mouth set hard. The tenement women shrank muttering away.

"Go home," was all he said, and I walked sheepishly in front of him to our house. My mother nearly fainted when she saw us enter together. Even then I did not realise that my father was so completely ignorant of my ragamuffin status. The discovery must have given him a terrible jolt. He sat down at a table, stood me in front of him, stared at me long in sinister silence.

Barefoot and in rags, I was also dirty and uncouth-looking, the more so because of my size. Further, I was scared stiff, which did not, I suppose, help to make me appear any the more prepossessing.

"Are you an idiot?" he asked at last. I said nothing.

Then he *roared,* ordering me to answer. I said I was not an idiot.

His next question was, "Why?" Promptly I said I *was* an idiot—line of least resistance—and ducked from the blow I expected. It did not come.

He groaned, painfully, instead, and kept silence for a long time. At last, wrinkling his nose in disgust, he took me by one shoulder with finger and thumb, and turned me round. Then he turned me back again, looked at my mother and said, "I presume this *is* our offspring?" She began to cry, and then there was another long silence.

"Well," he said at last, very quietly. "I always thought you were too good for a workshop. Now I think a workshop is far too good for *you*. Does this person possess any clothes?" he enquired of my mother. She nodded silently, and I was ordered to have a bath and sent to bed. Most of the night I stayed awake thinking that the boys in the Gallowgate were not so bad.

At six the next morning my mother wakened me. "Hush," she whispered fearfully. "Get up and dress. You have to go to the works."

She pronounced the words as if she meant that I had to go to the gallows. To me they were a magical incantation. The works! I shot out of bed and was dressed before my father came down.

He did not speak once, while we walked half a mile through the streets in the mist of the morning. Nor did he speak in the train while we went a couple of miles to Inchicore, where he had worked when I was a baby. He was employed there again, and it was to that "works" I was going. In the intervals of pretending to be depressed I walked on air.

It was exciting to get off the train with all those hundreds of men, to see other and still other hundreds coming, in four unbroken streams, into the great straggling works a couple of miles square. Locomotives hissed, the rattle and flash of machine-belts came from a shed, and I could hear a ponderous rhythmic thumping, like that of Park Head Forge, which thrilled me even then, although I did not yet know it was a giant steam-hammer.

My father told me, coldly, to wait, while he went in an office. Half an hour later I was at a machine, facing nuts. This meant turning them, in a small lathe, but the work required no skill, and I was left alone after less than an hour.

Beside me, three feet away inside a little railed enclosure, a big five-foot pulley hummed and sang, driving the main shaft of all the machine-shop. It was in one of the earliest stories I ever wrote; it was in a film story delivered only a few weeks before these lines were written. Perhaps this is the best way to tell how it impressed me. And I was being sent here for punishment!

There was only one man in the workshop. Boys were at the few other machines. Through the wall near me I could hear the most damnable and most intriguing noise. Boiler-shop, I was told.

Across a low wooden partition came ghostly flashes of light now and then, and the crunching of some potent machine torturing hot metal. Fifty yards away, in full view if I turned my back to the lathe, an enormous steam-hammer thumped and thudded on a big block of near-molten steel, twisted and turned by a red-shirted man who looked like the Gownseer of my mother's stories.

Miracle—when I made excuse to pass that way I saw its name. Cyclops! (Later it shocked me to find that hardly anyone in that part of the works knew what the word meant. But that morning I neither knew nor cared.) It and the Gownseer were in full view if I turned my back to the lathe. In those early days I turned my back to it often. Punishment!

CHAPTER VII

In the place where I first worked at Inchicore, half a dozen machines turned out screws, nuts, bolts, very little else. It was a small comfortable workshop, open at one end. Parts of the boiler-shop, the big steam-hammer, other work-places could be seen, with a murky background in which rows of smiths' forges faded away into the distance.

There were only six or seven boys in the place, and one machine-man, so that we came and went with a great degree of freedom. The manager was a white-haired old man, sour and distant, who never spoke except in rebuke. But he did not speak very often.

Quite early, from the workshop gossip, I learnt that he had been the manager of a large machine-shop, had got into some trouble, apparently through no fault of his own, was ending his days in the tiny sinecure job of managing the screwing-shop, as our place was called. By all accounts he had cause to feel sour. He certainly was, and we boys went in constant dread of him.

When dinner-time came, on the first day, I had no idea where to go or what to do. I had no money, no food, and did not know where to find my father. No one in my workshop knew him, nor did any of my enquiries help. Almost I decided to fadge my dinner! Except that I was not going to endanger my chances of staying in the works.

Eventually I discovered my father in a workshop about half a mile from my own. (I had been asking for Mr. James Phelan instead of Gentleman Whalen.) He shared his dinner with me, and I noted that his workplace was even more interesting than my own, then made excuse to return to work.

For several weeks I was very happy. The control of the machine, the mastery of the metal, when I had reached the stage of confidence and experiment, brought me a pleasure of body and mind which, since, I have only attained in the arms of someone loved or at the end of a satisfying story. I sang all day.

Almost from the beginning I got into the manager's bad books. It is easy to see now that I was precisely the kind of person on whom a bad-tempered old man would "pick," but it made me very unhappy for a while. However, I managed to forget his minor bullyings while I strayed around the vast works.

They were forgotten while I stared at tons of molten steel being poured in the foundries, gasped with delight as Cyclops thumped his billets of iron, glowed if I was asked to lend a hand, momentarily, in the boiler-shop. Moping around, like I did on the riverside, would be, I suppose, a practical way of describing my activities! I did not know anything about that.

Probably the place fascinated me far more than it did my workmates, because it was so obviously the opposite of everything connected with books and schools and problems in logic. My greatest thrill was in the iron-works, where rows of sweating smiths worked their will, miraculously, on steel and iron that responded as if they were rubber. I wanted to be a smith.

Again, as on Dublin dockside, I simply soaked in a million lovely impressions, without seeking a meaning anywhere. Every one of the other boys, I can see now, knew quite clearly where he would be and what he would be doing when he was a man. Such things never occurred to me, except when they came with a little twinge that reminded me of—of all the unpleasant times I had not succeeded in mixing with people. But the twinges were few, and fleeting.

One of my acquaintances, in say twenty years, would be the Gownseer, by Cyclops. His father was the Gownseer now.

Another would be a locomotive driver, as his father was—his "name was down" already, although he was several years too young. Yet another was to be a draughtsman, since his relatives had money and were prepared to pay a high premium. While I would not be anything. I would only look at Cyclops hammering, and watch the smiths.

One day I laughed out loud when I saw the whole thing clearly. They all had their futures planned!

Weeks passed, and I was still enjoying myself. Already I had made a thousand surreptitious experiments with the little lathe, turning out curious—and useless—objects in some degree resembling the watch-cases of my childhood days. But I always hurried to sneak them away out of sight when the old manager came round.

Chief blessing of our lives, I think, was that the poor old fellow hated the workshop. He watched the clock continually, went padding up and down, a couple of hundred yards each way, between his desk and the distant end of the blacksmiths'-shop, where there was a clock. He looked at that clock several hundred times a day. The habit made life tolerable for us, especially for me.

Then one day I broke a mandrel. This was a trivial affair, one that often occurred; the mandrel was a flimsy tool, easily broken, costing only a few pence at most. But the old man was in an exceptionally sour mood that morning, and threatened me with dire penalties if I broke another. Less than a minute later—naturally—the second mandrel broke.

The manager "sent me home." This was a particularly savage punishment of the time, for a man but not for a boy. A vindictive foreman could send a man home—that is to say he could deprive him of his work and his livelihood without dismissing him. There were always many men hanging around the main works gate, men who had been sent home, who dare not go away to seek another job, but who earned no money in the meantime.

For a boy, sending home was never used as a punishment, since it meant little more than a holiday for the youngster. But

I think the old chap must have been imagining himself back in his position of power—back in the days when frightened men could be turned white of face by the two words, "Go home."

With ludicrous pomposity, like the tough skipper of a whale-ship quelling a dangerous mutiny, he ordered me to go home. He ordered me to tell my father that he would send for me when a new mandrel was made. This, I think, was a cheap compromise with his conscience; there were dozens of mandrels in the toolshop. With my heart in my boots, and with the wreckage of my world again around my ears, I set out, very laggardly, for my father's workshop.

Just over five weeks later I reached it. What was the use of trying to explain to my father? A ballast train was pulling out just as I crossed the smithy yard.

A ballast train was the collection of trucks and living-wagons used by the gangs who kept the railroads in repair. Already, in my few weeks, I had learnt that the men of the ballast trains were rough-and-ready good-humoured fellows, leading a life something like a sailor's, although they worked near the cities, living often in the train and travelling much.

As the living-van at the end of the train passed me, I jumped. Again I was headed for the horizon—what was the use of trying to explain to my father?

The trained stopped at Sallins, about twenty miles from Dublin, and, after a cup of tea in the ballast van, I stepped off, crossed an embankment and walked along a canal. This was the Grand Canal again, of my seven-year-old memories. I followed the lonesome towpath.

Along the narrow track I stepped out smartly, whistled and sang, smacked my hands together from time to time, very happy because I had discovered myself at last. Now I was not going anywhere; I was just walking along the canal.

Country people, wandering, always walked along the canal out of Dublin. (This was a fallacy, but I felt quite certain about it.) Suddenly it struck me that it was the same canal from the Liffey, that it went back "all those miles"—actually it was less than twenty—to join the deepwater dock, went all those miles the other way to—oh, wherever it was.

Many of my friends and forerunners have emphasised the kind of feelings I experienced that day at Sallins. Those feelings stay, and are basic with, everyone like me for all our days.

It was, no doubt, a naïve and foolish preoccupation to look back along that canal, and forward along it, and be thrilled by the knowledge that it joined everywhere to everywhere else. Any sensible nine-year-old would know it did.

Yet even to-day I cannot ride the Finchley Road in London, come to the signpost marked "To the North," without feeling the same glow of satisfaction. Even though I know every inch of the road up to the Scottish border, where another signpost points down it, marked "To the South."

A naïve and foolish preoccupation. It appears to be fundamental with vagrant people. Explorers harness it, great road-makers capitalise it, cartographers choose their vocation because of it. Others merely feel it.

("I've been that Burma Road," said Eileen Bigland one day. "It goes to China. Right up from the bottom of Burma, over those hills and along towards Chungking at the end." Now, everyone who read newspapers, during the Second World War, knew that much. Soldiers, civilians, politicians, they all knew. But in so far as they used their imagination, in constructive thought about the Burma Road, they were doing in small what Bigland had done in large. But then, Eileen is a vagabond—no respectably conventional woman could have written those magnificent books of the roads.)

This part of my own book is easy to write, because I commenced, in effect, to write my autobiography that morning! For a month I wrote, every day, often several times a day, keeping a diary, interlarded with philosophical comments in verse.

It was very bad verse indeed: I can remember that much. Rhymed couplets, four anapæsts to a line, it consisted mainly of place-names, wishful thinking, and self-pity.

A recurrent phrase about seeking my fortune must be attributed to the influence of my mother's stories. The first section of her every tale ended with the words, ". . . and set out to seek his fortune." I was not very clear about how I was to do it— probably by finding a purse of gold on the canal towpath.

Come to think about it, my fantasy-objectives were far less clearly defined than Oilcan Odlum's job for the Christmas. Maybe there is a guide line to tramp psychology in the comparison.

The only items of value in the verses were the accounts of things that happened to me, and their effect on my mind. Half a dozen times there were references to "a child who looked like a man," which would seem very silly if the idea had not had a sound factual basis.

Three times, in my couple of months at the works, I had been jerked, unpleasantly, into the realisation that I had to be very careful indeed on my way through the world. Because of my size. Fourteen and a half years old, I appeared at least eighteen or twenty. Unless a person looked very closely, there was nothing to show that I was very young, reserved, imaginative, and gauche, far less experienced than the average fourteen-year-old of workshop or village.

Once, at the smith-works in Inchicore, I strayed around at dinner-time with some other youngsters. Most of my attention went into admiring the long, large workshop with rows of anvils, steam-hammers, and forges. Someone of our crowd threw a lump of coal at a group of smiths.

Suddenly I found myself confronted by a half-naked and wholly terrifying gorilla-like man, black faced and broken nosed, who doubled an enormous pair of fists and roared at me to "Come on." I nearly died with fear on the spot, stood trembling in terror, convinced that he would kill me with a single blow.

He probably could have done just that, too, for this was Bogey McCann, a dangerous rough-house fighter, notorious for miles around. I heard him hiss, and saw the huge fist drawn back to smash me, before one of the smiths intervened with, "No, Bogey. *No.* Can't you see he's only a kid?"

McCann stopped to peer, then stretched to shake hands with me, mumbling sheepishly, "Aw, bejaze, son, I'm sorry. Sure, I didn't know."

Another evening, on my way home from work, through Dublin, I came to the top of a steep hill, where a burly carter was in trouble with his horse and laden dray. The hill was a dangerous one, and I jumped in to help. We got the horse up, and stopped around a corner.

The carter protested when I tried to say good night. "Sure, I have to say thank yeh, haven't I?" he demanded. "Come on." I followed him into a pub. "If yeh hadn't turned up, mate," he asserted with a sententious headshake, "I'd a bin there till mornin' begod. Two pints, plaze," he added to the barman.

The pint of porter that was placed in front of me looked like a bathful of ink, but I simply had not the courage to tell the drayman I was only a boy. Although it nearly choked me, I gulped the porter down, said good night and hurried out.

The third stressing of my overgrowth was more highly significant, as some of my friends will say. One pay-night I had gone to the Tivoli Theatre, down near the docks where I had been a telegram boy. In the interval I went to the bar and had a bottle of lemonade.

A very beautiful young lady came across to me, smiling and obviously delighted. "Hel-*lo*, darling," she exclaimed, and I said hello. "Haven't seen you since Baldoyle Races," was her next remark, and I agreed.

She asked if she could have a lemonade, and I bought one. Then she had a gin in hers. After the interval she came back and sat in the seat next to mine.

No one so lovely had ever come into my life. She was much more beautiful and better dressed than my wealthy and almost fabulous godmother, than my opulent cousins, and she was nicer than my mother, or just as nice, when she held my hand and rubbed against me.

She looked like a blessed and holy saint. At first. Until I decided that at last I had found the beautiful girl who figured in all my myriad stories. Presently she looked at me hard, and patted me affectionately on the shoulder, as I would pat my son Seumas, before she went away.

A pretty little Dublin whore—I simply had not the foggiest notion what she was *for*. This, in spite of my Liberty experiences! She was, at any rate, a good sport not to hurt my feelings when she realised that I was a child carrying a man's body.

Those three incidents had taught me to be wary. It was necessary to remember that I could not "lark about" like other boys, nor go in for the playful sparring so common in work-shops. Above all, *I* could not expect people to make the allow-ances that are made, in time of mischief, for boyish ignorance or innocence.

So that when a policeman, on the canal bridge near Sallins, shouted "Hey," and beckoned me over to him, I thought quickly. What he saw, I knew, was a man in blue dungaree trousers, with a mechanic's blue jacket showing under his coat, with a notebook sticking out of a breast-pocket and a two-foot rule showing in the pocket of the dungarees. I had not known, until then, that policemen questioned tramps, and indeed all strangers on foot.

"Where y'going?" he demanded without preamble.

"Where am I goin'?" I repeated, in my most grown-up Dublin speech, realising in consternation that I did not know the name of a single nearby town. For a second I thought of saying I belonged to the ballast train, but dismissed the idea.

Then, immediately, I did what I have been doing most of my life since—lately with some small reward—I added up the present and most obvious factors and made them into a story. There was the canal. Here was I, a dungareed and obvious mechanic. Here was a policeman accustomed to canals and boats.

"I'm goin'," I announced, in a petulant voice, "*there*," pointing up the canal. "An' I'm comin' from *there*," pointing down it. "An' if annywan wants me bloody job they can have it."

The shade of a sympathetic grin began to show on the

policeman's face. "Ninety-seven's gone through, over an hour back," I went on, and he nodded. "Thirty-eight won't be along for another hour, near enough. So I'm footin' it to the locks." I fiddled with the steel rule, abstractedly stuck my pencil behind my ear, and blew loud snorting breaths indicative of contempt for the directors of the Grand Canal Company of Ireland.

"Aye," agreed the policeman. "I thought ye wuz a thramp when I seen ye comin' up the towpath. But then I could see ye wuz a canal man. 'Tis a fine day for walkin', anyway." We parted on a friendly level.

My instinct, and my technique as I afterwards discovered, were very sound. At that time policemen in Ireland simply threw selected vagrants in jail for a month without any protracted preliminaries. For the next mile or two after leaving the policeman I felt slightly uneasy, but decided to keep to the same story, at any rate while I was near the canal.

I had two shillings and twopence and a notebook. My father was far away, and the malignant manager of the screwing-shop at Inchicore belonged to the dead past. My mother would worry a little, but perhaps she might feel I was sure to return.

But of course I was never going back. Now I would seek my fortune all along that canal, right to the end, to wherever it stopped. The water was brown, everything was very quiet, there were fish in that canal.

It was October, but the sun was still shining strongly. There were strange round fruits on bushes, and some birds I had never heard before were calling in a wood. Two rabbits ran away. I saw my first squirrel. And what was a rhyme for Sallins?

That first night I slept in a field. Wandering people, I felt assured, somehow, always slept in fields. The place I picked by a hedge was sheltered, and the night was fine. But in the dark and the silence I was sick and lonely, and greatly afraid of I knew not what.

Later, I wanted my mother. Later still I remembered myself as very young, perhaps two, kneeling beside my mother one day, leaning against her leg, and licking her arm, so that she said, "What little dog is this that is licking me?" and I was very happy. Several things like that I recalled, with hurt.

On towards dawn, I awoke from a doze, in the blackness, to think about God and my wickedness and the secret sinful things I did for which I would be sent to hell.

Fear and despair and the curse of guilty difference and cut-off loneliness were on me, while the rustle of every night-animal was the approach of God, or the devil, or both, to crush me. I was afraid.

But I made my fear into rhymed couplets, four anapæsts to a line.

That night, I think, the Jim Phelan my friends call imperturbable, who only smiled coldly while those in power pronounced his doom, who wrote his epitaph in a well-tooled presentable sonnet from a death-cell, first began to come alive. Fear was in my life, and came near to me all my days. But he came so near that in time I knew him well, and looked him full in the face, and put him into anapæsts.

CHAPTER VIII

ON the first morning I was awakened early, by the angry screaming of a starling perched near my head. Probably I was disturbing him in some way and he wanted to be rid of me, I decided, as I rose. Cold and stiff, feeling very miserable and dirty, I made my way back to the canal-edge in the dawn.

Nothing was farther from my thoughts than that I was a tramp, but believing that life on the roads was terribly hard and harsh and isolated, I did not feel too happy at the thought of a lifetime spent sleeping in fields! After I had had a wash in the canal, and a drink of canal water, I felt a little better. When the sun came up I forgot about the misery of the night.

My two and twopence I spent foolishly, on food, in the first little town. (This, in Ireland of all places, where morality, religion, tradition, custom, and simple inclination make an open and unthinking hospitality the general rule, where even the lowest vagrant would scorn an English or American citizen's rations—in wartime, for instance. But I did not know anything about that.)

The canal, cutting through the loneliest parts of the flat bog-pasture country, was deserted except for an occasional passing boat. Of course, no beggars would travel such an unfruitful district, but I did not know that either. Pleased and happy and keenly observant, I stayed by the water, mooning along at what must have been a good pace, although I had neither need nor urge to hurry.

The names of the little towns come up into my memory, with all the music I had known, earlier, from perusal of an atlas. That part, I think, will be easy to understand and sympathise with. Many people must find pleasure, as I used to find it, merely in reading the names on a map of, say, South America or the Western States.

Someone wrote a song, humorous but with the master-touch of a hidden half-sob in it, of which I remember only the lines,

> *"And weekly from Southampton*
> *The liners white and gold*
> *Go rolling down to Rio . . .*
> *. . . And I'd like to go to Rio*
> *Some day before I'm old."*

The writer must have caught at some deeply buried and much involuted thread of the general consciousness, because the song was popular. For many, as for me when I was nine, there must have been magic in such names as Rosario, Rio Grande, Popocatapetl, Sierra Nevada, and Cheyenne. That first day along the Irish canal I found the same magic in place-names like Naas, Newbridge, Kildare, Rathangan, Monastarevan.

But long before I came to Monastarevan, in the early evening, I was hungry and did not know what to do about it. Here one could not fadge—there was only an empty towpath three feet wide. Only when I was ravenous did I strike away from the canal, depressed and miserable and despairing, to beg. BEG! It had never occurred to me that tramps begged.

My pride and self-esteem were gone, and I sank into terrible depths. Beg! Was this what seeking your fortune meant? My father was Gentleman Whalen, and I was Jim Phelan the great scholar—no, that was wrong; I was Jim Phelan the beggar. But *was* I to beg? Wave after wave of shame swept over me, as I skulked guiltily past the cottages, afraid to accost the people.

Finally, in desperation, I knocked at the door of a large house. A girl, well-dressed and about eighteen, opened the door, and I nearly sank through the ground. At any time I was shy enough with girls; now to beg from one! But I must have found the correct formula.

The girl and I measured one another with our eyes. What I saw was a pretty, friendly-looking girl, perhaps a doctor's daughter or something of the kind, not a farm-woman. She saw, I suppose, a big young mechanic, certainly not a local person or a farm-labourer. Probably I did not look too bad, in her eyes, since she smiled pleasantly and waited for me to speak.

"Can you give me something to eat?" I enquired, exactly in my father's rather up-stage manner. "I am very hungry."

The request must have come rather as a shock to the girl, but she recovered her composure in a second. Asking if I would wait, she went away, and I stood outside the door, feeling terribly sheepish and hoping no one would see me.

In a few minutes the girl returned with a brown-paper parcel and a smile. A second later, when I had taken the parcel and thanked her in very stilted language, she gave me a shilling. I hurried back to my canal, stepping springily again. Even more springily I stepped out when I had eaten the large meal—I can remember the cold leg of a rabbit *now*.

Thereafter, though, begging came no easier to me, and I was never comfortable, once, during all that particular wandering. But from sheer pressure of hunger I learnt, perforce, to use that compound of childish hope and helplessness which is every vagrant's passport to a meal.

Even the professional tramp is really a child, going away to look for a nicer world. However sophisticated he may become, fundamentally he is a hungry youngster coming home to his mother for dinner. Except that every woman in the world is his mother. The expert roadster's equipment consists, in the main, of a little psychological knowledge directed towards bringing the woman to realise it too.

It never once occurred to me that I might seek work as a way to avoid the ignominy of begging. Not once! But I hope most sincerely that no one will start to make hasty deductions from that statement. Because it had never occurred to me in my Glasgow days that I might go to work in Park Head Forge. While I know now, and anyone will know by this time, that I would willingly have paid to be allowed to work in such a place. The thing goes deeper than simple laziness.

However, I did not work, except twice. The first time was at a small farm near Monastarevan. My knowledge of Ireland, from books, and my acquaintance with the Irish language, were sufficient to tell me the place was historic. Strolling around, looking at the ancient town, I found myself in the middle of a conversation with a countryman.

Not understanding one-eighth of the things he said, I had been answering yes and no as he walked beside me in the middle of the wide street. Presently he summed up, "Well, we'll have a dhrink, then, to bind the bargain; an' ye can come out wud me in the car."

In a pub I was given a pint of porter and some bread and cheese. Those needed no questions, or answers, and I finished them off, although I had no clear idea of what it was all about.

The "car" was a farm cart. We stopped at a lonely farm, and I was introduced to the farmer's wife as "The b'y who's goin' to help wud the scrap o' whate." After another meal I went to bed in a barn, still rather vague about everything.

The next day I worked thirteen hours. The harvest was over, and they were bringing in wheat from a field, to make a stack in a yard. My job was to throw the sheaves, with a pitchfork, from a cart to the man on top of the stack.

In spite of my size and strength, that peasant nearly killed me. We finished that night, and he gave me a shilling. He at least had not been fooled into thinking I was much more than fourteen. Next morning, having slept in the barn again, I was so stiff that I could hardly move, and I only travelled the roads with difficulty. For years afterwards I hated peasants.

It is amusing, since nowadays in several countries I am called a famous peasant writer, really do know peasants well, and love them, and present their problems. But that first experience of sheer cold-blooded ruthlessness would have soured Maxim Gorky himself. I nearly threw the shilling in the canal.

During the day I got myself as far away from Monastarevan as possible, and that night I slept in a haystack near Tullamore. It was getting too cold, too late in the year, for sleeping in such places, but I had that to learn also. Besides, I did not know, since I never connected my Glasgow "stall" with the roads, that in England or Ireland the tramps always sleep in the towns.

Three weeks went in aimless wandering. Sometimes I struck away at random into the by-lanes, sometimes I glowed, as at meeting a long-lost friend, when chance brought me again to the canal. Always uncomfortable and awkward about asking for a meal, I drifted far down towards the South of Ireland.

My second experience as a workman resembled the coming true of all dreams for me. Late one night, in a small village, I came to a green where a circus-tent was being taken down. Hanging around, attracted by the flares, the shouting, the generally raffish atmosphere, I glowed when a big man asked me to lend a hand.

Here again my strength was an asset. Pulling down the tent, loading the poles and equipment, were not in the least like work. The big man hardly got half-way through his request whether I wanted a job, would like to "come on," when I agreed.

The outfit was small and very cheaply run, with awkward rustic "artistes" and scrubby horses. It looked like fairyland. The work was terribly hard, and we got hardly any sleep. But I did not mind, would almost have volunteered to set up the big tent by myself.

When, in a strange town—we only did "one-night stands" —with my heavy work over, I stood near the entrance to take tickets, to shoo away juvenile intruders, and watch the performance, my happiness was complete. Now at last I knew ... etc.

At the end of a week, just when I had earned my first wages, I left the circus hastily. There was a lovely and blessed saint here also, as in the Tivoli Theatre.

A dirty little drab, pulled by my bigness and probably sensing that I was new to women, she personified everything lovely of which I had ever heard or read or dreamt. Besides, I was growing up a little, and knew, roughly speaking, what she was for, and responded to her leads. After the packup one night, at her invitation, I went in her wagon.

Long before I had got past the stammering stage I was on the grass outside, being punched and pummelled by her man, a big, good-looking young fellow whom I had been idolising. The strong-man and weight-lifter of the circus, and a professional boxer besides, he all but murdered me.

I crawled away into a field until the circus had gone, and slept in a haystack afterwards. My first week's pay had gone too! . . . Afterwards I often wondered whether the whole thing was a set-up, an original way of obtaining free labour and no questions asked.

For several days I drifted slowly around in the County Limerick, recovering from my beating. For this period begging did not bother me—I ate at farmhouses, too listless even to be ashamed or to tell a story. Only gradually my strength came back, and I was thoroughly miserable. Twice or three times I thought of the red-shirted Gownseer beside Cyclops, but I put the thoughts away.

Then, drifting, I came to the Southern Railway at Limerick Junction. In the big shunting yard a train of wagons was being made up. It was a service train—one from the locomotive works. Almost I whimpered, and knew with pain where I wanted to go when I read the white-painted lettering along the wagon-sides—Loco. Inchicore. Loco. Inchicore. Loco. Inchicore.

Inchicore was only a hundred miles off, but it seemed many thousand, and all the more desirable for that. Just before the train moved off, I climbed into the guard's van, and told the man I wanted to go to Inchicore. Because I worked there.

"You're no railwayman," he stated at once. I persisted, told him what I was and where I worked. Finally he asked my name. "Hey?" he demanded. "Gentleman Whalen's son?"

It was the first time I had ever been really pleased to hear my father's nickname.

"Well, bejaze," the guard summed up. "I'll be hung, *an'* get the sack, if you're caught in here. But if you're goin' you're goin'." Next morning he wakened me, as we slowed at the signals above Inchicore, and I dropped off quietly at the upper end of the works.

Waiting around in a field until dinner-time, after I had cleaned up a little at a stream, I walked into my father's workshop. He shared his dinner with me without a word.

None of the other men, I noticed, seemed to see anything strange in my reappearance. Some more of my father's distant reserve, I guessed. He simply did not know how to gossip, and no one knew I had been away, only that I had been sent home by the manager of the screwing-shop.

After our dinner, my father and I went for a walk by the railway. Looking forward to a severe catechism, and perhaps a thrashing, I had decided to run away up the line if he attacked me, and jump a train. Jumping trains was now part of my philosophy although I had only ridden two, each by virtue of my being almost a railwayman. I watched my father warily.

He only asked if I had been home. When I said I had not, he told me to go, and to be ready for work the next day, as I had been "sent for" a few days earlier. The next morning I resumed work in the screwing-shop as if nothing had happened.

At home, too, I was treated as if nothing unusual had occurred. Whatever discussion there had been while I was away had evidently resulted in the acceptance of the sad fact that I was or had been crazy, that scolding or remonstrance was useless.

Only once, when we were alone, my mother cried, and kissed me, holding me very tightly to her, and I tried to say that I was sorry, while I wept bitterly too and promised to be good. Sincerely I meant that I would not make God angry by my secret wickedness any more, that I would be an ordinary boy, and lead a pure life like the holy saints of whom we read, and be good to my mother.

In a few days I was back into my ordinary routine at the works. Again, with my back to the lathe now and then, I stared half-hypnotised at Cyclops or listened to the command-shouts of the red-shirted Gownseer.

Much of my time, when the manager was not on the alert, went in making words to the clatter and clang of the black-smith's hammers, or the song of the big pulley by my side. For the rest, I was outwardly at least an ordinary working youth of Dublin in the early twentieth century.

CHAPTER IX

DUBLIN of the early twentieth century, versus Jim Phelan, was a bitter and prolonged contest. Dublin won. Which is to say that, from the view-point of the Irish outside the metropolis, I lost my immortal soul.

However, the consolation prize usual in such cases came my way. I gained the whole world.

Any attempt to tell about myself without also telling about Dublin would be useless at best, and at the worst a mean, small cheating. It would not serve.

That way I should make myself lofty-souled hero or craven fool, flesh-tormented ascetic or lust-consumed hypocrite, satyr or saint instead of an ordinary intelligent boy from the Ireland outside Dublin.

That way there would be little hope of understanding me or any of the queer crowd, poets and priests, artists and vagrants, writers and rogues, thrown out from the city over the last couple of centuries, the Dubliners.

Some of the best-known writers in the world have essayed the task of setting Dublin on paper. James Joyce and Liam O'Flaherty and Sean O'Casey, Kenneth Reddin and Conal O'Riordan, Sean O'Faolain and St. John Gogarty—the list would fill this chapter—all have known and shown that the city came first, that their own personalities were its reflection.

Involuntarily or of set purpose, each has told in report or by implication what the city has done to him. Each has given somewhere—or everywhere as in the case of Joyce—an account of his clash with the place called Dublin.

It is always a clash, when one of the outside Irish comes into contact with the life of the Liffeyside. None of strong personality can escape; he must be made or broken, if he be a stranger, if he be one of the Irish strayed in from outside.

That is all the secret. Few or none of the well-known Dubliners are Dubliners. Most are of the outside Irish, escaped and scarred survivors from the continuous war between Ireland and Liffeyside.

Their scars, shown boastfully or in sorrow to the outer world, mark the difference between themselves and those who have not escaped. The world calls the difference art, pictorial, histrionic or literary.

The story can be condensed into ten words—Dublin is not an Irish place and never has been. But since it is the capital of Ireland, the contradiction is not easily seen. For most of the Irish the difference is discovered too late. For others the shock of the discovery may last for decades, even decades lived outside Dublin.

If the Picts and Scots, those half-legendary peoples of ancient history, survived somehow in modern London and furnished most or much of its art; if the *Saturday Evening Post* and the *New Yorker* were edited and staffed by Piute Indians, someone would notice and comment. No one notices even greater contradictions in Dublin. This, in the main, constitutes what is often vaguely called the charm of the Irish capital.

There are few cities like it in the world. Hardly any other country has a chief city which, like a cuckoo in a nest, remains always alien. Only Hong Kong begins to approach the strange status of Liffeyside.

Since the latter half of last century, Hong Kong has been a meeting-place for the commerce and culture of half the world. School and church, office and barracks, steamship and locomotive, carried the languages of almost every known people. In the telephone book one might find, only a little while ago, German names and Russian, Japanese and French, British and American, Polish, Portuguese, Jewish, Swedish, perhaps a few Chinese.

The churches were Lutheran or Catholic, currency at one period was, fantastically, the Mexican dollar, the schools were French, Japanese, Russian or English. Hong Kong has been like that for several decades. Dublin has been such a city for centuries.

The small district, convenient for landing, at the mouth of the Liffey, has been invaded and peopled by temporary conquerors many times. Few of the newcomers ever spread far, for any length of time, beyond Dublin.

Outside the boundary, Ireland dreamed and drifted, changed from paganism to Christianity, dreamed and drifted again. Inside, Liffeytown swarmed and grew and changed.

Danes, English, Normans, Jews, French Huguenots, and Welsh made a mosaic, first superimposed upon and later embodied in a social matrix called Irish. The matrix was not Irish. But only the Irish people—outside Dublin—knew.

From the beginning of the attempts at conquest the waves of incomers were thrown back on themselves, again and again over hundreds of years, at Dublin. There was even at one time, according to the history books, something called The Pale, which was literally a fence between the cosmopolitan district of Dublin and the Irish outside.

The city has always been a foreign place, looked upon by the Irish—of perhaps less than twenty miles distance—as almost mythically strange and alien and sinful. That state of affairs does not exist anywhere else except in China.

No Dorset rustic would regard London as anything but a large, busy part of his own country. His equivalent in the Ireland of my time spoke of Dublin and England in the same breath. Three miles from the city centre, any country girl who met a "Dublin jackeen" expected to be raped on the spot. Except that she did not know the word rape, knew only that strange, terrible practices belonged to the wicked lands far away.

By and large, the Dublin people seldom knew anything about this, which was what made them so interesting. They thought they were Irish!

Three things marked the Dubliners off, sharply, from the people of, say, Sallins. Their average occupation, their language, their attitude to morality were all different.

Dublin was a manufacturing town, but within one mile from a factory you could find yourself among green fields, and travel a hundred miles in a straight line without seeing a factory chimney or a machine again. That was important.

More important was the matter of language. At one time, during a partially successful conquest by the British, the Irish tongue was abolished by law and English was made the official language. The law did not work very well; there are still whole districts where no English has ever been spoken.

But in Dublin the switch-over was made with ease. The change had some very curious results. For generations the Dubliners knew no Irish—or thought they knew none. For generations they did in fact use much Irish.

They used all the beloved secret little words for furtive acts and for things of which many men do not speak without embarrassed laugh or awkward turn of phrase. Those words are not found in the average Irish dictionary. Their equivalents are not found in the average English dictionary either, although every schoolboy knows them. But the Dubliners thought their particular words were English obscenity or English slang.

That held for long. Then it was discovered that there was a strange and beautiful immunity, applicable only to Dublin, for those who felt joy in the saying of secret things, openly and without penalty, as a release from the tension of a stern forbidding. To feel the potency of that release one need only read Rabelais or James Joyce. But the opportunity to enjoy it to the full exists in few cities other than Mexico and Dublin.

It is not at all the same thing as a Parisian taxi-driver cursing a foreigner in French. Nor does it resemble the case of a London citizen, drunk and truthful, using language for which he is fined in a police-court next morning. One may not use the strong monosyllables from Chaucer in a London street if there is a policeman about.

The Dubliner could and did use his words. No one could

object. He could talk like the hotspots of Chaucer or the satires of Juvenal without looking over his shoulder. The words, as far as he knew, were not English, were not Irish, were Dublin. Twenty miles away, in Sallins, only the village rake could imitate him, and he would have to be drunk. Dublin was different.

The attitude to morality, particularly sex-morality, was parallel. Men in Ireland married at thirty-five or so, without ever having seen the top of a girl's stocking. Girls averaged twenty-six at marriage, all the evidence being that they were virgins. Significant figures are on record.

The percentage of illegitimacy was astonishingly low, for a country where the people were healthy. Venereal disease was almost unknown. Homosexuality was a near-mythical story, about wicked lands abroad.

Sex and sin meant the same thing. No mother would dream of telling her daughter the facts of life, (a) because she knew little herself beyond farmyard empirics; (b) because she knew no words for the discourse.

In that state of severe frustration, sheer hard work on farms kept the majority out of the more dangerous neuroses. No reader will take me as eulogising this state of affairs, nor will anyone read here an attack upon it; merely a statement that it existed in the rural areas, that is, in most of the country. But in Dublin—that was another matter.

The average Dubliner, as a dozen books plainly show, was sex-conscious to a degree seldom encountered outside psychiatric wards. To start with, he was damned and different —chance encounters with country people told him that. Wherefore he went joyously to the other extreme.

Secondly, in his industrial city, he had the casual morality of Birmingham or Leeds, pleasurable because he had escaped from a restraint. His depravities were always carried off with a flourish; the fact that they were very harmless depravities indeed made the flourish all the more necessary. Again, even without touching Joyce, the reader can consult any one of a dozen books on Dublin.

The Parisian of fiction is supposed to be the worshipper *par excellence* at the shrine of Venus. One week in the Dublin of my youth would have made him feel like a celibate monk.

Farmers near the city had to leave the gates open on certain fields "for the wicked people," to prevent their other crops from being utterly ruined by the hosts of lovers. Along the canal banks, in the early evening, a pedestrian proceeded as in an obstacle race, so closely planted were the interlocked couples. One might hire a gay-girl for anything from fourpence upwards. Few wasted fourpence, in a city where so much finer loving might be had for a glance.

In such a city, any person who tried to keep the codes of the outside Irish, who accepted the sterilising restraints of the peasant morality, would have a very uncomfortable time indeed. Joyce and many others have told of their own clash with Dublin. The uncomfortable time was mine, to the full, from 1910 onwards.

Hell was a very real place for me, as it was for most of the other Dublin writers, those who won and those who lost alike. One did not have to imagine things—there were books. One, called, I think, *Hell Open for Christians,* was the only book in many Irish homes when I was young. As far as I remember, it had not the official approval of the Catholic Church, but it was far better known in Ireland than the Bible in other lands.

The author must have been very close to one of the more unpleasant forms of mania, was the kind of person who might have gained rapid promotion in Inquisition days, or spent his time skinning mice in his cell while jailed for sadism in the England of later days. He left few opportunities for misconception.

A miser, in hell, would have to count billions and trillions of coins, all red-hot. A drunkard had gallons of liquor, boiling, poured down his throat. Lazy people stayed in bed all day—red-hot beds, of course.

Impurity, i.e. the procreative act if unmarried, was the

greatest crime known to this writer. It will have to be imagined how he let himself go, in describing the technique of dealing with the impure, in hell. I believed it all. Furthermore, I was most certainly impure—or wanted to be. And I lived in Dublin.

A person in spotless cricket flannels, going down a coal-mine, with instructions to keep the flannels white unless he wanted to be tortured for ever and ever, would have been roughly in my position, at fifteen. Except that in my case there was also the sickening inner conviction that I could not get my flannels blackened even if I tried, had to be burnt up any-way, merely for thinking wistfully about coal-dust.

The dilemma and the conviction made me a sad boy. I was big and healthy as well, which made things worse. Now my work at the screwing-shop in Inchicore no longer sufficed. Nor did the pleasure of seeing Cyclops at work, nor the former miracle of making anapæsts that would sound like the clang of the anvil and sledge or the roar of the blast in the forge. Fear took most of the verses.

Worst strain, perhaps, was that I had to hide my thoughts and views. When the boys at the machines talked, I had to go quietly away, lest I be jeered into insanity like Bullock McGrath. When the men discussed the two main topics, legitimate sex and illegitimate sex, I had to be very careful not to look awkward. Jemser Gargan, who looked awkward at such moments, could not even ask the time without being reminded that he was a "mule."

The ordinary fledgling stage, of workshop or office any-where, was much more painful in Dublin because the moral trammels were infinitely closer on those who wore them. For one badly frightened of his father as well, and of most other things, as I was, the stage was torment.

Dick Merrigan, a shrewd, sympathetic clerk who was also a great athlete, must have sensed some of my difficulties and tried to help me. Twice he tackled me as to what I did, outside the works. Nothing, I told him. No football? No running? Did I box? Go in for cycling? No.

"But damn it, man," he burst out on the second occasion. "You must do *something*. If you don't do anything you're mad."

I nearly was, too. But how could I tell Merrigan that at night I walked for miles, on the dark roads, striding furiously at times and muttering foolish lines to the rhythm of my hurrying footfalls? In his view that would certainly have been mad. I thought it was myself.

The only difference, and it was a trifling one, between myself and a lunatic babbling his gibberish was that I muttered my words into rhythm, twisted and shaped at them, tooled them into anapæsts. That was all. Without the small pre-occupation I think I should have gone over the edge.

All the verses were story-form, fitted to ancient stock-ballad tunes, of which I knew many. From the ballad-singers and ballad-makers themselves I had learnt the tricks of crude song-narrative, of homely but efficient repetition, of refrain. On the night-roads around Dublin such activities canalised my thoughts away from danger-zone.

The thump-syllable of each anapæst came corresponding with a footfall of mine. That held the rhythm. Where a ballad-subject pulled me, or where fit-word and rhyme came flowing, the speed of my walking increased. Often I found myself tearing along.

One ancient tune must have had a dozen sets of words fitted to it at that time. It has always stayed with me, and I have many times used it in my work, although it is as old as the hills.

The original words went back at least two centuries, to the days when the men of the craft-guilds clashed in Dublin, often around the Liberty. The oldest version told of a pitched battle between the butchers' guild and the weavers' guild, in Meath Street, still a main Liberty highway.

> "*. . . we'll sweep an' we'll swing.*
> *We'll wallop a mosey down Meath Street in bloom,*
> *An' we won't leave a weaver alive in the Coombe.*"

Literary origins are always interesting. Perhaps this one will take prize as the most plebeian. In the years since the Dublin days I have written a few fair verses, sold a few ballads, and I could write this book more easily in anapæsts than in prose. Meath Street was the starting-point.

Years later, Geoffrey Toone, as a lorry-driver, sang the "North Road Song" in the film *Night Journey*. The ballad was built around a many-sided song of the lorry-men. But if Geoffrey had but known it, he was walloping a mosey down Meath Street all the time. I had done the story of the film with Maisie Sharman, and the Dublin anapæsts insisted on sneaking out.

NORTH ROAD

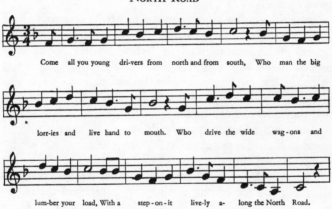

Come all you young dri-vers from north and from south, Who man the big lorr-ies and live hand to mouth. Who drive the wide wag-ons and lum-ber your load, With a step-on-it live-ly a-long the North Road.

The steel for the Clyde and the coal from the Tyne,
We blink as we steer them by factory and mine.
We blink at the wheel—but we keep to the code
With a—step-on-it-lively along the North Road, etc.

Speaking impartially, I should say it is not a bad ballad at all. Many of the lorry-drivers accept and will sing that version. Also I like it myself. It might have been written by Scutchy Callaghan of the Liberty.

But how could I tell Dick Merrigan anything about that?

Not long after I was fifteen, deliberately and coldly I "took to drink." Not knowing yet that liquor was an anodyne, I had it in wistful decision that thus one could be a man. It may have been a kind of compensation, giving me an advantage over the other boys, none of whom could drink without getting into trouble with their parents.

No one, I knew, would dare the familiarity of telling my father. Thus I was immune. On the economic side, I had at that time plenty of money, and could afford to spend much more than was necessary.

The money came in a way that very closely resembled my mother's finding of fortunes. The bookmakers provided it, quite regularly.

Some time earlier all of us in our family had started to back horses. Neither of my parents had ever gambled a penny before, which was unusual in Ireland, where horses were backed almost as a religious rite. But a positive epidemic of gambling had swept over Dublin, because practically everyone in the city had discovered a valuable secret, namely, how to find the winner in every race.

There was a noonday paper called the *Echo*, its sales roughly equal to the male populace of Dublin. The secret knowledge was connected with the *Echo*.

This knowledge, shared by everyone in the city, was that all racing and the editing of all racing-papers and the selling of tips and the publication of form-tables were swindles. Every race was fixed beforehand: the racing editors took care to put their silly readers on to the wrong horses, so as not to spoil the prices, the tipster gave out losers, for the same reason—were paid to do so.

Only the initiates and their cronies—those who knew what to look for in the *Echo*—got winners.

One ignored all the columns of form, all the discussion of chances. One passed by, in contempt, the list of horses given as likely to win. The initiate went straight to the day's programme, and found the secret marks showing which horses would be first, second, and third, as fixed by the swindling owners and editors and judges.

It was as simple as that. Starting with a capital of one shilling, my mother won a hundred pounds in a few months, and retired from gaming. I shall never forget her first bet—she backed Heroine, The Chemist, and Jerry M., all for one shilling. Two won at ten to one, the third at a hundred to eight. She went to her grave a firm and grateful believer in the system.

The system consisted in picking out the secret signs. Near the name of a horse a small rectangular black mark would show. A larger black would be somewhere on the line given to another horse. Still another and blacker sign might mark another name. First, second, and third. One merely wrote them down and went to the bookmaker.

The marks were the ordinary smudges and blotches and protruding "leads" of a paper set in a hurry. It will be hard to believe that a whole city gambled its earnings on the strength of such marks, but it is a fact; there must be thousands of people alive to-day who did so. I won quite large sums myself by following the system—which is more than I can say about others more scientific-seeming, which came to my later notice.

Many times since I have wondered whether the whole myth started from the bookmakers, perhaps with the help of a compositor or two at the printing works. If so, there is a beautiful irony, and a very Irish story, in the fact that prosperity descended from heaven on Dublin in those years, by way of the *Echo*.

Everyone won, except the unfortunate street-bookies. The "secret" was the talk of every pub, from Inchicore to Sir John Rogerson's Quay. In furtive and gloating whispers it would be discussed at first, then in more loud-voiced sophisticate boasting, as the whisky so kindly furnished by the bookmakers took a hand. The owners of beer-shops must have coined money at the time.

Thus I had always plenty of money to buy drinks. The experience definitely did me a great deal of good, giving me a fictitiously high standing in the workshops, where the other boys dared not drink or gamble except in a very minor and furtive way.

At night I would hurry home from work, wash, and go out to the pub to draw my winnings. After having some drinks I would just walk, sometimes in the quiet residential roads, more often on the dark country roads outside the city. Most of my money was spent on foolish small things, or given to beggars, but since it came regularly, it did not matter.

In my walking at that time I always had a story about myself, and was always just going to meet a lovely girl. Then in some magical way I would be ordinary, and not gelded at all, and I would hold this girl and love her and then go my way.

A dirty, mean little mind, I feel it must have been, because even my imagination-stories were always conditioned by the ever-present fear, of God and my father and of bearded men in forests and of strange black things that sprang at you.

I never got drunk. I never had a girl. I never had any friends. Books I hardly read, except a Juvenal sneaked from my father's room, and Dryden's *Virgil*—the sex bits.

Often I took a day off from work, pretending to be ill. Then I would go straight to the end of the quay, to where Dublin's river ended and the sea began, and sit on the steel bollard looking at the ships, blankly, or making foolish small verses about bowlines and hawsers and the sheer sea-wall.

Later I would have a pint in a sailor's pub, and listen to the men talking. If anyone spoke to me I generally answered in long-winded pedantic English like my father's, halting and hesitating because my head was full of dream-thought which found its way into my speech and made it almost impossible for people to understand me.

My habits of speech brought me into further unhappiness, deeper frustration. A live little factory girl made a dead set at me about that time. As far as I can remember she was by no means pretty, certainly not to be compared with the beautiful vision of the Tivoli music-hall. But she was good-humoured, very vivacious, and dying to be played with.

She did everything except rape me, but my strange "ejjicatified" way of talking frightened her off. This, too, was a cover-up on my part, I imagine, because I knew all the Dublin words for such an encounter just as well as James Joyce, probably for the same reason. I could have written a litany of sex, even in those days, in the archaic Irish phrases of the Liberty.

After that experience I drank more, and walked more wildly on the roads at night. In those days I think I must have been very close to madness.

A word about Irish euphemisms is necessary here. It is perhaps needless to point out that in a highly moral country like Ireland there were a good many cases of repressed or frustrated people going over the line of mind-safety. But no such thing as sex-perversion or sex-neurosis was known in everyday Irish speech—such things were always called religious mania. It may have been a misnomer. But I was getting near the edge of it by the time I was sixteen. Entirely by accident my father saved me.

At about that time he began to have some more of his visions of success and great achievement for me. Despite his previous experience of my complete unreliability, he planned my future again.

Theoretically, a boy could "rise" to be general manager of the whole railway system if he started in as an apprentice and not as a machine-minder or labourer. So that was what I was elected to do next. Now I was not going to be a judge or a famous surgeon—merely the manager of the Southern Railway. My father always had really ambitious ideas for me.

We had a long, stilted, uncomfortable talk one night, while he unfolded his plan. I listened to it all carefully, even worked up a certain enthusiasm at times. Because, of course, I could already see myself walking along the canal at Sallins next day!

Then he explained that he had had an interview with the secretary. There was no vacancy for a gifted engineer-apprentice at the time, which was a pity. Nearly all the top-grade jobs went to boys who had been apprenticed as engineers.

But the matter could be arranged, with a little difficulty and with a little extra study and application. One could, if deserving, reach the administrative office via another trade. So it was settled. I was going to be a smith. Mentally I cancelled Sallins, and hardly slept that night, I was so excited.

Next day I went to a big smith-works which looked like fairyland, and started to play with metal. Now I knew I had *always* wanted to be an iron-worker. There was no need for my foolish wailing and wandering any more, nor for the crazy muttering to myself, and no more of the biting unhappiness that kept me from sleep.

Power—I had it, by God, at last. The steel and iron answered my mind, went where I told it, turned and curved on itself at my bidding, and made a hundred miracles a day in cunning, impossible junctions that happened for all their impossibility. Again I was fortunate. The change came just in the nick of time to save me from a bad mind-twisting.

The heavy work, and the need to plan and calculate, plucked back the brain that was nearly going to seed. Although I never became a good smith, commercially speaking, that workshop was a place in which I lived. Perforce I was using my body and mind, no longer thinking in awkward romantic phrases.

Indirectly, that first year in the smith-works gave me back my intellect. I was just over sixteen; my education had ended six years earlier, when I was little over ten. In all the time between I had done nothing, except moon around and learn dirt-words and feel fear. Now I had to think again.

Besides, I found the art-school as a result of my preoccupation with metals, my power-dreams. Therefrom I found, in my own way, the world of cultural achievement towards which my parents had foolishly tried to thrust me. Except that for them such achievement meant money, and for me it meant life and happiness and sanity. What greater praise can I speak than to say I did not walk away from home for over two years?

CHAPTER X

My father's plans for me had, as usual, a slight but demonstrable foundation of practicability. For one thing, an apprentice at Inchicore had to go to school in Dublin, was allowed time off to go, had his fees paid by the company. I had forgotten that; certainly my father scored one point on me there, to my great advantage.

Any really distinguished student—such as, no doubt, I was going to be—got a chance to go in the drawing-office. There, if brilliant, he was given every opportunity to master the theoretical intricacies of engineering. After that, with query twelve promotions and scoring a hundred per cent. each time, he could get right to the top of the tree. In other words, the field-marshal's baton was in the haversack. I only wanted the haversack, namely, the anvil and forge.

However, when I went to school I naturally did my best. There was an entrance exam. The company paid our fees, but for people who made a high percentage entrance was free, the fees being paid by Dublin City. When I passed for free entry I was very pleased, then considered the matter at an end. Time spent in schools was going to be wasted, as far as I was concerned. My real interests were at Inchicore, in the smithy.

Then I discovered the world. The syllabus, I imagine, would make fairly ordinary dry reading to-day; for me it was strange and revelatory as the first peep through a microscope. After the first evening at the school I went straight to the nearest pub, drank several pints of porter, and sat there, arranging my thoughts.

There was a world, at the existence of which I had not guessed. People did and made things—not because they had to work at such jobs, but because they liked it. There were plenty of Jim Phelans—many of them, doubtless, cut by bearded men in forests, strange and different—who wrote words and painted pictures and did things with iron and bronze, who had been doing it for centuries. I drank my pints, and thought over all I had nearly missed.

There must have been many a thousand in Ireland of my time who missed it, and for my own reasons. Quite simply, I had not known that Juvenal was a man like myself. Nor that the statues in Dublin Art Gallery had been made by men, worried about their world and their difference, telling their worry in that way. Nor that the paintings in any church I knew had not been done by God, or by the priests.

That poor small "gifted" child had packed himself so full of words and phrases, of rhymes and reasons, that there was no room left for the lore of living men. I only knew books. Æsthetically, my age was still anything between four and six.

Probably legions of people were in the same boat—I cannot say. There are oil paintings of more or less value in every Irish church. But one did not think of them as the work of *people*. As Liam O'Flaherty, I think, has pointed out, for the majority such things are holy pictures and there is no more to be said.

In the same way, statues for me meant saints. Certainly I have the clearest recollection of being shown Saint Clement by my mother, in the church at Inchicore, when I was two, and believing, as she did, that the saint was there before us, asleep.

All other statues went into the same category. They were not talked about. Decent Irish people, like my mother, simply did not speak of such things. Similarly, the metal-work in a church was part of the church; it was holy, and not to be discussed. That was all.

Who or what was responsible for these ideas I neither know nor care. They existed, and still exist in many parts of the world, and they were very real for me until 1911.

My attitude to books was at bottom the same. In spite of my father's stories, and although I was a most expert liar, I fully believed that all novels and tales were true. (Incidentally, I still believe it—but from another angle!)

There were cleverly concocted lies, like my own, but the stories in the books were real. D'Artagnan and Jim Hawkins, Dickens and Scott and their friends, had all got into the strangest scrapes at one time or another, and the accounts of their troubles had got into print.

Lest any reader decide that I was a half-wit, or a complete lunatic, let me simplify. What student ever thought that his text-books on arithmetic or geometry had been punched out on a typewriter, by a man who ate and drank and slept, as these words are being punched out to-night? Who, studying Todhunter's *Algebra,* ever thought of Todhunter as a person? I did not.

All books, all pictures, all art, were equally anonymous and unearthly for me, at sixteen as they had been at six. Then I found out about this fellow Benvenuto Cellini. A smith, Cellini was. Well, a kind of smith—had I not before me the drawing of a pair of wrought-iron gates he had made? A smith, a man like me.

There was a class called Art Metal-work, which I had chosen almost at random. The work was divided. Sketching and precision drawing were taken in the art-school, practical work in repoussé, scroll-bending and the like in a workshop downstairs. Very soon I was being nursed and encouraged in both sections. Naïve, enthusiastic, and bursting with energy, I worked and never knew.

Dublin was a contradictorily democratic place at the time, and the City Sheriff was a mechanic from Inchicore works, Bob Bradley. Bob always "pushed" things for the Inchicore boys, was a great admirer of Gentleman Whalen, so again I had things made easy for me.

It meant that no one applied the strict letter of the law if there was a student extra in the sculpture class, or in the group who sketched the human figure, and one short at machine-drawing. (I hated machine-drawing.)

To study illustrations of Cellini's work, of all the fine things men had made in metal during the centuries since his time, to sketch them myself, feeling the thought behind the work and visualising the difficulties—this was better than working in a circus. I almost forgot about girls and God and hell. Until I strayed into the class doing "body."

My first study of a group of nudes was prurient almost to the point of orgasm. But I swiftly realised that there was much more to be got out of the subject. When I had talked with a few of the girls and boys, learnt that most of them wanted to be artists, I made up my mind. Now I knew at last what I had always . . . And so on.

I was going to get me a girl, like that girl of the yellow hair with the curls and breast, and take her in my studio where I painted pictures. Lots of artists married models. Or as good as.

When I had taken off all the girl's clothes—my four-year-old Marjorie must have been fairly persistent!—I would sketch her, especially all the nice bits. Then I would give her a good loving, and kiss her and play again. Then I would sell the picture and make another.

(Well, well. If anyone thinks that hefty sixteen-year-old was a shade peasant-crude, I will say I have lived in Montparnasse and Chelsea and similar places since, have watched with understanding sympathy the ways of my gifted young friends. Sure, it was not a bad ideal *at all*.)

But my immediate business was to know how and why men had made lovely things in copper and steel, to make, if I could, such things myself. General manager of the Southern Railway—pooh. But I was very glad my father's planning had brought me thus far.

The discovery of class snobbery was rather a jolt, and I bitterly regretted having abandoned my career as incipient

Great Man at ten/eleven. Brother Redmond's words, about hewers and drawers, often came back to me in those days, and I was sorry for my choice of ragamuffin status.

Sooner or later, each girl or teacher or boy acquaintance, getting to the edge of intimacy, would ask what I was, and I would answer a smith. "O-oh, a smith. It must be very interesting."

Of course I was not a smith at all, and was never likely to be, but—damn and blast it, Cellini had been a smith, hadn't he? Very well, then. Always at first I felt angry for being thus partly segregated, and had for a time a recurrence of the wretched isolation-feeling. But it disappeared in the excitement of the work.

Besides, I was five feet nine or more, weighed close on two hundred pounds, was clean and good-looking, with the erect carriage which is called the "Whalen walk" in some parts of Tipperary. The other boys did not really have much chance with those girls. If only I had not been cut by the man in the forest, they would have had no chance at all.

Already the bigness of my body, combined with my mental growth, was pulling me a little from my overwhelming fear of God and my father and hell and the black things that jumped out. While I was incapable of challenging the things of fear, at the same time I was losing some small part of my fundamental abject unhappiness. A piece of sheer good luck gave me the chance to awaken still more.

One night I had come home early from work, had no classes to attend, and was not inclined to roam the roads. On my way home I had had one pint of porter. Often I drank much more, but no one at home ever knew. (Liquor went with sex, blasphemy and atheism for my mother.) Lying on a couch, downstairs, I drowsed while waiting for my supper.

One of my sisters, passing, stopped and sniffed and looked at me curiously. She added up the beer-fumes with my stretched-out drowsiness, and announced in horror, "Why— Jim's drunk!"

While I was telling her not to be a fool, while my mother was weeping for the damnation of my immortal soul, my father came in, and was told. He was outraged, and dangerously angry. I was condemned unheard.

Unfortunately for my father, he had very obviously had several drinks. Not intoxicated, yet he spoke rather thickly, had had about as much liquor as I carried home most nights. But I usually kept my mouth shut—his job at the moment was to give a menacing lecture on temperance!

"What's this?" he demanded. "Drunk! Listen, you young ragamuffin——" I stood up quietly—I was terrified—and said I was not drunk, asked him to look at me and listen to the way I spoke. He roared me down.

"Listen," I said in turn. "You're the judge. Which of us is the nearer to being drunk? You decide." (Logic was always my strong point. It might have got me killed that night, though.)

That was the end of the talk. In a second I was down in a corner, the back of my head smashing against the wall, while God and the black dog and my father stood over me with their eyes blazing. Half dazed, nearly knocked out, I turned over to cry and crawl away.

There was a lovely girl, with yellow curls and a breast, in my thinking. During the tenth of a second while, stretched out on the floor, I raised myself to one elbow, the girl was alive in my mind. Slow hatred came up inside me too, for the mean, weasel-eyed, bearded man in the forest who had cut me when I was only a baby; there was rage for being wrongfully punished, because I was not drunk, for the day by the fountain when I had been knocked likewise, for nothing, for nothing, for . . . I sprang up and smashed back.

We must have fought for nearly a quarter of an hour, and my mother's sitting-room was wrecked beyond repair. But from the beginning I was not afraid of men in forests any more. I took the terrible blows—my father was a very powerful man and could fight—drank my own blood and liked it, smashed at him, blindly, for a long time, until at last I stretched him on the floor, and spat blood and saliva on his senseless face, and cried in rage and hatred for the baby who had been smashed down by the fountain that Sunday morning. My mother washed my face and got me out of the house.

My father might and might not have killed me if I had stayed, but I wanted to go—any way, anywhere—for the first moment. Then, outside the door, I asked myself quietly why I should go. There was not really anything to fear. If necessary . . .

Almost at once I heard my father coming out, and stepped swiftly into a doorway to let him pass, as I had often done in my ragamuffin days. He passed within a few inches of me, and went on down the street. I went indoors, and to bed. But I kept my clothes on, in case the fight should have a second round. It had not.

From what my mother told me later, it appeared that my father came in about an hour afterwards, washed his face, and examined his injuries. To-day I can imagine and sympathise with his horror, but at that time I merely rejoiced. He was badly marked, torn, and bruised, with his eyes blacked —how could Gentleman Whalen face the ignorant gloating gossip of the works?

He went next day to a doctor, told him he had kidney trouble or something of the sort. The doctor believed him, after one look at his face, and he did not go near the works until every sign of his injuries had gone. He never referred to the matter again, and neither did I. I did not roam the night-roads, nor make foolish anapæsts again, for a long time.

Nearly two years passed, bitter-sweetly, in a routine that did not resemble work, but in which I got a great deal done. I took everything they could give me at the school and asked for more, read an incredible number of books, without system or plan, simply taking them in fours or fives as my fancies changed. What did it matter if one here or there was not exactly what I wanted? Already I knew I could read much more quickly than anyone of my acquaintance.

Twice I wrote a story and sent it—to *Answers*. I treasured

the two rejection slips for long. In the practical class at the school I could already make things which, I told myself a hundred times, satisfied me as much as a girl.

Almost immediately after the fight with my father I decided that I was not "wrong" at all, and that it was all a mistake. Somehow I connected the two things, and as soon as possible I got me a girl, the first one that came.

In the Dublin of my days there was never any difficulty about getting a girl. One simply walked along and saw a girl and said hello. If she was not going to meet someone she went for a walk, in the Phœnix Park, or along a canal, or a little way out, into a field with the gate open. We went to the Phœnix Park.

The haste was slightly unfortunate for me. This was a factory girl, dull, blank, with just a few platitudes for conversation, but healthy and happy and knowing precisely why one went in the Park. Long before we got there we were eyeing one another rather doubtfully, both ill at ease because we spoke different languages.

Early, I found myself disliking her crude utterance, had not sufficient commonsense to realise that my problems were not related to the girl's diction. When we sat down I realised with horror that my stilted Sir Galahad speech was back, and that the lively youngster was regarding her big-bodied pickup as a freak.

We made no progress, and I left her, with despair on me again, because I had after all been mistaken in thinking I was like other people.

The next time I did not make the same mistake, but took out one of the girls from the school. This was no pickup, to be taken in a field and dealt with mechanically, but a girl who would have to be courted. Her middle-class prejudices would, in their own way, be almost as powerful as my own.

She had had no experience with men, came from a strait-laced and over-moral family like my own, except that they were upper middle class as well, which made things worse. That affair was headed for the rocks from the first moment.

In the long run I induced my moral counterpart to take a chance on love. She did, and I did not. My mother's morality was winning again.

That put me back nearly to breaking-point. My work was better, but the repetition of the sordid and embarrassing scenes had marked me. Now I knew I was not ordinary, and swore I should never try to be so again.

Nor did I ever any more make long, detailed, carefully secure plans to be a man, as I had done before, with only shame and frustration as the outcome. It would have been no use, and I did not care. A hundred times a day, a thousand times a night, I told myself I did not care. Sleep stayed away.

One night I lay awake as usual, downstairs in our house, with a raging toothache as well as my thoughts for company. Tossing and turning, I tried to be rid of the pain but without success. Finally I dressed and went out for a walk. The pain went almost immediately, but I continued walking, although it was two o'clock in the morning.

At a street corner a girl was standing talking to a policeman. She smiled as I passed, and caught me up after I had gone a few yards. Her first question made me jump, although it must have been merely conventional—"Can't you sleep, darlin'?"

Rather awkwardly, embarrassed, I answered her, and we walked along the street. She was very pretty: I could see that much without thinking of holy and blessed saints. But she also had a friendly and pleasant manner which surprised me, educated as I was to think of all town-girls as vile, demoniacal, and horrible.

Feeling very strained, I turned to go, heading back into the depths again, well knowing that I was so headed. The girl must have known much of what was going on in my mind.

"Sure, you're only pretending you don't like me," she said with a little laugh, and put one hand on my shoulder. "Won't you speak to me?" she pressed in surprise, then suddenly, as I tensed and worried and strained, with fear and revulsion and horror tearing me, she put an arm round my neck and drew me closer.

"Sure, you've never had a girl before. That's it, isn't it?" she urged, but I said nothing.

The pain and fear, in my strange twisted brain, made me want to strike her and run away, but the girl stretched her other hand, across my chest, and stroked me quietly, up to the neck and on the side of the face. There was a tasselled fringe on the collar of her coat, and my fingers twisted and kneaded at one of the tassels.

Hell and my mother and God and the black things and the bearded man were all together, while my fingers twitched at the tassel, until the girl laughed again, very slightly, and moved my hand.

"There," she said, and again, "There," as if I were a child. "That's better—sure, I have only one coat!" She moved my hand and looked in my eyes to smile.

It was a lonely narrow lane into which we had turned. Twenty yards from the main thoroughfare one might have been in open country. A pile of straw was by the wall at the rear of a stable yard, and I went in twitching haste to throw my overcoat on it.

The girl laughed again, at my choking eagerness, I suppose. Then she gave me back a kiss as wild as my own, and there was no more hell and no more black headless things to jump, nor any bearded men that mattered, only a girl.

I leant over her, trembling, afterwards, and we laughed together as I kissed her again. "*Now* do you like me?" she demanded triumphantly, and as I reached with my hands to answer her she added, "Come on home."

We went to a cheap, mean lodging-house where she lived. Half a dozen prostitutes and several drunken men were in the place, and it was frowsy and sordid, but to me of course it looked wonderful. A couple of hours later, when I was leaving, I gave the girl all the money I had with me, about four pounds.

It may have been that she was shrewd enough to know I would be generous, or that she was herself generously unthinking, or simply that she liked the look of me. A little of all three, I think, because she had not mentioned money from beginning to end. I walked on air going home. I was not wrong and different at all; I was Jim Phelan, and I was a man.

It will sound trivial, or even sentimental, to many of my friends, but I knew that girl had given me something much bigger than the fortune or fame of which I had read in books, something better than money, or saintliness, or scholarship. The dawn was coming up, over Dublin Bay from where the Bristol steamers went, and almost I stopped to talk to it. Already I wanted it to be next evening.

Love affairs, and real love, I have known much, since. But, naturally enough, I suppose, no one except one tramp girl has ever come so near to me, or given me such peace, as that laughing young gay-girl in a Dublin street.

In my clash with the Liffeyside city I had lost. As my mother would have put it, I had lost my immortal soul. My own thought was to take the other half of the quotation—I had gained the whole world. I could have sung, as I turned in at the corner by our house.

It was only dawn, a little after four o'clock, but to my surprise my parents were already up. My mother was in her accustomed place, by a table-corner, weeping bitterly. At first I could not see my father, but I heard a kind of strangled crying from beside a window curtain. Then I saw that he was sitting in a corner, choking with great painful sobs. Aghast, I stared at them.

It came out in the first few tearful words. Some neighbour, returning home late, had seen me with the girl, played Peeping Tom, followed us to the lodging-house, then hurried to my home, to wake my parents and deliver the cheerful news.

Their attitude can be understood, with a little difficulty. If I had been infected with leprosy and tuberculosis, had my arms and legs amputated, and was then carried off to a prison for lifelong torture, that would have been trivial, in their eyes, compared with the story they had heard. What could I say?

My mother's lamentations, for the loss of my soul, were dreadful to witness. My father rose, towering, and pointed to the door, with a dramatic gesture which would have been laughable if the unfortunate man had not been almost insane with grief for my loss.

"Go," he ordered, in a choking voice, and added no other word. I walked out.

By the time the sun came up I was four miles from Dublin, only then realising that I had not a penny in my possession or in the world. I whistled, along the canal, and it was Burns's song, which had only been words on paper to me before— "Oh, whistle, and I'll come to you, my lad."

CHAPTER XI

CALM, after the few miles' walk, I sat by the roadside to sum things up. Primarily I was pleased—there would be no more need for deception or pretence. All my life, since I was three or four, I had had too much of both. Now I was done with them.

For the first time I was not hurrying away, from pain or fear. There was nothing to fear in Dublin. Quite the reverse. I stretched myself and slapped my hands together like a school-boy as I repeated, quite the reverse.

A week or ten days, I considered, would suffice to blunt the edge of my parents' grief. They would be glad when I re-turned. They would soon be more than glad, when I was no longer a dreaming incompetent but a real workman. Now I might even fall in with my father's wishes, and work my way up to be general manager of the whole railway.

Why not? Chief barrier had been the fear-born certainty that I was not, and could never be, a whole man. That was gone and done with. Of course I would fall in with my father's wishes.

Pleased with my summary, I walked on. As surely as I know to-day, I knew that a phase of my life had closed. Tall, olive-green sloes made a lovely hedge, and I whistled along that road.

But I made the mistake that all of us except the saints and scholars make—I thought I was rid of the past for ever. As well might a man go tramping a year in the tropics, then reach temperate latitude and decide that, because he has come to cool

123

at last, his blood has not been thinned nor his face burnt brown.

However, my philosophising lost itself in an abrupt recall to fact. I was ravenously hungry, and I had no money.

By that time I had covered about ten miles, and was in the middle of a cattle-grazing district where there were few houses. I recalled my reactions of shrinking and shame, on that tramping-day nearly four years earlier, when I had first decided to beg.

But this time I felt nothing of the kind. This time I was not begging—I was only going for a walk. Smiling and confident, I asked for food at the nearest house.

It was only a small cottage, where a farm-worker lived, but without hesitation the woman led the way into a kitchen. Her husband, shirt-sleeved, was just sitting down to breakfast, and a place was laid for me.

The couple were plainly puzzled by my appearance and manner. Well-dressed, but unwashed and unshaven, speaking correct English, good-humoured, but obviously penniless and a beggar, I cannot have conformed to their experience of tramps. Quite early they abandoned the attempt to place me.

The man had put a hundred indirect questions—indirect because the Irish custom is not to enquire about another person's business, but merely to find out. The simple truth, that I was just walking, had no money and no job, did not know where I was going, left him even more mystified than before. After a final cup of tea and a friendly parting I followed the road at random.

Having dawdled a further few miles, I felt little urge to go on. Back towards Dublin my inclination lay, not off at hazard along the bog roads. Perhaps I could walk a circle of a hundred miles or so, then get back to the city and really start life at last.

My only three cigarettes I smoked, loitering pleasurably in a wood of beech and oak near the roadside, and was still quite clear that my goal was in fact behind me. To-morrow, or in a few days, I would return home, to love and help my parents, finished with the black miserable past for ever.

My mother used to tell that everything one did or thought was written on a great manuscript in heaven. This is not the place for me to argue about it—I have believed even stranger things in my time. But if I had a celestial biographer that morning, he must have been amused.

Kicking about among the dead leaves, I made me a poem as I had always done at such times. And not once did I grasp the significance of what I was writing, nor feel the flat contradiction of everything I thought about myself.

This is what came out of the oak wood:

VAGRANT

I am an acorn. In the roar of the rain and the heave of the gale was I born, and a million like me were asleep on the parquet of mould in the whispering cool of the forest that brought us to life.

Isolate, desolate, vacillant, feeble and small, as we lay in the shivering shade of the lords of the wood, puerile and impotent we.

Somewhere, above, was a sun. Somewhere, below, was a soil. Errant we fared, to the kicks of the wind, for the sun and the soil were the right and the spoil of the lords.

Tremblingly, upward, we gazed at the day. Faintly and feebly we asked, "Why is a Forest, and whence?" But, peering, we strained for the brightness that chequered the shade and, asking, we stirred for the warm that came down on the mould.

Stunted and stifled by cold-casting limbs, still did we waken and rise, straining and stirring to hold by the beam that came down.

Thus did we press, when the cycle of time had completed its destinate round, to the smile of the day and the kiss of the wind. When the limbs that o'er-pressed us were rent, when the cristates that crippled us tottered and fell, then did we stare on the stars. Then did we drink of the day, in the light-streaming love of a radiant sky and owned not the forest—but were it.

Here, had I but recognised it, was a later version of the poem from my four-year-old days, which I had sung by the roadside on my first runaway from Inchicore. To be consistent, I should have called it, "Far away my many parties."

But—it was many years ago, and I was not consistent. The next few miles of road passed like a landscape on a cinema screen. Not until evening did I beg another meal, and I slept in a haybarn instead of a field. Then it was morning, and I had known a new thing—real sleep.

Several days went in aimless wandering, in a blank and peaceful somnolence. Any of the sociologists I knew later would have labelled the burly young fellow of those days as a typical, shiftless, workshy drifter. Probably there were other explanations, but it is true that I did not think of working. Until by accident I looked in a mirror, and saw a filthy, battered tramp.

The well-cut suit for which the Dublin bookies had paid was creased and dirty. At embarrassing moments, pocket or coat-collar would give evidence about my sleeping places, by shedding a shower of hayseeds. Scrubby, awkward-looking whiskers disguised my face. The expensive hat with which I had left Dublin was battered into a most villainous slouch, and my boots were thick with crusted mud. A clean-up was imperative.

At the next big farm I asked for a job, and worked two days. My pay was only five shillings—farm-labourers in Ireland were very badly paid—but I slept and ate at the farm, and was able to borrow a razor and clothes-brush. So that when I came into the city of Kilkenny my money was still intact.

After a total expenditure, for lodging, food, and cigarettes, of half a crown, I rested up for a day and purchased my outfit. Razor, soap, comb, collar, needles and thread, with a small cheap towel to wrap them, cost less than my remaining half-crown. With threepence change and my traveller's equipment, I walked out of Kilkenny on the first road that offered.

It occurs to me, here, that in the year of writing this book I earned twelve hundred pounds. Also that, on occasion, the income-tax authorities have indicated, uncompromisingly, large earnings of mine. Yet I have gone on the road, without any money, more than once in recent years.

I went penniless, as ever. But I went fully equipped for tramping. Here is the itemisation of my latest outfit—razor, soap, collar and handkerchief, shoelaces, buttons and collar-stud, clothes-brush, needles and thread, with a small cheap towel to wrap them.

The additions may prove that I am becoming sybaritic. Or they may prove that, without knowing it, I was already a genuine road-goer when I bought my kit in Kilkenny.

Certainly it never occurred to me at the time that I was a tramp, although one incident brought up an awkwardness. Near nightfall, on the second evening after Kilkenny, the names on a signpost gave me a jolt. I was in Tipperary, in the district where my relatives lived.

It only took me a second to decide—I was not going to see any of my friends while I was a wanderer on the roads. I remember walking, in the dusk, straight through one small town and three villages, at all of which I had been an honoured visitor when I was thirteen. Then I slept in a haystack—it may have belonged to some cousin of mine, and probably did. Next day I hurried away from Tipperary, earnestly as I had once hurried towards it.

Meeting with the Southern Railway, in the county Limerick, brought the curious inverted nostalgia I have known all my life. It also brought the realisation that I was at least theoretically a railwayman, and might ride to—somewhere. The guard of a goods train made no demur about letting me travel in his van, and I walked out into Cork city at midnight, possessed of threepence and greatly interested.

Cork was a wonderfully cosmopolitan place, when glimpsed for the first time in the middle of the night. Across the street was a Turkish name on a shop-front. A few yards off, a street lamp showed the words "Coiffeur des dames." Near me, in the window of a store, were strange spiky fruits I had never previously seen. Here was the big world come to put its foot on my doorstep.

Knowing that Cork was on the River Lee—and I knew little more about it—I turned downhill at the first crossing of the streets. A policeman halted me for questioning, in the darkness, but my Dublin speech and railway jargon helped me out, and he was satisfied. One incident of the enquiry might have come straight from the Middle Ages—needing a better look at me, he struck a match and lit a small candle.

We said good night and, as behoved a workman going about his business, I struck off smartly down the dark street, without the faintest idea where it went. Presently I came to a river, and had to throw in a piece of white paper before I could see which way it flowed.

Upstream would be streets and houses, which I did not then want. Downstream would be something like Dublin riverside. Keeping down, I came at last to deserted wharves, with an occasional dark and silent steamer alongside.

Unexpectedly, it began to freeze hard. The question of a sleeping-place became urgent, but there were here no stables or haystacks. Nevertheless, I had to find somewhere quickly —I could feel the cold biting into my body more keenly every moment.

In desperation I hailed a watchman, snoozing in the galley of a steamer, and asked him to let me sit at the fire until morning. But he was part grumpy, part frightened, and refused with many sheepish explanations. Back on the quay, I lifted the tarpaulin from a pile of cargo, but the sheet was frozen stiff as a board and creaked in my hand.

Anyone may laugh at me for what I did next, but in all probability it saved my life—I camped out. On the public riverside of Cork, open to pedestrian or other traffic, and theoretically patrolled by the police, I camped out.

An iron roof covered a small square of pavement at a place where, apparently, dock workers or such people had their meals. There was a wide wooden seat against a warehouse wall, with the iron roof over it. That was all; the place was open on three sides, was the public footwalk.

A loose tarpaulin at one end made me a windscreen and a corner. A big bundle of wood scraps collected on the quay gave a noble fire. When I found a rusty square of tin, to back the fire and reflect the heat into my corner, I knew luxury, and slept stretched out on the seat. As far as I know, not one person passed during the night.

A combination of good luck, logic, and instinct brought me my breakfast. Further, they brought the realisation that I had been a naïve young fool to go lighting fires on the quayside, risking a month's imprisonment. Leaving my camp before full sunrise, I drifted towards a place with tall chimneys and occasional pleasant Gownseer-like clangings.

It proved to be the engine-house of a factory, one stoker tending four fires. When I walked in by the coal-door, he merely grinned and said something about the cold. Then, after a single shrewd glance, he asked if I had been out all night.

He whistled with surprise, and was genuinely perturbed, when he heard I had been out in the frost, but he guffawed again and again when I told about my camp-fire. Then he nodded to a large notice on the wall, which told of dire penalties to follow if a stoker allowed any unauthorised person in the stokehold.

"Sure, I wouldn't turn a dog out on a night like that," he summed up. "You should have come in." I had passed the place, in the dark, on my way down to the quayside.

While we talked, the stoker had been boiling a can of water. Presently he gave me a sandwich and sat me down to several cups of tea. But he made me keep away from the fire, lest the cold should bite me when I left.

From his anecdotes, I gathered that he was accustomed to riverside drifters, and he asked no personal questions whatever. Then, when I was leaving, he "lent" me a shilling. Lent! What diplomat ever approached that stoker for tact?

The difference between two million pounds and one million pounds is less than the difference between a shilling and threepence. Warm, after a good sleep, with my breakfast eaten and one and threepence to spend, I smacked my hands and stepped out, on a bridge across the river. Cork city was exclusively mine, riverside, steamers, and all.

The opposite bank was much the busier. Stores and warehouses thinned out into a large open space called the Marina. A huge foreign-looking steamer was discharging a cargo of timber, and lower down was a ship with a flag I did not know. Cork was maintaining its cosmopolitan status for me.

My chief reason for prowling along the Marina was that it looked the sort of place where one might be able to clean up. I did not want to go up the city looking raffish, and one cannot wash or shave in a river—if it runs through city streets.

An incredibly cheap café had a rough toilet attached, and in a few minutes I felt clean and smart enough to face the city police. Also I would have to face a landlady of some kind, because I intended to sleep in a bed that night. Wherefore I kept my shilling intact.

Then I nearly lost the shilling after all, did in fact lose it. On my way back up the river I passed a group of men playing cards for pennies, and had the idea of at least doubling my capital. Presently I was wondering what the factory stoker would say, when I turned up that night, to sit by the fire. I had only twopence.

My luck turned, but after an hour I had only a shilling and sevenpence, so I decided I was not going to find any fortune on that riverside. A loafer told me where I could find a lodging. He named three rates, and seemed surprised when I chose the most expensive, one where a bed for a night cost a shilling.

On the way to the boarding-house I passed the street of many nations which had been my first glimpse of Cork. The Turkish name was genuine enough, but it was the trade-name for someone's sweetmeats, Hassan Effendi or the like. The "Coiffeur des dames" was an ordinary little hairdresser's place. My exotic fruits were pineapples, then a rarity in Ireland. The Phelan imagination had been painting that street for me!

When I found the "stall," I had to answer as many questions

as if I were a suspected criminal, and the "stall" free. A man and his wife, both very prim and grim and precise, interrogated me as to my respectability and my intention to work in the city. At last they condescended to let me stay, and I paid my shilling.

When I said I would go to my room and have a wash, they both stared in perfect silence. After a very long pause, the man said I had to be in by half-past ten. This, apparently, concluded the business discussion, so I left, having made certain of the address.

On the Marina I had a large bowl of pea-soup for a penny. It tasted like badly burnt rather dirty brown paper, and the accompanying loaf, which also cost a penny, was rubbery, but I had no complaints to make. Later I loitered along the river.

Dock-work in Cork appeared to be carried out in the most primitive manner. Thus, on a coal-steamer, instead of an iron tub hoisting a ton or more at a time, as in other ports, a small basket full of coal was heaved up. A large man then placed it on his shoulder, walked gravely down the gang-plank, and tipped the basket on the quayside.

In the same way, the timber-ship was being unloaded by hand. Carrying perhaps a thousand tons of timber, the steamer had three double gangways out. Up and down each pair of planks, a stream of men moved constantly to and fro, one docker going aboard empty-handed, his mate descending with a log on his shoulder. The whole business seemed incredibly foolish and wasteful.

I remarked as much to a man who sat near me, with three others, watching the ship. To my surprise, he glared menacingly, and told me in a threatening tone that they wanted no bloody polismen on that waterfront. The other three supported him.

Mystified, I could see that I was likely to get a pair of black eyes, or to go in the river. In haste I explained that I was an engineer—a railwayman from Dublin—and knew nothing whatever about dock work. The plea of ignorance made my peace, but only just in time.

Cork was different, that was all. The dockers, all huge men, were banded in a sort of mediæval guild. By sheer pugnacity, and by complete loyalty to one another, they kept the port as they wanted it.

They wanted it without machines. Foolish strangers, from Dublin or elsewhere, who had bright ideas about machinery, were likely to sample the pleasant waters of the River Lee. I made no further comments on the man-handling of the cargo.

Rambling around the city, up and down the hundred hills, I tired myself but enjoyed every minute of the prowl. Then towards dusk I drifted back down the Marina again, to have a big bowl of tea and another of the rubbery loaves.

Work had ceased, and when the little café closed, the riverside was very still. Now and then a dim figure passed, silently, between the tall warehouse walls. A distant chime clanged down the darkness—the Shandon Bells I had known only from song and poem.

Out on the river a small tug hooted, friendly beams of rose and emerald reflected from the water. Far down the Lee someone sang. The many stacks of timber, in the open spaces of the Marina, threw a hundred curiously shaped patches of shadow. That waterfront pleased me.

A man came along the quay, singing loudly, and in a few minutes I was deep in friendly talk with a young fellow in sailor clothes. From Hull, he was a quartermaster or something of the kind on the timber ship, was very drunk, and apparently liked Ireland a great deal.

We swore eternal friendship several times by the riverside. Then for a moment it looked as if I would have to prove my amity at once. Two small and very slinky-looking Chinese came silently out of the shadows from the direction of the city, and I braced myself to stand by the drunken sailor, if necessary.

My imagination was away again—they were two quite ordinary firemen from the young fellow's ship, and seemed rather proud and pleased when he spoke to them. I gathered that quartermasters and Chinese firemen made little contact, except after the sampling of much Irish whisky.

It was settled, over and over again, that I was going to

Stockholm, where the steamer was bound. My friend dismissed the difficulties with a wave of his hand—he would put everything right with the chief engineer, would get me signed on. It seemed possible that he might do exactly as he said, since he was a thoroughly friendly chap.

But of course there was the possibility that next morning he would have forgotten the whole incident! So I convoyed him to the ship's gangway and saw him aboard. Only then I remembered it was after ten, and hurried away to my lodgings.

The landlord and his wife reminded me, rather grimly, that it was very close to half-past ten. A short lecture on the evils of walking around city streets followed, with many side references to the need for respectable boarding houses to keep themselves respectable, and for dwellers therein to appreciate their privileges. Then the landlord took a candle and showed me to my room.

Unlocking a door, he ordered rather than invited me to enter. Six small beds were around the walls of a fairly large room; this was the total accommodation. Four of the beds were already occupied, by unkempt and unmistakable tramps. Waving me to a fifth, the landlord proceeded to undress, and took the remaining bed. Then his wife called from outside, and a moment later she locked the door, leaving her husband inside with me and the tramps.

The couple seemed to be completely crazy, but next morning one of the tramps told me it was the best stall in Cork, for anyone who had a shilling. That was after the door had been unlocked and the host let out for his breakfast.

My own breakfast came from my remaining coppers, and thereafter I sat around on the timber-piles, looking at nothing in particular, dreaming and drifting. Well on in the afternoon I realised I was hungry and had no money. That in turn reminded me I had no shilling for my grim hosts, and I decided, vaguely, to walk out of Cork.

Begging in a city would not be the same thing as calling for a meal at a farmhouse. One would have to ask people for money, in the streets, and I could not do that. Very wistfully

I wondered where the tramps from my stall got their shillings each day. It seemed that Cork was to be the last city I would visit, because now I should have to drift along the country lanes again, within reach of farmhouse kitchen and haystack, until I went home.

On the quayside I met one of the tramps from my lodgings, and he shared a big parcel of food with me. He had begged it from the galley of a ship, and we divided it there and then, on a pile of timber. I felt very foolish and embarrassed, to be eating in public, but apparently my companion did not mind. Presently he asked if I had paid my stall and I said yes.

His opinion of my veracity showed in his next two remarks, when he told me to look out for the police if I was walking about all night, and volunteered the information that my suit might well pawn for thirty shillings or more. On that note we parted.

Plodding across the city, in the early evening, I came to a large open space where an amusement fair was in full swing. There were roundabouts, a steam organ, and side shows, and the place was already crowded. Loitering around in the light and warmth, presently I noticed a big man watching me.

Wearing a smart navy-blue suit and a hard black hat, he was clean-shaved, and powerful looking. Mentally I placed him as a policeman in plain clothes, who had spotted me for a stranger and was keeping an eye on me. Accordingly I nodded and smiled, giving him a chance to talk if he wished to get the enquiries over.

His name was Tom Dunne, he said, and it was his first time in Ireland, although he was an Irish-American from Seattle. Chief engineer of an oil-tanker, he had been looking forward to the trip to Cork, was enjoying the city greatly.

The story sounded wrong, and I suspected a rather crude police trap, in which I was doubtless expected to steal the foreign sailor's wallet or something of the kind. My suspicions were confirmed by the fact that the man's American accent could have been cut with a knife.

We had a drink, then another, and gradually I realised

that the accent was real. Simply I had never heard western American speech before. We had other drinks, many, I having the pints of porter to which I was accustomed, Dunne engulfing large quantities of whisky.

He was a very likeable fellow, about forty-five, and I could not at first decide whether he was extremely innocent or very tough. Having a large roll of American money in his pocket, he enjoined me to see him down the waterfront, for safety. In other words, he elected as escort the very man who *might* have been expected to knock him on the head in the dark and take the roll.

Perhaps, though, Tom Dunne really had learnt a lot about people, in his thirty years at sea.

After a very wild evening around Cork, we staggered down the quay at a late hour, both very drunk but capable. Several times we arranged that I was to sleep aboard the tanker, and sign on the next day, but I said good night at the gangway-foot. Then I lurched in the dark, Dunne steadied me, and we repeated our thousand pledges of comradeship. Finally we talked our way past a watchman, and I curled up on a bunk in a nearly empty fo'c'sle.

In spite of my Dublin dockside experience, I had not realised that the chief engineer of a steamer was such an important person. Next morning I was given my breakfast without question, Dunne sent me a large slug of whisky, and I was signed on as a fireman by midday.

Vague and incompetent as ever, I did not consider the facts that I had no kit and was no fireman. Indeed, I did not even know the name of the steamer, until I saw *Narraganset* on the papers I signed. However, I appreciated the three sovereigns I was paid in advance.

On that night's tide we went down the river, but I paid no farewells to the Irish coast. I vomited continually, not from sea-sickness, but from the effect of the oil-fumes, and I must have been running a temperature before we were twelve hours out.

Somehow I managed to keep on my feet, but my head and

lungs were bursting. Medical science had not then discovered allergy, and I did not know, as I know now, that I was dangerously allergic to oil-fumes, petrol-exhaust, or anything of the kind. Like the others of my crowd, I thought I was a nuisance and a softy.

The *Narraganset* was less than two weeks at sea, but it felt like many years. The moment we tied up, at Galveston in Texas, I decided to walk away. None of my home-leavings had ever cost me such a strain.

Unwilling to clear out and leave Dunne to think of me as a mean vagabond, I tried to explain, but of course it was useless. The big fellow genuinely liked me, and was disappointed. I recall some remarks of his, dogmatically philosophical, about drifters. They hit me hard, but I walked away nevertheless.

Wide water separated Galveston from the land to the east and, knowing nothing of American geography, I started to walk around it. Two days later, jaded and still walking, I came into Houston. But the wide water was still to the east and my journey had not begun. Vaguely I thought that Florida would be over there, and the Suwanee River, with New York a little way to the north.

Really it was only a few inches on an atlas. I did not yet know that the whole of Ireland would fit in one small corner of Texas.

At Houston I managed to get some American money for the remnant of my three English pounds, and strolled, largely confident and at random. My drift-instinct was developing, and without discomfiture I found the slightly rakish district where casual strangers came and went.

A tramp with whom I talked made open guffaw when he heard I had been walking. From his manner, I concluded that I was a simple fool. Apparently no sophisticated person walked.

After he had attempted to swindle me out of my few dollars, and after I had explained that I was a professional boxer from Ireland, we got on well. He had many packets of food which we could share, it being my function to stand some drinks. Then, when I had bought a bottle of whisky for the road, he showed me how to ride in what I called a goods wagon.

This is a wholly impossible feat in Ireland, for a very simple reason. A loose door-fastener would always be dropped into place, by some railwayman, because a swinging door might catch a platform. Thus, a tramp who rode in an Irish goods wagon would stay inside—until some official let him out.

I think my companion was really a clumsy blunderer, and that we took foolhardy chances, but of course I did not know at the time. He was the cicerone, justified in his boasting, since we rode for a whole day on the Southern Railroad without molestation.

A thoroughly detestable type, this vagrant prejudiced me against tramps for a long time, and the meeting with him was a serious disillusionment. Anti-social to the edge of insanity, he searched incessantly for opportunities to inflict mean and trivial injuries on persons unknown.

A small bracket was fixed inside the wagon, where a man might hang a lamp when working. My fellow-traveller worked hard for nearly an hour to wrench it off. On the floor at one end of the wagon was a pile of light, fragrant wood-shavings, comfortable bed for a tramp; he urinated on it three times, gloating.

A mean, thin snigger, sheepishly malicious, came from him after each such performance, accompanied by some phrase of pseudo-justification such as that *that* would show the bastards. Gradually I began to wonder if the man was mad—I had never seen anyone like him before.

Then he picked up a tin from which we had been drinking, and deliberately washed certain parts of his body, again with the same falsetto snigger of malice. Gloatingly he spoke the thought that later tramps would drink from the same tin. Casually I told a sanguinary story of my boxing days in Dublin, and he seemed to see the point, for he kept quiet for a while.

Besides his other twists, he was rabidly homosexual. I did

not know what that was either, at the time, but I knew there was something wrong. Rabid is the only word, since he plainly knew I was in a dangerous temper, could knock him cold with a single blow.

Even in spite of his knowledge, with fear in his eyes, but with the silly titter on his lips, he persisted. I laid him out, and stood over him waiting for the expected fight, but he stayed insensible at the end of the wagon. When he recovered, he lay where he had fallen, and then, at a stop, he cleared out without a word.

Still the deep dirt of him came to the surface, for he left the wagon in such a way as to draw attention to me, turning back to wave and call good-bye. Knowing nothing of the difficulties, I was settling down with my whisky-bottle when a hoarse voice roared, "C'mon, y'sonofabitch. What're ya ridin' on, hey? What're ya ridin' on?"

Panic-stricken, for I was worse than inexperienced, and my late companion had told a hundred blood-curdling stories about "shacks" or brakemen, I stood up to look out, not even understanding what the man had said. It is embarrassing and laughable to remember now, but possibly my grave and serious manner saved me from the shack's anger.

I said, "Pardon?"

The brakeman nearly choked with rage. In all probability he had never before heard such a speech from a tramp.

"Pardin!" he bellowed. "*Pardin,* y'sonofabitch! I'll——"

But by that time I had caught the basic Irish in his voice, and turned on my best "ejjicatified" Irish accent, realising clearly that I might get a bad beating if the man was not impressed. When he identified me as a Dubliner, I knew I was safe.

In pretended grumpiness he closed the door, after threatening me with castration and other things if I smoked. Then I sat without food or water, with nothing except a half-pint of whisky, for close on twenty-four hours as I judged. Later, when the train had been stopped for a long time, I crept out, into the darkness.

After losing myself a dozen times in a big railway-yard with a maze of tracks, I emerged on a quiet street with warehouses. Afraid to walk through the strange town in the darkness, I loitered. Although I had three and a half dollars, I was dubious about going in search of a lodging, since I did not know what time it was, what the town was called, nor what the police might be like.

It was warm, and I waited without moving far. Then, sooner than I had expected, it was morning, and I drifted until I came to the side of a huge river. Even I knew it could only be the Mississippi. Careful prowling, an examination of wall-notices and advertisements, told me I was in New Orleans.

A mighty breakfast cost only twenty-five cents. Then I promenaded—there is no other word, for I was enjoying the incredibly attractive city with every atom of my body. I strolled by the river, back to the city centre, down the streets by the riverside again.

The tramping-verses of a few years earlier had contained many place-names. But I nearly made a song from the names of the streets in the west of New Orleans that first morning.

Even to-day, thirty-odd years later, there is a music for me in the mere list. Claiborne, Willow, Clara, Magnolia, Robertson, Freret, Howard, Liberty, Rampart—they all gave on to the same main road, with the thrice-apt name Felicity.

At the bottom was Shakespeare Square, never without a dozen tramps. Then, having passed enough thrown-away fruit to feed all the vagrants in Ireland, one came to the river. It looked much bigger than the Atlantic, and after the quiet river-wharves of Cork and Dublin there seemed to be hundreds of steamers. One heard more laughter than in many a theatre. Further, and important, the place smelt like my memories of Dublin fruit market.

Almost from the beginning I made Howard Street my spiritual home, sauntering up and down until even on the first day people knew my face. There were girls in Howard Street.

Many of them were just whores; to me they seemed like houris. Perhaps the reader who has known the hell of my first eighteen years will understand how the people appeared.

Howard was really three separate streets, all in a straight line and having the same name, but varying almost as much as if they were in different countries. One part was keeping up appearances, gaudily, as if all the people came from theatre or circus; another section was an ordinary busy shopping-place; a third district had many negroes. The place I chose as a lodging had all negroes except myself.

My choice was unusual, but I neither knew nor cared, drank in the talk and the stories. At the earliest moment in the morning I went off to prowl by the river.

There were many tramps on the waterfront, most of them dilapidated and frowsy-looking. Several made friendly approaches, in what I later learnt was the ordinary way of the road, but, rather hastily generalising from my solitary specimen, I avoided them. Big and burly, and I suppose tough-looking in my dirt and my strange clothes, I had no difficulty about repelling advances. Several days dreamt themselves away.

The ruin of my clothes worried me a little. My only suit, navy blue, much more expensive than Irish workmen usually wore, was filthy with smears of oil and grease. My solitary shirt was grimed, and I had now no money to buy another.

Several times in the first few days I decided to take a job; there were plenty. But it was so easy to drift in New Orleans —the place is a paradise for drifters, rich or poor—that I postponed the decision each time. Then, insanely by tramp standards, when a young Englishman gave me two dollars, instead of keeping the money for a bed, I squandered it on a shirt and handkerchiefs.

Relatively clean again, I sat, most of the time, looking at the water, at the busy riverside and the people on Felicity.

Again a sociologist would have written me down as an unmitigated work-dodger, but really I was working very hard.

collecting a million impressions of the river and city. On the printed papers of modern civilisation one cannot write, in the space enquiring about occupation, "Examining New Orleans and the Mississippi River." That, however, is what I was doing.

Although I was always just about to take the plunge, I never plucked up sufficient courage to beg in the streets. Joe Jarrett, the young Englishman who had given me the two dollars, stood me a drink each time we met, often passed me the few cents change in a matter-of-fact way. That helped.

Once a very effeminate Portuguese—the opposite of my tramp-friend, as it were—gave me a packet of cigarettes and three dollars, in exchange for a sock on the jaw. And once an Irish policeman warned me not to let him catch me bumming around the block, and gave me half a dollar.

For the rest I merely lazed. If I could pay I stayed at my Howard Street place; if not, I stayed out, and the difference was nil. Food came almost without asking.

For all I know, I might have stayed on that waterfront until now if it had not been for young Jarrett. A ship's fireman from Lancashire, he was of about my own age and bulk, did not drink much, was very friendly, and talked every time we met. The second time we encountered one another he offered to fix things for me if I wanted to sign on their steamer, but I was not greatly interested. Until I heard they were going to Scotland, to Glasgow—I had been thinking in terms of American ports—and changed my mind quickly.

The "fixing" required little effort, although one of the items, which included a union card as an extra, cost Jarrett a further five dollars. However, I was able to pay him that afternoon. I still have the union card—at the present date my arrears total close on a thousand dollars.

Everyone concerned knew I was a drifter—one look at me would have sufficed for that—but nobody minded much. A large tolerance in everything is the mark of New Orleans.

If the cities had personality, as Kipling wrote, and if New York were an insurance broker, Paris a *restaurateur*, London a

merchant, and Dublin a bookie, New Orleans would have
been a drifter, a dreaming lie-about, a casual glancer at muddy
rivers.

When I had paid Jarrett I had not enough money for even
the cheapest suit of clothes, so I bought overalls in which I
could walk without being spotted, at least immediately, for a
tramp. Then I had one very pleasant perambulation of
Howard Street. Next night we were going down the river,
and I had more than my fill of playing Gownseer in front of
a furnace.

Firing a steamer—a coal-burner—is heavy work. But even
at that I played. Literally, I played my way across the Atlantic,
and I can feel the smooth skin of the long hand-polished steel
slice now. Smooth as the barrel of a fountain-pen, the handle
glistening as if made of mirror-glass, beautifully balanced, it
was a real Gownseer tool for play.

Of course, I was not staying in that stokehold, nor in any
stokehold, for life. It may have made a difference.

When we docked at Glasgow, my first visit, ludicrously
enough, was to the Gallowgate. Then on the second day I said
good-bye to Jarrett, swopped addresses, and made for the
coal-lading wharf, where I had climbed the *Zillah* five years
earlier.

One of the Robinson steamers—those with the precious-
stone names—was bound into Dublin, and once again I had no
difficulty. Next morning we tied at Sir John Rogerson's Quay
—to be met by a roaring crowd of angry men.

A dock strike was in full swing, coal was a blackleg cargo,
and I had arrived on a coal-steamer. Dublin was putting out
one of her left-handed welcomes.

With some little difficulty, trading on my acquaintance with
cranemen, coal-heavers, and dockers, since the Post Office days,
I managed to assure the boys that I was only an illegal passenger. An hour later my mother was crying quietly but
happily, saying nothing, and my father spoke in distantly
friendly fashion of everyday trifles, before he left for work. I
had been away less than eleven weeks.

It had seemed like years of pleasurable wandering, and there was a stirring of happiness in the thought that nothing whatever had changed except for the better. Two days later, back at the works, the feeling persisted. Place and people appeared strange as a play on a stage. Nearly everyone, nearly everywhere, has appeared like that to me ever since.

CHAPTER XII

THERE is an Irish phrase about a man "leppin' out of his skin," used of one markedly alert and pleased. It describes my state exactly, for the period when I resumed existence in Dublin. Now *this* was a city—and I had nearly missed knowing it.

Life was very pleasant and I grew fast.

Perhaps no one will laugh when I tell that almost at once I resolved to get married. My resolution may have been pardonable, perhaps innocent; it was certainly most seriously formulated. Perhaps because my knowledge of the factors involved was nil. I had not grown up; I had happened suddenly, one morning at two o'clock. My knowledge was nil.

Before one plans a holiday or chooses a play to see, one has first decided on a vacation or a visit to the theatre. To that extent, and to that extent only, I was concerned about marriage.

Not that I was to be in love, or become engaged, or marry any particular girl—just marry. The basic peasant seems to have been emergent in me as well as in my father. Fortunately I had no money.

A word is necessary here about the economics of apprenticeship, in the old world of craftsmanship which was already nearing its end in my youth. Nowadays, in civilised countries, the craftsman has no place in everyday life. We have relegated all his work to machines.

In countries like Ireland, even in my adolescent days, the

end was already in sight if people had but known. But no hint of that end was glimpsed by the majority.

Life was still organised on a handicraft basis, and people planned affairs, years ahead, in terms of personal contacts and craftsmanship. The stage-coach operators of Britain and America must have done the same thing, in the days when the railroads were new.

It is amusing that I, who have never planned anything except a book or a film-story, should have sensed the approach of Nemesis. One day a machine was brought into Inchicore smithy, and admired by all when it was set up. Ten minutes later I remarked to the smith-manager, and to Gentleman Whalen, that *that* was the end of Inchicore ironworks. Both smiled tolerantly.

Neither they, nor any of those who so carefully planned the futures of their sons and their grandsons, had the slightest inkling that their world was already falling into ruins around them. Yet a fletcher—that is, a maker of arrows—seeking a job at a modern arsenal, would be less out of place than a crafts-man in a present-day factory. And it is less than forty years since the first drop-hammer came to Inchicore.

A single example will serve to illustrate the change. In my apprentice days, the hinges of a railway wagon were forged by an expert craftsman, who was paid a pound per set. Thus, if he made ten sets in a week, he had ten pounds to divide between his hammer-man and himself. That was craft. It had grown up over several centuries.

The drop-hammer, an American invention, came at that time, to prove that my father and all the fathers were wrong. Working at a drop-hammer, an unskilled labourer, not a crafts-man, could make a set of the same hinges better than they could have been forged by any smith in the world. For that work he received and was well paid with—eightpence.

But the fathers could not read the writing on the wall. Millions of apprentices were still bound, each certain of life-long employment in a pleasurable and satisfying craft, certain of being paid two or three times as much as a labourer, certain of a status too—for the word tradesman did not yet mean the person who delivers the milk or groceries.

An apprentice received, in return for his five or seven years' service, a piece of property then considered invaluable. He gained the knowledge of a craft and the right to work in it. Compared with this priceless gift, money was considered almost negligible. Certainly no one ever thought of giving any to the budding craftsman.

As a consequence, one might see a young near-engineer of twenty-five or so, more than mature in almost everything, whose total income would hardly suffice for a modern schoolboy's pocket-money. The apprentice was supposed to live, and did live, on his parents. At eighteen I was paid seven shillings a week, and many of my contemporaries had less.

In a sophisticated and unrepressed city like Dublin, this often had embarrassing results. (It should be borne in mind that birth-control was almost unknown.) I knew more than one burly and potent apprentice of twenty-odd, not yet a moulder or smith or engineer, married and set up by his own fireside— complete with cradle alongside—on five shillings a week!

In Dublin the approach of a birth did not necessarily mean marriage. But apprentices could not run away from their futures. Wherefore many apprentices married, while still dependent on their parents.

I was not sufficiently in love with marriage for that.

Besides, unplanning my future as it were, I thought it very unlikely that I should ever finish learning to be a smith. Not for a moment had I ever thought of being an ironworker for money. The apprentice went to "a pleasurable and satisfying craft." Those were the operative words as far as I was concerned. In my mind no state of affairs existed in which I could not continue to live on my father.

Pleasurable and satisfying—it meant making things, like the quasi-watchcases I used to turn out on my lathe in the screwing-shop. It meant making things, if I could, like the old art-ironworkers and Benvenuto Cellini. It did not mean earning a living.

If ever I thought, for a second or two, about the things I might want to do, I considered vaguely that I might sell stories. Had I not two rejection slips? Very well, then. Meanwhile I lived at home and could not get married. Even then I was a thousand times embarrassed by my lack of money.

My former financial helpers, the Dublin bookies, had failed me too. The magic secret of the *Racing Echo* was losing its power, probably because the giant strike had tied up everything in the city This was the historic labour clash of 1913, which gradually spread until it affected most of Dublin and a great part of Ireland outside.

Sean O'Casey and others have told, in story and drama, the history of that strike, and no descriptions are necessary here. Only two phases of it need comment, since they concerned me personally and were important in my development.

Dock-work, haulage, tramways, and everything of that kind stood still for months. Before the coming of James Connolly and Jim Larkin, the people of Dublin had been very quiescent and servile, perhaps the worst-paid work-folk of western Europe. Now Labour was an organised force.

Making demands, and apparently possessing the will and power to enforce them, Dublin claimed a living from Ireland. This was a new thing, not only to me, vague and uninformed and youthful, but to large numbers of Dubliners besides.

Naturally, quiet and frightened people wanted to stay outside the labour struggle, stand apart. It did not work out that way, with the result that, for a year, Dublin was like no other city in the world.

At Inchicore, for instance, a couple of thousand men were employed, a large proportion living in Dublin. Since tramway work was a blackleg activity, and since travelling in trams carried a stigma, these hundreds made the long trail to and from the city each morning and evening on foot.

They walked, with anathemas on the strikers, the employers, the Labour leaders, and the strike-breakers, distributed about evenly. But they walked.

Human nature being what it is, if a tram driven by a police-escorted strike-breaker, and carrying a few "blackleg" passengers—from Inchicore—became a centre of attack, the weary and bad-tempered men who had been tramping were quite likely to feel suddenly virtuous, and join in the mêlée.

Trams were wrecked. A couple were burnt. Defaulting workers and the police who escorted them were trounced. Working people in turn were trounced by the police. Those untrounced, although not directly concerned, naturally felt pleased that they had not been so unprincipled, or mean, or simply foolhardy, as to antagonise their friends in the transport ranks. Thus the strike spread.

It spread until it was no longer a struggle between certain employers and certain working-men. Practically it became a fight to the death between the business men of Ireland and the city of Dublin.

In the savagery of that time, it seemed logical and natural that the employers should next loose a force to terrorise Dublin itself, if they could find one. They found such a force and, since Ireland was then a British colony, not even a dominion, the finding was easy.

Enormous numbers of the Royal Constabulary, an English-armed police then used in rural Ireland, were drafted into the city. Thereafter blood flowed at random and in plenty.

One had been accustomed, in Dublin as elsewhere, to the sight of strike-breakers going about their work, with police to protect them, occasional object of attack by angry strikers. The 1913 clashes were not at all of that nature.

Seemingly the Royal Constabulary, or whoever directed them, had decided that the uniformed man with a bludgeon ran little risk of wasting his efforts if he slugged any Dubliner whatever on the skull. Pragmatically speaking, they were not far wrong. The news-files of the day make fairly grim reading.

Thus, at almost any hour of the day or night, one might run into a bitter and bloody fight between a body of Constabulary and a group of the citizens. The Constabulary wasted no words. If a man wore clothes other than police uniform, he might expect to be bludgeoned anywhere, at any time.

Unless, of course, he too had acquired a bludgeon and got his blow in first. It was a hard school, but Dublin was quick to learn. The clashes became bloodier and more frequent.

Naturally there were many amusing incidents—amusing, that is, to everyone except the persons concerned. Some of them are still recounted in the Dublin pubs, among journalists of almost any political hue, radical Labour men, or strictly unpolitical citizens of over fifty.

At College Green, in the heart of Dublin, one night an elderly Englishman, cultured and apparently wealthy, spoke to me about what he rightly called the savagery of the city. He gestured in serious disapproval to the nearby raucously-roaring crowd of people, armed with sticks and paving-stones, who gave way and advanced, gave way and advanced, before the batons of an equally raucous crowd of Constabulary. While I tried to explain that the Dubliners had no choice but to fight back, the tide turned our way.

Grabbing the stranger's arm, I jerked my thumb and showed him the way to run, but he shook off my hand with quiet dignity.

"Preposterous," he was saying. "The whole thing is mere hooliganism on both sides. The police should be——"

I never heard what the police were to be, for at that moment a brisk young constabularyman felled my companion, and swung the club to deal with me next. But I was a bigger and heavier man than he.

Besides, he did not know that, like practically everyone from Inchicore ironworks in those days, I carried an iron bar in my coat-sleeve.

But the funniest story, from the Dublin Labour man's point of view, may have been at least in part apocryphal. It concerned William Martin Murphy.

William Martin Murphy was regarded by the transport men and many others as the arch-enemy of organised labour in Ireland. (He was, as the name implies, Irish of the Irish himself, which rather emphasised the Larkin-Connolly dictum that capital had no patriotism.)

With enormous financial interests in the growing industries of the country, Murphy could count on the support of the British organised forces like the Constabulary. Confronting him was Jim Larkin, leader of the Dublin workers. The two exchanged everything but bullets.

Railways, steamships, coal, tramways, were among the principal Murphy properties. In a strike which began with transport men, naturally Murphy became the centre of the employers' field. Since he also owned several newspapers, which of course took an anti-Labour line, a thousand curses came to him, later, even from people who knew little or nothing of the Labour movement.

One night, the radical version of the story ran, Murphy was in O'Connell Street, chief thoroughfare of the city. On one side were his newspaper offices, on the other his hotels, in the middle were his tramways, all at a standstill, all surrounded by grumbling groups of sullen workers.

In that year the gathering of groups in Dublin was not permitted by William Martin Murphy, or by the Royal Constabulary, which meant the same thing, as the Labour man would point out. Wherefore from every side-street other groups of angry police flourishing batons came rushing out, and the evening fight was on.

Murphy watched, while the tramway men were clubbed, and clubbed back, but hurried forward when an enthusiastic young constabularyman felled an old apple-woman. "Not those, Officer," the radical raconteur would allege him to have said. "Not apple-women. Those tramway fellows over there. *Mustn't* club women. The forces of law and——" At which stage the young rustic bludgeoned him.

A hard felt hat saved the Murphy brain, and the capitalist scuttled away. At the corner of Abbey Street, near the office from which, daily, the Murphy press poured a flood of praise for the Constabulary, a sergeant leant against the wall drinking from a whisky bottle. Murphy, having first noted that the sergeant was baton-less, stated his complaint and reissued his orders.

"Begob, sor, ye don't say," protested the sergeant sympathetically. "So he hit th'oul wan with the battle?" (A baton was always called a battle—perhaps not too incongruously.) "An' then took the battle to yerself, is it? Boys, oh boys, sure that's terrible, sor, terrible." He straightened himself against the wall. "Well, sor, I haven't no battle meself I'm sorry to say, but——"

Whereupon he cracked the bottle on Murphy's head, kicked him in the stomach, and strolled away to earn further praise from Murphy's newspapers. The Labour man would generally finish his story by saying that when Murphy recovered consciousness, in hospital, he telephoned Jim Larkin and volunteered to join the Transport Union.

The two stories will serve to picture Dublin of the time. No other city, this century, has known similar experience. London and Paris, Liverpool and Chicago, San Francisco and Detroit and Sydney, have all known bitter and bloody strikes, fierce clashes between capital and labour. The Irish episode was of an entirely different nature.

It was, for some reason at which more than half the people could not even guess, an attack upon Dublin exactly comparable to a military assault by an enemy.

That was the city in which, while I was "leppin' out of my skin," I grew. No simple term like anarchy or chaos will describe the state of affairs. It was nightmare. Law was at an end, destroyed by the bludgeon-bearing officers of the law. In the eyes of the constabularyman, a workman on strike was a maniac homicide. Aged women, children, the bed-ridden— and in one case a dying man—if they were Dubliners, were treated as maniac homicides too.

Only those came unscathed who knew, and could laugh at the knowledge, that there was no quarter. Or those, and they were many, who were humorously prepared to play the game of tip-and-run with pick-handle or paving-stone, a cracked skull the penalty for not running in time. Or those who learnt, without any great anger or with even a little amusement, to carry an iron bar in a sleeve.

Someone set out to teach Dublin a lesson. Dublin learnt—
but not the lesson intended.

Out of this turmoil came the beginnings of the Irish Citizen
Army. Organised by James Connolly and Jim Larkin, with the
assistance of Captain Jack White, it was, in the early days, like
the Constabulary of the opposite side, an organised force of
bludgeon-men.

Armed at the commencement with dummy wooden rifles,
for the legal and laudable purpose of physical training and the
acquisition of dexterity in manly exercises, the I.C.A. somehow managed to be on the scene whenever the Constabulary
were applying "battle" instruction to the Dubliners. The
wooden guns, being slightly longer than the batons, proved
useful at such times.

Very shortly afterwards, this force was turned into an armed
and disciplined body, and came in time to be an important
factor in the Irish War of Independence. But in the blood-
spattered months of 1913, the I.C.A. was, quite simply, a direct
counter to "Murphy's men."

Politically ignorant as I was, and knowing nothing whatever
about the rights and wrongs of the Labour movement, I still
had the keenest admiration for the hard-faced, big-fisted
dockers and carters of the Irish Citizen Army. Whenever a
"battle" anticipated my iron bar by a second or so, my admiration for the I.C.A. was even keener.

Those interests and—counter-attractions, I suppose I should
call them—cut across my rather hazily made plans to have a
real mind-life now that I was freed from the torment of fear
and worry and the feeling of inferior incompleteness.

Inevitably the studies I had intended to resume fell into
abeyance. Still I managed to come at a few books and attend
an occasional class. Doubtless the sympathetic reader will count
it as evidence of a passion for learning that I often arrived in
the classroom with a sore skull or with blood on my knuckles!

As an apprentice, I was still compelled to attend the school
in Dublin, was allowed to leave work an hour or so earlier for
that purpose. But—the road to the school skirted the fringe

of the Liberty, and there were nearly always two or three mass-fights in progress to make me forget the classes. Besides, one did not always get as far as the Liberty.

Best, perhaps, is to quote here a typical dialogue between two law-abiding citizens of the time, neither perhaps an ardent sympathiser with the Labour cause. To a smith at Inchicore works a friend might approach towards evening for gossip.

"Looks like rain, Mick."

"Aye." (Pause.) "I wish the bloody strike was over, that a man didn't have to thramp the sthreets into Dublin, and could ride the bloody tram, ordinary."

"Aye, indeed. A lousy road, into the city, on a wet night especial. (Pause.) There's a meeting at Inchicore Cross just after knock-off time."

"Oh! Should be good. They say that big Daly fella's a fine speaker. If it's not too wet——"

"Me, too. They say Jem Larkin'll be out here himself, speakin' to-night."

"Uh-huh. *That'll* be broke up, of course. (Pause.) There's no way of gettin' past the bloody polis at Inchicore Cross. That means the long way round, for anyone that wants to miss the meetin'."

"Uh-huh. An' I hate that bloody back road, on a wet night."

"Me, too. (Pause.) To hell with them. I'm going by Inchicore Cross."

"Sure, sure. (More briskly.) You'll be shoeing a shaft, then?"

"Aye."

"Make it two."

Shoeing a shaft was, like the making of my watchcases, simple but uneconomic and illegal. It consisted of selecting a new sledge-hammer handle, a piece of hickory about four feet long, shaped to the hand and thickened at one end. A short piece of iron piping was made red-hot, slid on to the thick end of the hammer-shaft, and water-cooled firmly into position.

Equipped with two of these, the pair of citizens could start on foot for their distant homes, might even risk paying a call at the Labour meeting *en route*, to hear the fiery, world-famous orator Jim Larkin. Since a shod-shaft was a foot longer and a pound heavier than a constabulary baton, the Inchicore worthies often reached home almost undamaged.

The Constabulary attacks on districts like the Liberty were not only ludicrous but completely perverse. For one thing, the average Liberty man did not work a great deal. Further, if he did work, he would be very unlikely to join the ranks of organised Labour, was indeed nearly always on the anti-popular side, at that time demonstrably the stronger.

Besides this, a large percentage of the Liberty people were, in one way or another, semi-dependent on the British Army. As a consequence they were, by and large, opposed to the strike and the strikers.

None of those things saved them.

Citizens of the Liberty were, from their avocations, more than prone to group and gossip in the slum streets. In 1913 that meant the "battle"—in every sense of the word. There were amusing corollaries. Some of the Liberty people, in every land, know rather unconventional things about fighting. Many a constabularyman in 1913, braced to tackle a Dubliner with a stick or stone, cursed the alleys where people used such unsporting engines as eye-pepper, hatpins, or broken glass in socks.

For an apprentice who was not a striker, was bound for the Art Class in a technical school, but had to cross the Liberty, the taming of Dublin brought many distractions.

Of course, I could have gone the long way round. To avoid the clashes, it would only have been necessary to go a quarter of a mile or so out of my way.

Some of the things I have felt impelled to set down here already, and many to come, bring me sadness or shame or at least embarrassment when I recall them. But I would much wish to set down here, on the other side, the recollection that I never once went the long way round, to avoid the battle-men. I was Jim Phelan, and why should I? To hell with them.

Writing several decades after the fact, I still have nothing to add to those last four words.

Thus, in less than a year, and mainly as a free gift from the Royal Constabulary, I acquired, like many another Dubliner, a dexterity in the technique of what is often called a rough-house. Many a law-abiding citizen, of later years, has expressed unmistakable disapproval of me, and of others my age from Dublin, some of them writers. Bewailing an occasional swift transit from logomachy to mayhem, they have debited me with a violent temper, labelled me a savage.

This is wrong. I was always afraid, and am always afraid even now. Merely my body-responses were trained, in the myriad unavoidable clashes of 1913. The citizen must blame conditions in 1913 Dublin, or the Royal Constabulary, or William Martin Murphy, not me nor yet the cheerful nocent ruffians of Dublin's Liberty.

At the time, of course, I knew nothing of all this, and my principal feeling was one of shame. In what will (rightly, I think) be classed as a ludicrous snobbery, I had a kind of double or even treble existence among my fellow-students, especially among the girls.

Nearly all the teachers, and all the students I met, were ordinary middle-class people, knew little or nothing of real life. For them, a striker was a maniac homicide, the Royal Constabulary were the saviours of the city, Jim Larkin was a criminal lunatic paid by the enemies of England. Did they not read those things, daily, in the papers owned by William Murphy?

For all my ignorance, I knew better than that. But I lacked moral courage.

In the art class, when I attended, I would be at great pains to hide the fact that, perhaps half an hour earlier, I had been roaring defiance, charging or fleeing from the batons, in the back streets of the Liberty. I would even pop into the Art Ironwork class downstairs, where a forge was in use, and where an extra bar of iron would not be noticed, to hide my brain-protector.

One night, on my way out through the main hall after school, my treasured bar went jangling and clanging out on the tiled floor. Everyone, including my middle-class girl friends, obviously thought that, for some obscure reason, I was stealing a short iron bar from the forge-class. Of course there was no possible explanation I could put forward. Least fitting of all would have been the truth!

The incident nearly got me into trouble at the school, and I had resigned myself to being thrown out. A chat with Bob Bradley, the sheriff of Dublin, in the fitting-shop at Inchicore, put matters right. But I brought my iron bar to school no more. Perhaps it was just as well. A pen is lighter.

The narrow escape from being expelled from the school steadied me, for two reasons. I was much preoccupied about a girl in the art-class, of whom I had thought much and wistfully in my torment-of-incompleteness days. There was a girl at Inchicore too, of a different type, towards whom I felt myself turning. But the Dublin girl interested me more. Also, I did not want to be expelled from the school until I could make the things we drew, or until I knew I could not make them.

Always, fresh as when it had come to me with startling suddenness, the realisation that the metal-art paragons had been made by men, just men, brought a strangely powerful thrill. Some of those fellows had been dead for years, but there were the beautifully reproduced drawings of the things they had made. With their names on.

Here in Dublin was a teacher to show how one might understand and copy the drawings. Downstairs was another teacher, a practical man, who could at least start one on the way to make things like them.

So I did.

Two or three times already I have invited the reader to laugh with me. Now I do not want anyone to laugh at all. I made a beautiful wrought-iron cross for a grave, with a thoroughly attractive little art-metal fence to surround it, and I felt very proud indeed.

I had put such loving care and labour into the grave-irons

that I felt thrilled, and awed, and noble, at the thought that they would stand, a worthy and unmistakably personal monument, as long as iron should last, over my father.

Sometimes I wonder what Benvenuto Cellini was thinking of while he did that metal scroll-work of his.

A few months passed, during which I paid more attention to school and people, less to the brawls of the Liberty. But the wild, imperative, driving force of the previous year was lacking for the school. Although I knew keen pleasure for every moment of my studies, I no longer grabbed for the knowledge as a starving man clutches food. I was an ordinary young man now, for a while, and that was the difference.

The books did not yield up, either, as they had done before, all the treasures of the world made ready especially for me. I still read avidly, voraciously, but there was something lacking and the books were no longer my life. Books had their place. But in that first year of my growing I did not want only books: I wanted girls.

Now, only the blind, the halt, and the lame, or those who thought bearded men had done things to them in forests, had need to be without girls in 1913 Dublin.

Fortunately, I can summarise the conventions of courtship in my Dublin, for British or American people, very briefly. The ceremony known colloquially in some part of Britain as a christening-marriage, and in the United States as a shotgun wedding, was almost a commonplace among many sections of the Dublin populace.

In some countries the phrase is used that such-and-such a girl has fallen for a such-and-such a young man. Meaning that she is greatly fascinated, completely in love with him.

Precisely the same phrase was used in Dublin, decades before it got to England or America. But it did not mean that a girl was very much in love with a named young man. It meant that she was going to have a baby.

Girl and man became friendly, went around together for a few months. Then one evening, tearfully or with a laugh, the girl made announcement *re* probable increases of population.

Whereupon, in many cases, the young man borrowed his fare to Liverpool or Glasgow and vanished for some weeks or months.

The occurrence was common. In many districts it was at that time regarded as ordinary and usual. Indeed, the malignant gossip one might have expected at such a time did not even flourish, barely existed.

A had fallen for B. Ergo, B was working in Liverpool. Or alternately, if the girl happened to have two or three hefty brothers, or if the young man were an apprentice, who could not run away from his trade and his whole future, A had fallen for B and B was going to stand for it. That last phrase is exact and literal quotation.

It was as simple as announcing that a political meeting would be held at some point on the homeward journey, and then enquiring whether the other person would be shoeing a shaft.

Partly because of my largely romantic reading, partly from the very real overhang of my mother's morality, but mainly I think because of the Sir Galahad speech-and-thought habits which had so long been mine, I felt the strongest disapproval whenever those subjects cropped up among my acquaintances. They cropped up often. This was Dublin.

I was very censorious about such things, although I had developed a dislike and contempt for sentimentally moral books. Books of any kind no longer sufficed as a substitute for living. I had been too long held under.

The forge-work helped, but not enough. How could it—I was five feet ten, a big, powerful, upstanding youngster, with a great confidence in myself and a vast leeway to make up.

So I was walking up a narrow lane near Hazelhatch one morning, headed for the main south road, and with Dublin twelve miles behind me.

It would be quite untrue to say I was disinclined to get married. Even though I was not in love with anyone, knew little or nothing of love because of my youth and inexperience and my queer mental make-up.

Neither would my devastating poverty and my complete dependence on my father have deterred me. Had I felt inclined, I could have found ways and means.

Yet, because of my fastidiousness, and the bigness of the fellow inside me who was trying to get out, even one christening-marriage or shotgun wedding would have nauseated me. With two on my hands—I drifted towards the main south road.

For long, I have considered Robert Burns a much-maligned man. Only those like myself know the full inner significance of the lofty, moral, Sir-Galahad-like phrases which appear in so many of his poems, addressed to one girl or another, and generally serving as a substitute for a wedding-ring.

CHAPTER XIII

HAZELHATCH is a tiny place, away from a main road in a peaceful pasture-land, an ideal district for one, meditative and quietly strolling, to appraise his situation, evaluate recent events, and decide on his plans. Quietly, I strolled. But that was all.

Brutal, heartless, unscrupulous, sensual and selfish and especially mean, with other and numerous terms of similar import, occur to me as likely to be used, by many, for description of my conduct in walking away out of Dublin. Naturally I cannot argue about it, since my opinion would be worthless.

All I have to record here is that the incident was ordinary, for Dublin, that I never once consciously thought of it on the first day. Neither did I consider where I was going, nor what I might do. The pine-trees by the road were pleasant, and the call of a wood-pigeon soothing. Then presently there was my old friend the canal.

Crossing the canal, I came by a by-lane to the main south road, and, so far as I knew, my journey was at an end. I padded along, quietly and without effort or haste, dream-calm and with a horizon bounded by the next bend, in a world that included only the visible few yards of dusty road. Already, there is no shade of doubt, I was a tramp in the making.

One informed may know a tramp, however well dressed and however cultured, by his eyes, or by his conversation. But the chief, unmistakable, ineradicable mark of the roadster is his walk. No complete and lasting change of it is possible, and there is embarrassing amusement when (as in my own case) it clashes with a strongly marked individual gait.

Basically, I have an erect, free carriage, common to all our family, known and labelled as the "Whalen walk" in parts of Tipperary. When I am working, stay a few weeks or months in one place on business, when I am temporarily a respectable citizen, people in a dozen cities know my walk, and it is the Whalen gait.

But after half a day on the road I am back to the pad, the quiet pad that is only going five yards, but will eat up miles by the hundred on occasion. It came to me first, and pleasantly, that morning on the south road of Ireland.

Perhaps a Buddhist monk, or a Lama, might be able to explain. Every tramp I have questioned says it is just that a fellow goes quiet and blank, looking at the road and liking the sound of his footfalls, and then he's at the next town, without noticing. That definition will serve for the time being.

There has to be peace inside, a freedom from the worry and strain which, for professional purposes, the tramp has to pretend he knows. Then contemplation, not of one's navel but of the tiny surrounding patch of road-surface.

Not a very useful or practical occupation, by any modern standard. But that is all of it, notwithstanding the evidence of Kipling and Service and all the others who did not know.

It would be wrong, though, to think that a tramp does not see the road or the movements around, because he is preoccupied by the rhythm of his own footfalls, hypnotised by the eternal swift-rushing towards him of the particles on the road-surface. He sees everything, but in tiny instalments.

For a good many years I have worked on and off in films. Where the cinema-patron sees only lumps of scene measuring perhaps several hundred celluloid feet, I, like the others, have had to know the story almost foot by foot. That is how the tramp sees the road and sees life.

Apropos, many tramps, from Jack London (who was one of the first) down to Jim Tully and myself and a dozen others, have been efficient film-script writers. Could it be that the fundamental foot-by-foot outlook of the roadster fits them for the job? Even if not, the coincidence is amusing.

Thus it can be accepted as the literal truth when a tramp says he knows every yard of the road from Plymouth to Aberdeen or from Boston to Miami. The rod-riders and blind-baggage climbers of the United States, true, know far less of the highways than the average motorist. But foot-padders are as numerous in America as anywhere else, in spite of what the degenerate told me at Houston. No surveyor, no roadmaker or cartographer knows the United States as they do.

Blank and blissful, then, I dreamt my way down into the boglands of central Ireland. Twice, at intervals of a week or so, I had to work a day at casual labour on a farm, to get cleaned up, but that was all the work I did. It had been a pleasant surprise, on my last wandering, to find that one could eat and sleep at a farm where one worked. Now I remembered and used the system.

It was a very convenient system indeed whereby, for spreading a few loads of manure, hacking a hedge, or milking a few cows one could, every week or so, eat a few hearty regular meals, enjoy a smoke and friendly gossip by the fire, get cleaned and brushed, gratis, and get out on the road with a few small coins at the end. I liked it.

My first cow-milking was funny. At a large farm—where I had really only stepped in for my breakfast—the farmer offered me a couple of days' work. I was to clear a long drain, which was simple and straightforward, also I was to trim a thick privet hedge with a hedge-slasher. This last was a very ordinary, unskilled job, except that I had never seen, let alone handled, a hedge-slasher before.

However, I managed the slasher, since, as I have always maintained, a man who can use any tool can use all tools. But besides these jobs, it was taken for granted without discussion that I should help each morning and evening to milk the many cows.

In spite of my peasant background, I had never milked a cow, except very clumsily at night in a field with the Liberty boys from Dublin. It looks easy. The reader is invited to try.

On the first morning, nonchalant and genial, I entered the milking-shed. A girl and a man had already started, and a row of cows, five I think, had been left for me. I finished my cigarette in leisurely fashion, really keeping alert to pick up hints.

The other milkers used a short looped rope to tie each cow's hind legs while she was being milked. That seemed common-sense. Given a pail, a one-legged stool, and a rope, I approached my first cow and tied her back-ankles together, making certain the rope would not slip.

A wicked slash across the eyes from the animal's tail was my first hint that anything was wrong. Then I thought the nearly frantic animal was about to fall on me, from the crazy way she tottered. Eventually the girl showed me that the legs should not be tied, but noosed loosely in a figure-of-eight.

Still ashamed to admit that I was bluffing, I roped the first cow properly, and started to milk. Nothing happened, except that she nearly blinded me with her tail. I tried again, and nothing happened. When I was about to admit defeat, and get out on the road, the other workman finished and went to the next shed.

Promptly I made the correct peasant-Rabelaisian jocular remark to the girl. She laughed.

"Wisha, sure ye wouldn't get far on the wrong side of *me*, either," she came back mischievously, and the last word gave me the clue.

Cows can only be milked on the starboard side, God knows why. I had been expending my good energy on the left bank and finding the stream dry.

In two days I could milk fairly well. But by then I was leaving.

It was spring, and the weather was delightful for walking. I moved lazily into a lonely part of the country where the farms were smaller and the boglands wide. Gradually I felt myself a tramp, and did not care. I wrote a hundred worthless poems, but not one letter of any kind.

One of those trivial-important incidents, those brief but memorable moments of experience that come once or twice in everyone's life, came to me there in the bog-country. One morning, pleased and stimulated, I had been looking out over a couple of miles of brown heathery turf-bog at the road on which I stood, as it went straight and white, like a long pier narrowing away into the dun and mist of the distance. Then I lay down and fell asleep on the grass-verge in the sun.

"Here's the polis." The words came, in a girl's laughing voice, two or three times before I was fully awake. I rubbed my eyes and stood up.

A black tinker-caravan was halted a little way farther on, and two brown-faced, obvious tinker-girls were standing beside me, laughing at my startled expression. Dressed in bits and scraps, with shapeless shoes, hatless, and not over-painfully clean, they were both good-looking, the taller one extremely so.

She repeated her joking remarks, while I stood there and we looked at one another. I asked their name, and she gave it, with a brief account of their future movements, which she seemed to assume I required.

Without possessing or needing any conceit at that time, I knew girls looked at me twice. The taller one read my eyes, and similarly, instantly, knew that she in turn looked good in them. She repeated the scraps of detail about the way they would go, added the information that there was only their father with them, looked at me again.

Words were unnecessary. I knew I need only stretch one hand to be a married man that night, with a home and a wife and a future. That is, if one can so name a black-covered wagon, a tinker-girl, and an eternal wheel-creaking down the bog roads.

I let her go.

Anyone who knows my story *Quest* knows how the brief episode was possibility-packed, and what I did with it. I let her go, and that night, wakeful, I cursed myself for a weakling, vacillant fool. Sometimes I wonder . . . Let it pass.

For a few days I enquired about the wagon, at the places the girl had named. But each time I heard they had gone on. Then I forgot the incident. Thirty years later I remembered it, and wrote *Quest*. No good stories are made: they are part-remembered. That I think is why *Quest* is a good story.

Presently I must have been feeling, and looking like, a tramp, for one evening a very solid and sententious farmer lectured me, self-righteously, on my many short-comings and general worthlessness. (His own sterling qualities naturally emerged by contrast.) He had given me a lift in his farm-cart into a small village, and utilised the opportunity.

"So there y'are on the road," he stressed, more than once. "And ye'll never get off it, never. Ye're just a tramp now, a big, good-looking young man like ye, and ye'll never be anything but a tramp. Aye, indeed."

He drew the horse to a halt, and I alighted at the village cross-roads, while he drove on, exuding self-satisfaction. He knew all about tramps, and all about honest workmen, that farmer.

That night, as became a solid agriculturist of established position, he relaxed, and patronised the drama. Meaning that he paid ninepence admission to see a play presented by a travelling dramatic company in the little village hall.

At the door he did not know me again, although I collected his ticket, and I have no doubt that he applauded the dramatic intervention of one Shaun, at a critical moment of the drama. I was Shaun. Perhaps, after all, my farmer acquaintance only knew about honest workmen.

Ireland was at that time, and later, a paradise for little dramatic companies. Strangely enough, there were very few amateur groups on the road; nearly all were strictly professional "fitup" affairs, of the traditional barn-stormer type.

All carried stage, scenery, and props with them (hence the generic name fitup), and status varied from those who played in large town halls, provincial theatres, or even occasionally in a big city, to the smaller outfits which confined themselves to the villages.

The company, "straight from prolonged success in the West End of London," to which I had attached myself, was one of the smallest. We never stayed more than one night at a place.

Shakespeare himself would, I think, have been proud of those troupers. Performing daily miracles of adaptation, study, and make-up, not to mention negotiation and financial adjustment, they drifted from point to point, differing only from the tinkers and tramps in that perforce they travelled by rail—and worked.

It came my way, afterwards, to see convicts at work, many times. But I never saw any convicts work like those actresses and actors. The smaller the company the harder the work. Only the "lumpers," the tent-hands of a big circus, laboured harder.

My interview, examination, testing, engagement, and instruction had occupied perhaps six minutes. The baggage-man of the little company had left without warning. Unerringly, the stage-manager's trained eye had picked me.

We haggled about wages for some time, his version starting at one pound per week. Eventually we compromised at thirty shillings.

Then he told me I could borrow a pair of trousers and some boots from the prop basket, for that night's show, and intimated that I might get myself cleaned up without delay.

I had not known that the baggage-man played all the small parts, sometimes two or even three in the same play. Feeling very self-conscious, I put on my first grease-paint. No one took the slightest notice of me, and after the first minute I belonged to the company.

Thus I managed to be Shaun well enough. But that was after I had first helped with the fitup and scenery, lugged the various wardrobe baskets into position, arranged chairs in the hall for the audience, fiddled with bad, cheap footlights, collected the tickets at the door, and learnt my part.

There was a strange, almost eerie, feeling of being at home. Long before my first entrance, some ninety-odd minutes after my engagement, I felt as if I had been working with the people for many years, and had never known any existence other than fitups. Nor was there much time for self-analysis.

There was little pause for reflection at the end, either. Before the final curtain was down I was already working. All the wardrobe baskets had to go out again, by the back door, to be loaded on a wagon and taken to the railway. Scenery followed as it was finished with. The fitup itself had to be pulled down and loaded when all was over.

Then all the company went away to their lodgings, leaving the stage-manager and me to convoy the outfit to the railway at Clara.

When we had loaded all our equipment there, it was long after midnight. We were to catch a train at eight o'clock next morning. I had no lodgings, no money, no breakfast for the next day.

Apparently the stage-manager was accustomed to such conditions among newly-joined baggage-men, for he made no move to do anything about it. When I asked for some money he was horrified.

Salary call, he informed me, would be at eleven o'clock on the following Saturday. (Everything was a call. There were train calls and rehearsal calls, reading calls, and salary calls. I believe the colloquial reference to a pub-crawl was originally an actor's joke about calls.) The advancing of money to strange baggage-men, however gifted and however fortunately acquired, was seemingly unthinkable.

But this was Colonel Shaw, manager as well as stage-manager and also owner of the outfit, a thoroughly good sort and a hundred per cent. trouper. He took me back to his own digs, where I stayed and had supper and breakfast. Shaw paid the bill. But of course he deducted the sum at next "salary call."

While we yarned on the first night, I asked if it was always such a simple matter to get a baggage-man who could play small parts. Did he really depend on taking the first rustic, or tramp, who came along—and what happened if he got a succession of no-goods?

Casually dogmatic, he told me that troupers were a type, and that he could pick one a mile off, had known I was just right. He added the information that if I had not happened along, he and the "boys" would have had to handle the baggage between them, share out the small parts as best they might, muddle along somehow.

Then, as I frowned in perplexity at this sudden revelation of what I really *was,* Shaw hastily assured me that good baggage-men and small-part players were really ten a penny. But that, I suspected, was lest I set a new value on my services.

All the crowd were jolly and careless people, none of them having the slightest pretensions to culture except one. A very ponderous and distant chap, named Ronald Murtagh on the bills and called Mick Sweeney in the dressing-rooms, contrasted sharply with the others.

Sweeney, although a youngster, spoke and behaved precisely like a middle-aged lawyer in a family drama, or like a heavier and more pedantic Gentleman Whalen. In off-hours, on the second day, he discussed psychology and similar matters, of which I had read a good deal, but of which I had no applied knowledge.

Overawed, I set myself, assiduously, to benefit from the chance of talk with him. But on the third day he commenced to repeat all the bits he had used in the beginning, went right through, verbatim, then coughed ponderously, looked wise, and remained silent.

I found out from one of the girls that Mick was all but illiterate, that he had been the baggage-man before the chap I had replaced, had learnt the "culture," seriously, word by word, as he would have learnt a small part, from a *Pears' Encyclopædia* picked up in some casual digs. An even greater joke was that the first "big" part Mick had ever been given, when he ceased to be a baggage-man and became a character actor, actually was the part of a family lawyer!

Several times in the next couple of weeks I saw Ronald Murtagh play the part; every inflexion of voice, every pause— and many of the turns of phrase!—came exactly as if Mick Sweeney was talking over coffee in the digs after the show.

Poor Mick. Probably there was never so thorough and sincere a disciple of Thespis before. One could almost swear that he *dreamt* in the legal-gentleman rôle. Another Irving may have been lost when he was killed quite early in the First World War.

Fitup life in the villages and small towns was thoroughly enjoyable, even although our company was tenth- or twelfth-rate. In the first days I discovered, with some surprise, that everyone of the company, from Shaw down to the youngest and last-joined girl, had the tense imagination and dreamy lack of realism which I had thought was my own particular curse. To this day I have not answered the question whether they had all met, or thought they had met, bearded men in forests.

Continuous half-intoxication, without liquor or other material stimulant, is the only descriptive phrase applicable to them, and to all of their kind I have known. With a swinging chanty or a roar of coax-and-command, one can bring workmen, or soldiers, or sailors, into the state for a few minutes. People in love will know it for hours at a time. Writer or artist will attain it at the end of a satisfying work.

These poverty-stricken, half-educated, over-worked actors and actresses were in the condition continuously.

Later I met many of the top-rank figures in the theatrical world, often found the art-drunkenness absent. Either the nerve-state named has nothing to do with the theatrical profession, quâ profession, or—or I had better leave the subject there.

Several years seemed to pass, doing "one-night stands" in the tiny towns. By the calendar, I was in the company for just under three weeks.

At Borris, in the County Carlow, I got drunk, which was

normal enough. In the dressing-room, following a financial discussion, I had a row with Shaw. That, too, was normal enough, as was my assertion that I was quitting. Such things happened almost nightly.

But frozen stares of horror, from all, and a drawing away as if I smelt of manure, followed when it was seen that I meant it. Quitting just before the show was apparently unheard of. Which only made me the more decided.

But I felt very shamed and foolish and lonely, drinking in a nearby pub during show-time, completely unable to maintain the bluster, even to myself. Next morning, when they had gone, I felt as if I had stolen their underclothes or eaten their dinners.

Looking back sometimes, as we all do, I can find many things to bring shame and regret. But even the big things go down when I remember my drunken meanness to my friends, that night at Borris. I walked fast on the road out of Carlow County, hurrying away.

Then lazing my way south, eating at the farms and rapidly becoming a tramp again, I felt thoroughly dissatisfied with life and with myself, almost resolved on a return to Dublin. For the first and only time in my life I read a "Situations Vacant" column.

This was in the *Irish Independent,* which at that time served, in Ireland, to replace the English *Stage* and *Era.* In Shaw's company I had learnt that much, and I looked eagerly for advertisers requiring small-part players or a baggage-man-cum-character-actor. There was none, and after a couple of days I ceased to bother.

Presently the dream-drift of the road took me again, until I came into Waterford and started to crawl the waterfront as I had done on Cork's Marina. The city was simply crowded with drifters, expert cadgers for the most part, compared with whom I was the veriest simpleton, and by the second evening I had decided to leave.

A big Norwegian steamer interested me, and I thought of going to Norway or wherever she was bound. But the people were hostile and suspicious—I never got even as far as the galley.

One other big steamer, from England, seemed to offer chances of going somewhere, but again I was frozen out. Waterford was so full of penniless drifters at the time that any steamer could have shipped a stokehold full of firemen without even the formality of an advance. The place was depressing, and its police were efficient and sceptical.

Then I had an inspiration, and went uptown to the offices of Murphys Limited, a small local shipping company. As far as I could see, there was only one of their boats in the river, but nothing was certain. I tried out my idea.

Briefly, I had compared myself, physically and personally, with the horde of waterfront drifters, and found them wanting. If only I could get speech with someone, anyone, at Murphy's, a girl for preference, that steamer or some other steamer was mine.

As between conceit and good psychology, I think the latter gets the preference. That is my honest opinion, because only a maniac, or a fellow who really has something inside him, can work up a "gude conceit o' himsel'" when he is a penniless and hungry tramp.

My luck was in, for I spoke with the chief's secretary, a cool, pretty, capable girl with wide, nice eyes and a smile. After a minute's talk, I knew those eyes were not seeing only an untidy lie-about tramp. That girl was competent and brisk, but she was a girl, and knew about men. My luck was in.

One would have thought I was booking a passage on a luxury liner instead of seeking a "shove" to—wherever Messrs. Murphy's steamer happened to be going. The tact and adroitness of the girl nearly floored me.

She was several years older than I, but my bulk and experience matched us, and it required almost as few words as the tinker-girl had used, to make it clear that she liked me, and wanted to be friendly and helpful. For her the rest was routine.

Half an hour later I left with a note for the skipper of the little steamer, had a supper aboard that night, and next day was down in a stokehold again. But this was a coal-burner, and there were no gaspings and headaches. Two days later I stepped blissfully and innocently out into Le Havre in France, to find it a Gethsemane. That is, for a drifter without any official documents.

I have used the wrong word. Even then, in the early days of the century and before the first world war, France was a positive hell for a person without papers. Even then the stamped and signed document was already a fetish.

Nowadays everyone, in almost every country, fills in many printed forms when engaged in any major activity or movement. In my youth, the people of Ireland, England, America, had no such duty.

For the vast majority of the people, the only official document known or used was a birth certificate. Hundreds of thousands did not bother even with that solitary specimen. But in France the printed form had even then begun to smother the lives of the people.

One could not check in at a small hotel, make a rail journey, cash a money order, pawn a watch or visit a brothel without being prepared to meet a demand for official documents. Coming from Ireland as I did, and knowing only the widely-tolerant and personal approach of seafaring folks and American harbour officials, I swiftly found France a nightmare place.

It seems clear to me, and I think one could prove, that all this monstrous paper blanketing and formality frustration, taken for normal towards the middle of this century, had its beginnings in France. Because of the proximity of France and Germany, from the clash of ideas between their rulers, the plague of meaningless suspicion arose.

The mad search for a salve to the suspicion, in the fiction security guaranteed by correctly inscribed official papers, followed swiftly. France and Germany were smothered.

Now the whole world is being smothered. In the year the second great war ended, at a time of dire dearth and emergency, eight hundred and fifty thousand tons of paper were used for printed forms with neat blank spaces for the people to fill in. There were practically no books that year. Because there was no paper.

It is not for me, a tramp off the roads even if I can write an occasional readable story, to tell the people who own the billion neat rows of houses and the million neat factories and offices how to run their world. I know nothing about it. But if the best that normality can offer is a fair share of eight hundred and fifty thousand tons of printed forms, I prefer to know nothing about it.

That first night, having been badgered and startled and warned a dozen times, I decided to make for England or Ireland next morning. They seemed far more desirable than paradise. But next morning I changed my mind, and struck out to walk south.

Again, as at Galveston, I had only flimsy and incorrect notions of the geography. I was, in fact, at first convinced that Le Havre was in the south of France.

When a drifter told me it was a thousand kilometres to Marseilles, I thought he was joking or an imbecile. But I wanted to go.

I had an idea, based on I know not what fragments of heterogeneous reading, that people in the south would be more open, more human, less *formal*! It is amusing, now, to recall that the hazy generalisation was justified.

The professional tramp, as known everywhere from Hong Kong to Copenhagen—both ways round—does not exist in France. It would be rash to say that no single vagrant has ever ridden a train illegally in that country. But I think that if ever in the past one did attempt the feat, he is still sitting in a cell somewhere, a hoary penitent, answering questions.

Even the most inferior and juvenile officials asked, or wanted to ask, thousands of questions. Skill in lying was not of the slightest use either—they wanted it printed and signed. Bitterly I reflected that if only I had been a pick-pocket, a bag-snatcher, a drug trafficker, or a white-slave trader, I would have had reams of papers, all correctly filled in, and the gendarmes would have saluted me.

Now I skulked. Several times I went by night, blindly. I had twenty-two shillings in English money, which I was saving for some dire emergency, but if I had dared to face the uniformed men, I would have paid my rail-fare.

Begging a meal was easy, in the rural districts—for me. But I soon discovered that no Frenchman could do as I was doing. My casual food came only because of the small amusement (it became my stock-in-trade for several days) which arose when the people discovered I could hardly speak French, was an Englishman, and then almost immediately discovered that I was an Irishman, sometimes even before I told them.

At that time there was hardly any heavy motor-transport on the French roads, and to ask for a lift in a private car brought hostility, suspicion, a torrent of awkward foolish questions, and a glance over the shoulder for a gendarme. Hitch-hiking, I should say, came about equal to rape in the French consciousness of that day.

Paradoxically, a great deal of the awkwardness comes from the eternal and irrepressible friendliness of the French people. They are not really a form-loving and businesslike people— they are forced by law into pretending to be so.

Where an English-speaking official will say something like "Fares, please," his French equivalent wants to start off with, "Ah, well, I suppose I might as well have the fares, if there are any. Go to, let's have them. By the mother of God, I'd better collect those fares, eh?" Something of that kind is behind even the curtest and snappiest attempt at pidgin officialese in France.

There is hope for such a people yet. One day they will stuff the form-fillers, top and bottom, back and front, with their own forms, and roast them on a fire of official documents.

But in my first sample I saw no sign whatever of anything

but jail for a paperless man. The basic, friendly gossiping escaped me, although the only lift I had on the road came in that way and not through asking for it.

Near Arles, a big motor-lorry drew to a halt by a little roadside stream where I had been kneeling to drink. Such vehicles were few and far between in France at the time, were almost unknown in Ireland except for a handful on the main roads. So I stared, and of course did not dare ask a lift.

This is a nostalgia in remembering the green flapping tarpaulin, which made the wagon look like some battered tramp-ship of the roads, the pleasure I felt in its size and in its nearness when it stopped. The driver filled a can at the stream, after the inevitable few gossiping remarks.

When he had placed me as an Anglais, and then as an Irlandais, he chatted on while he unscrewed the radiator cap and filled up. At an early stage I mentioned that I was going south, but with little hope of interesting him. I had already been humiliated, and nearly terrified, in my early attempts to seek transportation.

Quite to my surprise, he nodded to the seat beside his, adding a word I did not know, with a questioning accent. Apparently it was the name of a town, for he tried another, but I did not know that either. Then, impatient but still friendly, he guffawed and slapped me on the shoulder.

"Sud," he shouted in pretended despair. "Côte de Provence." Even the generic terms meant nothing to me, but I began to move towards the cab. "Midi," my companion almost screamed, and waved his arms.

I nodded emphatically and got in. But I had been talking for several minutes in my Christian Brothers' French, and we had covered several kilometres before I realised that my friend had been telling me he was going south.

He told me later—with difficulty, for my ears were quite unaccustomed to French—that he was driving for a rich man. But the richest, he insisted with impressiveness and awe and something else, nameless, in his voice.

First a farmer (but of the smallest, God), and then the owner of a tiny wine-press business, his boss had, it seemed, organised something like a co-operative among the small farmers in the district of Var.

The lorryman himself used the phrase describing the organisation as something like a co-operative. Early farm produce, early flowers and late flowers, rough wine and sometimes the grapes themselves, were handled by the merger of little farmers.

It was a co-operative. Except that my driver's boss took most of the money. The something else that had been in his voice came out more clearly, an unmistakable snarl of hatred. Hastily I attempted to tell about farmers' co-operatives in Ireland.

From there I went on, halting for words, to describe the Irish equivalent of his boss, a type with which every Irish writer of the last hundred years has been preoccupied. (Anyone may find him in my own story *Shay Peen Ella*, or can meet him more fully and better described in Liam O'Flaherty's *Famine*.) Then I boggled for a word, since I did not know an English equivalent for the Irish term.

The French had no word for the type either until that day. The lorry-driver and I tried for one, a dozen ways, he growing more and more excited as I described the wolfish rapacity and almost maniacal greed of the Irish farmer-shopkeeper-carrier-moneylender in the last century.

That was he. And *that* was he, and *that,* the driver insisted, panting in eagerness, and recognising a portrait of his boss, but we had no word for it.

At last I told him the Irish term—"gombeen." He seized on it at once, muttered it a hundred times, with varying maledictions, announced over and over again that *that* was his boss, *le gombeen*.

He dropped me on the outskirts of Toulon, and the last word I heard, as he headed away on the main road, was "gombeen." If the term is not part of the Provençal dialect by this time, there is no truth in dialectical philology.

Toulon thrilled me. It would have thrilled me still more if I had not been terrified of the gendarmes, constantly aware of the fact that I carried no printed talisman. But even in spite of my worries, I revelled in the crooked town, the citadel, the new harbour and the old one—a beckoning place, this, one of the few in which I have ever wanted to stay.

The tall, strangely-shut-up-looking houses came with a jolt of surprise and pleasure after Le Havre and Waterford and Cork. On in the evening I began to remember (or rather misremember) scraps of my reading about Toulon, and prowled the quay with a zest similar to but more intense than that of my prowlings in Dublin or New Orleans.

That old fish quay is a fascinating place for anyone from anywhere, I think. To an unpractical and dreamy person like myself, it held far more of comfort and caress than any idea or reality of home, anywhere, could hold.

Twice I have mentioned the twisted nostalgia of the tramp. In practice it means such things as I felt on the quay of Toulon that evening.

It meant that there was an iron bollard, from which I could look out over the harbour, read the names on the small boats, and drift off into something more vivid than any dream on the thought of the sound of the names, with the dusk-pictures of the tall strange houses and the gay strange shop-fronts to back them.

Drifting, I looked out over the water, at the other iron bollard on Dublin riverside and at the thirteen-year-old who sat there to look out over Dublin Bay at me. I looked forward, too, and saw many a picture which, in later days, I knew to come alive. Hamburg docks, for instance, I saw quite clearly, and years afterwards the false-nostalgia came when I looked at them in reality. I even saw Guatemala.

A mystic might have called it a visioning, but even then, although a dreamer, I was no mystic. There was no visioning, because in my forward glimpses I saw no sign of Jim Phelan the writer, nor any hint of men with guns. There was no steel and granite torture-house of a jail, nor any pale, salaried man who earned his pay with a hangman's rope.

The dream-drift of the vagrant is more practical than any visioning. Cats and dogs seem to do the same thing, and I think all people know the experience, even if vaguely and for a short time, when perfectly calm for a few minutes, looking at a fire or something of the kind, perhaps on a much-desired holiday.

The drifter keeps contact, as busy preoccupied people only seldom find time to do, between his future self and his past, through many and varying presents. The quay at Toulon would, I think, induce the same dream-state in almost anyone.

Of course it would! It comes to me that half the world must have enjoyed something of the same feeling, from that same place. Because it seems certain that scenarist and director both were influenced by the very environment of which I write, in making the simple, elemental little film, *Quai des Brûmes*.

That evening I did not move from the *Quai* until nearly dusk. I did not wish to go in search of a lodging while there was still sufficient light for me to be conspicuous. Besides, there appeared to be no scarcity of places.

At the *Gare,* a friendly porter sent me to an address, giving me his name and telling me to use it. By the time I found the place, an enormously tall, white-stone house in a silent street, it was almost dark.

I rang the bell, and after a moment there was a click. Fumbling, I opened the door, but found there was no one inside. Feeling my way down a wide, long hallway in the dark, I came to the foot of a stone staircase.

This, too, was in darkness; but at the very top of the house a light showed, a head looked over the balustrade, and a man's voice enquired what I wanted. Twice I shouted up—the house was very high—that I wanted a lodging, and mentioned the name the railwayman had given me. At last the voice instructed, "*Montez.*"

Feeling my way up the dark stone stairs, making a hundred theories about the possibly sinister inhabitants, uncertain whether at any moment I might not step over an edge and break my neck, I came after a long time to the top. A very friendly-looking and smiling Frenchman emerged from a door to meet me.

"Pawnshop?" he enquired pleasantly.

CHAPTER XIV

WHEN the Frenchman put his wholly unexpected query, I did some quick thinking.

Here was a man accustomed to strangers, perhaps meeting a good many English sailormen. When they were in funds, they would stay at a more expensive place than his. He would only know them towards the end of a stay ashore.

When they came his way they would be short of money, would want to pawn a watch or coat in order to have resources for the last day or two. The patron had spotted me for a stranger, taken me for an English sailor, noted at once that I was hard-up. So . . . "Pawnshop?"

The whole train of thought took perhaps a fifth of a second. I have often thought in that way, or at even greater speed. Everyone has, at one time or another. A person is tensed up, receptive. He hears a phrase, perhaps even a single word, and in a split second the whole situation is plain.

So I shall have quite a substantial moiety of my readers with me, to understand the first minute of that first encounter at Toulon.

All the way "down France" I had been wish-thinking myself, while I wrestled to understand people, into a belief that in the south my Irish-French would be more comprehensible. Because, I reasoned, the people of southern France would be different, would speak differently from those of Le Havre and the towns between.

The south would be a kind of French Yorkshire, and its speech would be the French equivalent of an Irish accent! So I would be able to understand it more easily.

The joke on me was that all my wistful hypotheses were correct. Midi speech is to a Parisian what a Sheffield or Tipperary accent is to London. But now I had it exemplified, and I did not recognise it. My midi landlord asked in the friendliest way if I wanted a *pension*. And I thought he said "Pawnshop?".

Fortunately the landlord ignored my attempts to explain.

The place was incredibly cheap and very comfortable, the people good-humoured and friendly. It was no tramps' stall, that was clear; but it was cheaper than many of the twentieth-rate places I knew.

The patron and his wife and I talked until late, and the comfort-glow made up for the language-limpings. I slept well, in a beautifully clean bed, had a good breakfast and a thorough clean-up, the whole for little more than a sixth of a tramp-stall cost in Cork.

At breakfast, when I opened up a little about my lack of seamen's papers, identity documents, or anything of the kind, the landlord frowned at once and shook his head in a thoroughly depressing negation. I would be "pulled" that day, he told me, and made an expressive grab at his own coat collar.

In Toulon, he explained, because of the Government dockyard, the gendarmes had to be strict. The people, too, he added, and looked me over uncompromisingly.

While I was wondering what the British Consul would have to say, and reconciling myself to a month in a French prison, my host mentioned that Marseilles was different. If I could get to Marseilles—his tone implied a myriad doubts—I could perhaps get a steamer to Ireland.

He seemed to take it for granted, without any discussion whatever, that a person who found himself without papers in France should get out as quickly as possible—if he could. I was inclined to agree.

Not very optimistically, I skulked out of Toulon, keeping to the little streets paralleling the main, headed for Marseilles and Dublin, but without any great hope of reaching either.

Less than two kilometres out of Toulon, purely on instinct and in complete certainty, I waved to a big private car. Flagging cars was completely unknown in France and England at that time, but I *knew* it was my car.

Nowadays, from the make, speed, colour, road position, and general state of a car, in the few seconds while it is oncoming before I decide to wave or let it go on, I can deduce much about the driver or owner. That morning outside Toulon I was only beginning to feel my way. But I knew, against all the laws and customs and codes of France, that the people would be right. They were an American couple.

We talked, animatedly, all the way into Marseilles. At the end they noted my name, and gave me fifty francs, and hoped, sincerely I could see, that we would meet again.

That was thirty-three years ago. Somehow I think they will be alive and will see this, will read my thanks for the ride and the fifty francs, but most of all for the talk.

Before I had been an hour in Marseilles I realised that my Toulon landlord's optimism about the city had been baseless. Probably a Marseilles landlord could, with equal reason, have told me Toulon was better for a drifter.

Already I had had questing glances from three gendarmes, had only avoided query by a smart business-like gait, knew that if I met any one of them again the interview would be short and the sequel protracted. Down the wharves I was afraid to risk asking a question, drifted luck-hunting.

My fantasy was that I would meet someone like Joe Jarrett, or walk plunk into some steamer I knew from Dublin, or meet Tom Dunne from the *Narraganset*! That I did not add the further detail of first finding a thousand pounds in gold, in a purse on the quayside, may perhaps be noted as evidence of a stern and pragmatical realism. Or perhaps only as evidence that I was not yet completely crazy or yet completely a tramp.

None of the fantasy-items materialised during the day, and I walked myself weary without speaking a word. Towards evening I found a rough lodging-house, without any great difficulty except that of depending on my eyes alone, since I knew that street questions in my funny French would attract attention to me.

In the first half-hour at the lodging-house, two people had tried to pilfer the two francs I had shown as all my wealth, one small but very tough and completely degenerate French-Italian had sought a fight with me, one very filthy effeminate had tried to attach himself to me and my two francs. I debated going out into the night, but knew it was madness to attempt walking about. Fortunately, the place quieted later, and I slept with few interruptions.

Next morning I was ill, vomiting and with a headache that nearly floored me. Looking back, I surmise that it was ptomaine poisoning, from some of the cheap and filthy food I had eaten. But that morning I was convinced I had, somehow, acquired some mysterious and horrible disease from the filthy bed and loathsome surroundings. I crawled along the quays, not caring if a hundred gendarmes asked for papers.

Looking hopelessly and lackadaisically for an English ship, I passed the word *Halcyon* on a steamer's bow, automatically dismissing it as a French word. But I could feel her, could even smell her as English, several minutes before I saw London on her stern.

Any commonsense psychiatrist would have rated me low-grade imbecile at that moment, for I could already see myself in England. Indeed, I could hear the thump of the steam-hammers at Inchicore. This, because I had smelt and felt an English ship. It will sound infantile to many. In fact, it was merely the beginning of the boundless, insatiable optimism of the tramp.

However, I was brought swiftly back to earth when I spoke to the first of the *Halcyon's* crew. He jerked his thumb shore-ward and told me to ally-toot-sweet in French even worse than my own.

Mick Brennan was my saviour. I cursed his bones later that day, but he was my saviour, none the less.

Brennan, in spite of his name, which is straight Irish, was a russet-haired Welshman from Cardiff. Friendly, and with a

pleasantly cynical grin, he interrupted my first few remarks
with a statement that that would be all right—he could square
things. I was to see him later in the afternoon at a *bistro* he
named.

There were no hitches, and I went with the *Halcyon* to
Wapping, down the Thames from London. But first, before
leaving Marseilles, Brennan took every cent I possessed—
forty-four francs and one English pound. I had not known that
friendliness included such things.

Of course Mick was quite right, as I can plainly see now.
But that night I could gladly have poisoned him.

For one who read as much as I did, Wapping was a dreadful
disappointment. I had been expecting something which would
at least approach the waterside at Toulon or Marseilles. Instead, there were high dead walls and narrow, muddy, house-
less roads, with a distant and unpleasant-looking background
of slum.

Pubs were many, but mean and dirty, and another fantasy
of mine went by the board. Already a tramp at heart, an
opportunist by inclination, a beggar by philosophy, I had been
visualising Wapping as a Golconda, a kind of bigger and better
Liberty, where sailors predominated, and where I, a *kind* of
sailor, might—might like the people.

There would be rows on rows of pubs, all more or less like
Chalker Doyle's of Dublin, where the alley-slinkers of the
Coombe gathered to celebrate, where girls danced on the pavement, to music from melodeon or banjo. And where one elect
would be lucratively welcome.

Wapping showed nothing like that. It was strictly business.

I had read too much of Harrison Ainsworth and Captain
Marryat when I was a child. The place of which I had memor-
ised the features had vanished half a century earlier, had been
on its way out of existence even while the stories and songs
were being written.

Now I was, so to speak, looking for Dick Turpin on the
road to York, or expecting to see a pony-express rider in
Cheyenne. My disappointment was profound. Inchicore in

perspective gained attraction. And I had still no money.

However, I did at last in fact find a tavern like those I had mentally pictured. But by that time my state of mind was such that I simply refused to believe the place was there. It looked *wrong,* now.

A large pub—two pubs at least, on top of one another—clung precariously to the river wall, overhung the water. Dark little ferry steps were on one side, a patch of shingle showed with the low tide, and a most villainous-looking boatman, Rogue Riderhood to the life, slunk up from the steps and went into the public bar.

Inside, two large rooms adjoined, and were filled with customers. Parrot-cages and models of yachts, a vast photo of a tattooed girl, a couple of full-rigged ships in bottles, met my eyes. There were many sailors, some of them foreign. This was most definitely better. I had been unfair to Wapping.

My hopes of acquiring a shilling for a stall began to disintegrate when a stony-eyed barman fixed me with his eyes the moment I entered. Since I had not even the price of a drink, I had no *locus standi,* no right of entrance, as it were. Fortunately, two firemen from the *Halcyon* were drinking with a crowd of others. One waved, and brought me a pint of beer. Standing on the edge of the crowd, I began to think the pub interior marvellous.

Then and later I discovered that it was really a show-place, a survival from the old days. Remaining, when all the rest had gone, intact among the grim warehouse walls and formal dock-sheds, it had almost become a "phoney" resort, equivalent to Ye Ollde Englysshe Tea Shoppe or Deadwood Dick's Quick-fire Saloon—and Soda Fountain.

Then a sentimental but shrewd proprietor had realised that the place would be a gold-mine, if left alone. He had saved the "improvement and alteration" money, and the place was still a gold-mine. Artists and especially writers came to see, but the genuine sailormen also came to drink.

Even that half-compromise with my preconceptions pleased me. But in the early part of my first evening I was acutely conscious of the passage of time and of the fact that I had no money. This would be no place in which to walk about at night, and Wapping would be less casual than Cork about camp-fires on the riverside.

Then one of the firemen told with gusto how I had come out of Marseilles without papers of any kind. Various reminiscences followed, and presently I gave a jocular account of my journey down to Toulon. One and all damned the French mania for reading bits of paper. Other beer came. I was accepted, was drinking with my peers in a Wapping pub. Great happiness came with the beer.

When the *Halcyon* man enquired about my finances, I told him simply that I had not a cent. Seemingly the situation was familiar to him, for he promptly produced a shilling, but without passing it over stood looking at the rest of the group.

Another pint of the watery beer was brought (I had been "trained" on the muddy heavy beer of Dublin), and a little while later the fireman passed me a comforting collection of small coins. The boys wanted me to stay and drink with them, were all easy-going and friendly. But they had themselves all been adrift at one time or another, knew my problems about lodgings and the rest even better than I did myself. After a final drink I left.

On a tram, bound London-wards, I found I had eight shillings. This would have been two days' pay for a ship's fireman, almost a week's wages for an Irish farm-labourer, would more than suffice to get me through London.

A policeman in the city directed me to a lodging, where I paid sevenpence for a bed in a separate little room. A chime sounded outside, before I fell asleep, and in spite of my disillusionment at Wapping, I remembered all I had read about Bow Bells.

It was a sevenpenny bed in a multiple stall, but I nestled into it satisfied. Presently I would see Banbury Cross, and the Banks and Braes of Bonny Doon, about which Robert Burns wrote, and Shenandoah and Hamburg Docks and Guatemala. London first, though. And here I was.

Luxuriously as if I were in a palace, I stretched, and dropped away into a bliss-jumbled picturing of delectable scenes, past and to come, visual miniature-samples of the lazy loveliness the world had to offer.

Last picture of all, after the tinker-girl had said "Here's the polis," and smiled at me, after the bustle and thrill-gaiety of the fitup crowd had emerged for a second, after the shipping-secretary's quiet smile had faded while a dozen gendarmes peered around street-corners in the eternal quest for papers—last picture of all was the genial friendly face of my Toulon landlord, clear as it had been at the moment and as I can see it now, welcoming me with the singularly un-French-sounding word, "Pawnshop?"

I do not know whether I would have been counted as just, or unjust, or merely neutral, but I slept peacefully all night.

Next morning before inspecting the city I made my best toilet. This was easy. The only purchase I had made in France, with the butt-end of my fifty francs and my English money, was a startlingly bright green shirt. This was the sole remnant of my French fortune. Mick Brennan had taken everything else.

A thorough clean-up at the lodging-place cost me a penny. Then I threw away my hat, which was dirty, bought a collar for fourpence, carried my coat on my arm, and presently started to "walk down London."

For one such as I (although I did not yet know anything much about myself) the district in which I chose to walk, down Charing Cross Road, was precisely right. Knowing nothing of the English capital, except dateless romanticisms about Old London Bridge and the sound of Bow Bells, I might just as well have started in some other direction, walked for days in the wilderness of houses.

As always, when in a place I liked, I commenced to write a song about that street. Years later, and in a jail-cell of all places, I finished it—"Walking down Charing Cross Road." Later still I discovered that a dozen song-writers had been intrigued by the same theme.

The place was delectable in ways which perhaps meant nothing to hundreds of casual passers-by, but which were strong drug to me. It was not merely that there were many places where one saw music and song-sheet, straight hot from the brains of the makers as it were, although that meant much. Nor that there were book-stores in plenty, although that meant more.

There were other angles to that street. They are still there, and I still find a new one, every decade or so, when I return to remember and compare.

Down the narrow streets to one side could be glimpsed a district which, unmistakably as if its people screamed the news, was the exact counterpart of Liberty-Dublin. The sight of it brought little pleasure-jolts, but although I had read of it in a score of books, I did not know I was measuring Seven Dials.

On the opposite side of the road, lane and alley and narrow street led away to a still more colourful district, where foreign-looking men stood on street corners and women un-English of garb went by. A single Chinaman, hurrying about his business, completed my picture of exoticism. I did not know then, nor for years, that I was looking at Soho. But I liked it.

With such places to either side, with the book-stores and the music-shops in the middle, and with all the powerful pull of London exerted on my hairspring imagination, I felt like a far-wandering pilgrim come home at last. Except that the home-town was a strange place.

My eagerness and the keen pleasure of my questing must have shown in my face and walk. Also the French shirt was *very* green, and I had been burnt brown on the roads of Ireland and France. Outside a bookshop a stout, middle-aged man eyed me over, twitched the beginnings of a friendly smile and glinted a twinkle of welcome in grey wide eyes. I halted, uncertainly.

"You look," he said in a friendly manner, and smiled, "just as if you'd stepped in for a minute, straight out of Devonshire."

With only vague ideas of what or where Devonshire was, I accepted the speech as an amity-gambit. We talked a while, and in some seven minutes the man had the whole story, of everything that is in the preceding chapter—except the two shotgun weddings. Although he was more than twice my age, we got on beautifully.

I took him to say his name was Wales, and told him I had never been in Wales, yet. He laughed as if I had made a good joke, and said neither had a lot of other people who'd have liked to. Missing the point of that, I felt awkward for a moment, but he spotted it at once and put me at my ease, going on to ask a hundred questions about Ireland.

He knew Jim Larkin, and James Connolly, asked questions about the previous year's strike, showed keen interest when I talked about the Liberty. Then he switched back to my recent walking, and asked where I was going.

When I told him I did not know, but perhaps up north and then on to Dublin, he laughed again, asked suddenly if I had ever read Jack London. He gave me a list of books when he heard I had not, and told me not to miss *The People of the Abyss*.

It is an embarrassing thing to remember, but all this time I had been estimating that a genial old gentleman of this kind, who obviously liked me and so completely understood things, would most probably give me half a sovereign when we had finished talking. Perhaps he read that in my face too!

"Go down and see Wilson at the *Daily News*," he said suddenly. "He's a nice fellow—you'll like talking to him. Tell him this fitup and cow-milking story, and about having no papers in France and the rest. He'll be glad of . . . Can you write it?" he enquired, after a second's hesitation, and I said I could. Then and there he gave me a note for the features editor, wished me luck, and asked me to write him—again without giving me a name or address.

Later and at long intervals we met many times, and he was always the same genial, greying man of that morning. Once, when I was fighting hard in the literary market, he helped me out with money and practical tips. Once he warned me about a publisher who was "on the edge," would have taken me over the edge along with him. Caroline, the girl who knew more about his literary business than he did himself, vetted contracts for me at a critical moment in my professional life. Also, at a still more critical moment of my financial life, she sent money to a girl I had perforce left stranded.

It was a fortunate meeting, that morning in Charing Cross Road. Elsewhere I have written of the memory-clusters which mean so much for mental health. The talk with the stranger that morning centres one of them. Even though I did not know his name, except Wales, and it would have meant little or nothing at the time if I had known.

Peak of the pyramid is a note he wrote me when I published my novel *Museum,* perhaps the nicest line ever penned from an old writer to a young one:

"DEAR JIM PHELAN. *I have just finished your novel* Museum. *If ever anyone else attempts to write a novel on the same subject, I shall re-read yours. Cordially,* H. G. WELLS."

Praise of my books generally leaves me cold. Sometimes it irritates me. But I like that line from H. G. W.

At the *Daily News* office I felt, in the first minute, as if I were back in my telegram-days, snooping around in the newspaper offices, looking for stories in chance-read wires. Swiftly followed the inevitable fantasy, and I was away again, riding the kinky imagination, into a hundred realms of opulence and success.

There was no discussion, inside the mind of me. The thing was settled. I was a writer—one might almost say a *great* writer, for surely no one else had ever walked down that wretched road from Le Havre without papers. What doubt was there? Had I not a note from the grey man? Had I not seen delectable roads? Very well, then.

Anyone who has ever seen a factory-worker, just after he has been paid, stepping out springily on his toes, slapping his hands together from time to time, laughing in boundless good humour at every small jest of the revered and beloved comrades who, an hour earlier, were only the chaps he worked with—anyone who has seen this mystical change, and knows it to have been wrought by the receipt of some few coins or pieces of currency-paper, knows how a fantasy-follower goes, and how I stepped into that office.

Of course, if the reader has ever made silly-fool fantasies himself or herself, the understanding will be easier.

The features man was all Wells had said. He extracted the full flavour of my narrative of wandering, showed by a question or two that he sensed all the minor possibilities, grinned in wistful envy at a few points.

Then, with precisely two quietly spoken words, he punctured my fantasy-balloon and brought me to earth with a bump.

"What emerges?" he enquired at the end of my talk.

Emerges! What the . . . Knowing nothing of news-making, I had not known such a question was inevitable. I boggled.

Of course I knew better than he, but I did not know I knew. Not then nor for long had I the wit to answer that *I* emerged, and that was the story. He promised to "get in touch with me," and I plodded, leaden-footed, back to my lodgings.

When I had eaten, and had wandered a little around the river, I cheered up and forgot about my brief and blasted career as a writer, my ruptured reveries. Instead of moping, I went early to bed, and was out in the streets before even the London sparrows were awake. I plunged into the maze of streets and headed for Dublin.

CHAPTER XV

To this day I am proud of the fact that, steering by nothing but instinct and the sky, asking no questions after the first few had shown me that no Londoner knows anything whatever about London, I went straight to the place where the main north-west road forks off.

There were then no motorists' signposts such as one knows to-day. All the others were worse than useless. London is some twenty-four miles across, from north-west to south-east.

No citizen of London knows anything about main roads—why should he? A stranger might walk for a week, or even for a month, through the endless rows of houses, without ever finding an escape from the labyrinth.

By the shortest road, there are thirteen miles of streets between Seven Dials and Barnet, where Watling Street strikes off towards Chester and the north-west. I might have ridden a tram for much of the way—if I had known even one name of a place. Not knowing one, I padded on, with an occasional sniff at a street-crossing, and came before midday to Barnet and Watling Street.

There was a most definite thrill in passing the last house, seeing the green road ahead. This in spite of the fact that I liked London. Roads always look better. I was going to Dublin, and it might have been at the next cross-roads from the way I stepped up that first green mile.

Within the hour I had made friends with a tramp, the talk with whom slowed my gait to a normal padding. This was the first vagrant with whom I had ever talked much, although I had seen dozens in Cork and Marseilles, scores in New Orleans and Waterford. My first venture, with the degenerate on the Southern Pacific, had prejudiced me. This Watling Street man was different.

In the very beginning he attempted to beg cigarettes, then struggled hard for a drink, or even a few coppers, but I met each request with a nonchalant and obvious lie, to the effect that I was penniless and would myself be glad of a little assistance. Thereafter we got on well.

It may be taken as an axiom that no person who gives a tramp anything, however trifling, can hope to be treated with human respect or met on a basis of equality. (As well buy expensive drinks for a hostess in a night-club and then expect her to be friendly, or give one sausage from a string to a prowling dog and hope he will ignore the remainder.)

My road-companion was called Toaster Dick, and at first sight appeared to be about sixty. He wore long hair and beard, had the old-roadster crouch, and behaved in general like an ancient, but after the first few minutes I knew he was a young man. From his talk—of having joined the army early in the Boer War—I reckoned him to be not more than thirty-five.

Toaster and I made friends—as far as tramps do, which meant that we agreed to keep together for a while. The arrangement delighted me because, in a vague way, ever since New Orleans, I had been hoping to know a real tramp. Two others came my way that first morning—I had a worthy trio of masters, but the lesson was brief.

Near a village called Mimms, where a narrow by-lane came in from Elstree, Toaster hung about for a few minutes, without explanation. From his glances up the lane one would have thought he had an appointment, and that his man was late.

Less than a quarter of an hour after we had arrived, two tramps came down the lane from Elstree. Toaster talked, and I learnt their names—Joe Ockley and Pimple Simmons.

Toaster and they had not met for nine weeks. All three had arrived at the lane-corner within fifteen minutes of one another. Pride was mine, even for being allowed to witness such a meeting.

First I had not wanted to be a genius. Now I was not even sure that I wanted to be a writer.

When the boys had left, down the by-lanes for Enfield and Essex, Toaster suddenly seemed to become weary of me. All our projected double-travelling had gone by the board already. Somehow I had done wrong, or Ockley and Pimple had suspected or feared me, and passed on the feeling, for Toaster made flimsy excuse to turn off on a by-road.

I never saw him again. But I met Joe Ockley many times, wrote a story about him years ago, an article about him years later, and tried to sell a photo-feature based on his life when I met him, twenty-nine years after that first meeting, still walking down Watling Street.

He was an ancient-looking, ragged, whiskered man that first day. Either he is now over a hundred years old, or his whiskers were even better camouflage than Toaster Dick's.

Up the road to St. Albans, after my "friend" had left, I fell in with another friendly tramp, Irish I believed, although he said he came from Liverpool. We also were to go together up Watling Street, I to join him on the listin-leg after we had done a bit of parson-thumping at a nearby place called Colney.

It sounded far more attractive to me than the dressing-room talk of the fitups, and I know no higher praise.

The parson-thumping, as I had expected, meant scientific fadging at vicarages. Near Colney there were three, all good according to Jemmy Suttle, my new mentor. He went into the first, and emerged in three minutes with a sixpence. After a decent interval I opened the garden gate and went up the path.

Unfortunately I did not know the tramps' first rule—to have a story ready and be prepared to make instant adjustments. When a pleasant-faced woman came to the door I simply goggled. She stared. So did I. She spoke first.

Then and there I learnt my own particular variant of the tramps' first rule, which I here pass on, for latter-day roadsters and for all whom it may concern. It is far better to let the other person tell the story for you. Nearly everyone wants to.

Nowadays I do not tell stories for sixpences. I sell them to film-producers or editors. But the principle is the same. Half a dozen times I have evolved and sold a good film story, a score of times I have polished—and peddled—a feature article, all on the interruptions and emendations of the person I set out to impress.

That day at the vicarage the woman smiled at my awkwardness, put me at my ease, asked if I was hungry, and gave me my sixpence. At the other two vicarages I said little or nothing either.

Jemmy had warned me at the last place not to say I knew any clergyman whatever, anywhere, especially at my home, as "the bloke puts the pump on then." I said practically nothing, and got my sixpences.

Coming into St. Albans, Jemmy popped aside twice, at large houses, each time returning with a shilling, each time announcing that the houses were "no bottle" for me. I did not insist on proof of my incapacity. But I felt hurt just the same. It would have been interesting to try.

We stayed at a lodging-house, where we paid sixpence each and shared a bed after we had eaten our supper in the common kitchen. There were five other tramps staying that night, and one man who was contemptuously dismissed by Suttle as a young mug, with the emphasis on the adjective, although the man was nearing fifty.

Next morning after breakfast, out in the streets of St. Albans, Jemmy said the K.R.R. would be best for me. The depot was away in Hampshire, and I could hammer the leg right up the road, maybe to Brum, as the scream would not be out for more than four days. He would do the Tillery for the same reason, and we could keep together until the scream was ahead.

If it had been Greek, or Gaelic, or even Toulonese French, I might have extracted some sense from the explanation. As it was, I did not understand one word. Wherefore I nodded comprehension, grunted agreement, made wise faces, and started slowly up Watling Street. Jemmy explained that the office was the other way, in the market-place.

Only when we reached the market-place, only when we came to the office itself, the wealth-project made itself clear. Apparently it was a well-practised branch of craft, for Suttle seemed quite at home with the details. We were to join the British Army, take our few days' advance-pay, desert, and go to the next town at once, repeat the process there, and go repeating it up Watling Street until things got too hot for us. That was the listin-leg.

Turning down the nearest lane, with a muttered excuse about finding a lavatory, I hurried away. In roundabout fashion I got back on to Watling Street again.

Then I went fast, up through Hockliffe and Dunstable, to keep ahead of Jemmy and his own particular "scream." I was ashamed. Also I was disappointed with Jemmy and with myself. But I could see I had no future on the listin-leg. I had not the necessary courage!

Up the road I met and spoke to many tramps (they averaged one per five miles or thereabouts), but kept away from anything like companionship. The second night up from St. Albans I stayed at Towcester, having covered more than forty miles in the two days.

No "working" tramp, I found out, would attain one-third of the speed. Logically enough, I suppose. The sportsman passes many rabbit-warrens to reach the place where he is licensed to shoot. The pot-hunter stops, because he is on business, to interview the first rabbits that show.

At Towcester (it is pronounced Toaster, like my ancient-seeming friend's nickname) there were half a dozen tramps in the lodging-house, and I listened eagerly to the technical talk. Besides detailed discussions of territory and prospects, there were also statements of rights, of pre-emption, of free and untrammelled choice as to direction and terrain.

The frankness and freedom, the fearless and unhampered assertion of manly right, would have delighted one of the people who write vagrant verses and romances of the road.

Thus, a flimsy-looking tramp with a cough and a whine said he was going to work the back road from Towcester to Northampton. A bulky man with an under-slung jaw said threateningly that anyone who didn't want their guts kicked out better keep off the Northampton road next morning. Thereafter it was fairly and democratically agreed in amity and comradeship that the bulky man was going to Northampton—first.

Being first was apparently important. Many people will not tolerate two tramps in a day, may even set the dogs on the second. Having read much about the brotherhood of the road, and having seen my moron from Houston, I liked those discussions. The reality was far better at bottom, and far more attractive than the slobbering falsities of the sentimentalists.

Partly because I was not going anywhere, partly because the information that I was going straight on had eliminated me as a possible competitor, partly because I could have knocked out any of the six, I enjoyed those Towcester discussions.

The grey-haired young mug who had been at St. Albans was here again at Towcester, although I had not seen him on the road. He was a pariah.

The tramps ignored him, or treated him with open contempt. His clothes were searched, in the common bedroom, before he was fairly asleep. He did not dare any objections, and was off on the road at dawn.

Like many people, I had taken it for granted that the average tramp was an itinerant out-of-work tradesman or labourer. The writers had misled me rather badly. Because the timid man was the only work-seeker of our company.

All the way up Watling Street I enjoyed myself. (Tramps go up Watling Street: motorists go down it.) I had one lift from Weedon to Cannock in a big furniture-lorry, and one from Stoke-on-Trent almost to Warrington with a cattle-wagon, shortening my journey by more than a week. For the rest I walked, fadged, parson-thumped, and stayed at tramps' doss-houses.

Long before Warrington, no one would have taken me for

anything but a tramp. Even a very young sociologist would have hesitated before adding me to the unemployment statistics.

The gait and the outlook of the roadster were mine, and I liked them. Mainly because I thought they were not mine, because I wore them as an amusing disguise, I liked them.

North from the Potteries there were many genuine work-seekers on the road, but they always went past with some shamefaced, awkward, crudely phrased question as to where there was work or whether such and such a place was good for employment. I did not know and could only say so. The regular tramps hardly bothered to say as much.

The work-seeker is always called a young mug, whatever his age, until the day when he abandons hope, becomes a beggar in desperation, turns tramp by chance, learns to live on the road.

Some of them never learn, become loathsome objects of dirt and disease, infesting the tidy roads and destroying a decent tramp's chance of food or coin by revolting and nauseating the housewives.

They make themselves a nuisance to the police in the towns, frighten the children in the villages, dirty the doss-houses, and depress the company at night by croaking their eternal wretched queries about work.

The sociologists think those people are tramps. The tramps hardly admit them to be human. My vote, if I have one, goes to the tramps.

At first glance, the roadsters' treatment of these unfortunate people seems heartless. But of course there is a causation. There are perhaps twenty versions of a tramp's song telling the facts. Hundreds of tramps must have altered and hacked at it, in the decades since the growth of the industrial cities brought the work-seekers out on the highways.

Probably the best rendering is that given by Kaye Newton, although I remember hearing the thing, in a cruder and more outspoken form, twenty years before Kaye was on the road.

It is the cowboy and the tenderfoot, the old campaigner and

the rookie, the craftsman and the botcher all over again.

Every professional artist and writer knows the incalculable harm that is wrought, in the respective fields, by eager amateurs, hungry botch-workers in a hurry to acquire a few pounds, half-paid and half-informed interlopers.

Meaning no harm, acting in all ignorance and innocence, such people wreck and ruin a thousand good works of art every year, antagonise art-agents and editors, cheapen the vocation they only barely think may be theirs—take the bread out of the professional's mouth without even putting it into their own!

The trained tramp is an artist, a professional, a keen and meticulous worker in his chosen field. To him, the brawling and blundering work-seeker is the wrecker—taking the bread, etcetera. The young-mug song comes from the bitter bottoms of a hundred vagrant hearts. Here is Kaye Newton's distillation.

PAD'N IT

"Oh, the young mug strides along the highroad gay,
  Making mileage like a race-track team,
  With a big swag swinging and the hobnails ringing
While he sweats in every sunshine beam.
But the old grey tramp takes the by-path way
Where the cottage women smile for a song.
Neither grim nor gaily, for his nine mile daily
He goes pad'n it, pad'n it along.

"Now the young mug loads a pile of household gear,
  Clinging tightly to his home-town ties,
  To the worn-out slippers and the two stale kippers,
With a blanket for his best-kept prize.
But the old grey tramp has no junk load queer.
(Hauling lumber on the road must be wrong.)
When the old pipe's going that's a home hearth glowing
While he's pad'n it, pad'n it along.

"Then the young mug moans because the road seems bare,
  Always wonders if he'll soon reach town.
  While he hides and hurries or he wilts and worries
When the women at the house doors frown.

200

But the old grey tramp knows that grub comes fair
And that charity is still going strong.
So a full-faith beggar with a flat-foot swagger
He goes pad'n it, pad'n it along.

"When the young mug's wandered for a few years more
He decides to take his own good time.
So he's done with worry and no more he'll hurry
And his gear is ditched in roadside slime.
Then one more grey tramp raps the farm back-door
Or goes wheedling the church-going throng.
Down a by-lane lowly goes an old man—slowly
Pad'n it, pad'n it along."

Thoughts and things like those occupied me, up the road to Warrington. I enjoyed them, as part of a delectable experience, because I believed they were passing pictures, fragments of a life other than mine. They were no part of me, nor I of them, in my mind.

From Warrington I rode "flash," i.e. paying my fare, into Liverpool, already felt myself in Dublin as soon as I heard the people speak. No one, so far as I know, has commented on the resemblance between the speech of Dublin and that of Liverpool, or better, of Birkenhead. Somewhere, some time, the influences must have been the same, for Merseyside speech is as foreign to Lancashire as the Liffeyside accent is to the Ireland around, and the two are almost the same.

At the biggest lodging-house I had ever seen, where there were literally hundreds of tramps, sailormen, waterfront drifters, young mugs, and itinerant navvies, I got thoroughly cleaned, put away my tramp interlude as part of the past, and mentally glanced across the Irish Sea. But first I went in search of Joe Jarrett.

At the address he had given me, a huge and hostile old man told me Joe was away—Callao, he thought. He added neither information nor invitation, and I left. Joe had told me about his father, who had beaten him to a pulp and sent him to sea as a man—at fourteen—merely in order to take his advance-money. Disappointed, I went looking for a Dublin steamer.

My fare would only have been seven shillings, travelling "deck," but the purchase of a ticket did not occur to me, although I could have earned the seven shillings in one day. It looks like simple addition, but is not really so. The abbreviated mathematics of the drifter have the greater logic.

To earn the seven shillings I should have spent five. Then, even if I had faithfully saved the remaining florin—instead of buying a book or giving the two shillings to someone—I should still have to earn seven further shillings, next day. Even then I would not have had my fare, but would have had to . . . And so on. The shortest way, and the most scientific when all is said and done, was to find out where the Dublin steamer docked.

Over the stern-rail of the *Eblana,* a boat I knew well at the Irish end of her run, I saw an expressionless, wooden-looking face I recognised. This was Archie Anderson, whom I had known for several years, although unaware that he was a sailor on the Liverpool run. I had an idea that Archie belonged to, or was a hanger-on of, the Irish Citizen Army, had encountered him many times in the Dublin riots of the previous year, knew he was one of Jim Larkin's men. He nodded, perhaps a quarter of an inch, when I indicated that I wanted a "shove."

Since the *Eblana* was a passenger steamer, with all the usual routine of ticket-checking, gangway supervision and the like, a shove would have seemed to be out of the question. So it was, but for anyone with a friend among the crew it was easy, since the deck-passengers, not being allowed in the saloon, generally crowded, thus making a convenient cover for anyone not intercepted in the first few yards.

Archie was coming ashore, the steamer not being out-bound until that evening, and we drifted among the dockline pubs, gossiping. Presently we went a mile or more, through the city, to "do a bit of business," which meant that Archie collected four revolvers, stuck them in his pockets, and went back to the ship. My guess was that he did the miniature arms-trafficking as a small private side-line, Ireland being then a gold-mine for anyone with his opportunities.

In that afternoon I learnt more about the small traffic of small arms than I learnt from a dozen "exhaustive" books on the subject and a good deal of later experience. The revolvers Archie carried had come from Buenos Aires, where one could then buy such things as easily as watches.

They had been carried by a sailor, and sold at a profit to a lodging-house keeper in Liverpool, who sold them at a profit to a man in the Seamen's Union, who sold them at a profit to Archie. I did not know where Archie would deliver his hardware, or the extent of his particular profit, but guess and deduction were easy for anyone from Dublin.

Archie's complete "open-up" came as a surprise. I had known the same kind of thing often before, with other people, but coming from the taciturn Anderson, the completeness of the exposition, the taking for granted that I was reliable, were almost startling.

Twice already, in writing the last few lines, I have had some doubts about telling how thoroughly and immediately Archie, a rebel and a smuggler, trusted me with his secrets. It was not that he was naïve, nor over-trustful. A seasoned schemer, he showed then and for years that he knew when to keep his mouth shut. That day he told everything.

People have always done that with me, still do it. For years now I have taken it as a commonplace to be given a casual lift by an ordinary motorist, to talk for five minutes with him about trivial matters, and then to have him unfold the story of his life, with all his most intimate secrets, before we parted.

There is no room for doubt that I possess, in marked degree, at least *one* of the qualities necessary in a good psychoanalyst. Neither is there any doubt that I might have amassed a huge fortune as a blackmailer !

Like the eternal freshness of the truth that ordinary men like me built Milan Cathedral, like the perennial power of the tree-felling picture with my many parties, and the delicious novelty of reading a signpost to Santa Fé in Missouri or to Llandudno in some tiny village of Essex, this fact that people tell me things perpetually fascinates me.

There is no need for me to inform anyone that I advance no nonsense about being psychic or anything of that nature. Nor am I such a fool as to claim that I am exceptionally sympathetic. There is nothing like that. But people tell me things.

I.R.A. men with the noose or bullet awaiting them have opened up, even before they knew guarantee that they might. Conspirators of every kind have unburdened themselves. But I do not merely refer to those who, from a knowledge of my history, might have been expected to regard me as trustworthy. Crooks, thoroughly cynical writers, hard-boiled business men, detectives from Scotland Yard, and one from the F.B.I. have done the same.

Let me top that edifice with a finial. English jailers, grim, steel-faced, monosyllabic men, have wrecked their most sacred personal and professional rules to tell their inside stories. In the whole world of humans I know none less likely to conform. But they conformed.

Archie seemed to take it for granted that I knew all the main principles involved, so to speak, and that he was merely filling in details. A few years later he attended to many such minor details, for me and for others. Later still, in a chapter of my novel *Green Volcano,* wherein the minutiæ of small gun-running were shown, I simply gave a picture of Archie. That was easier than writing.

Back at the dock that evening, we went up the crew's gangway. An eagle-eyed man was at the head of it, but the single phrase, "Right, Dick," short-circuited all query. A minute later I was mingling with the deck passengers.

In Dublin, where we arrived in the middle of the night, I went to a cheap hotel, stayed for a more thorough clean-up rather than present myself at home as a returned vagrant. When I did arrive at the house, all my family were casual and friendly, even my father treating me as if nothing had happened.

The cleaning-up, I remember, assumed almost religious importance in my eyes. My parents had never seen me untidy or looking like a tramp. They never knew I was one—neither did I, of course. Generally, when I was away, the family assumed that I was working in Glasgow or London "or one of those places."

Inchicore's guesses seldom went much nearer. The truth was unthinkable. An apprentice and a tramp were two different kinds of people. I was an apprentice. Very well then.

Two amusing memories of the homecoming recur to me. The moment I appeared, my mother put the question she always asked when I returned from "abroad." Her first words were an enquiry whether I had brought any money!

This was not merely mercenary. Or rather it was not directly mercenary, but a reflection of my mother's fundamental beliefs about the seeking of one's fortune. It implied a basic conviction that one day I would walk in after an absence, staggering under a large leathern sack packed tightly with golden coins. That particular day, well knowing that all things considered I had just cause to be proud, I produced two shillings and threepence.

The second contingent memory is of my thoughts immediately afterwards. After all, two and threepence was not really a lot of money for a man to bring, after an absence of . . . Then I began to count days and weeks. I felt as if I had been away at least a year. In all, my wanderings had lasted less than four months.

The brevity of the interval jolted me into remembering my near-commitments and the dual reason for my departure. I need not have bothered. One of the girls had been married a few weeks earlier. The other ignored me. Just then I wanted to be ignored.

Quiet contentment would have served as a label for my life during many of the following months. No longer astrain and eager, I studied a good deal nevertheless, and read much fiction for pleasure. After a while I wrote an account of the journey from London to Liverpool and sent it to the *Daily News* man. He sent it back. The 1914 war had started in the meantime, but I think he would have sent it back, anyway.

This did not worry or depress me, as I had no urgent wishes of any kind at the time, was healthy and satisfied and ordinary. Sometimes I thought of the things I had learnt on the roads, but never with longing and never imagining myself as part of such a life.

Inevitably I looked around for girls, and found them. I found no intellectual companionship, but its lack did not trouble me. I was not seeking it.

One disappointment came when I remembered and wrote a story Joe Jarrett had told me. He too had fought with his father, but had lost, and had been sent to sea, too young, for some thirteen pounds profit. Knowing nothing of the effects the war would have on fiction, I wrote this, very neatly, with an ordinary pen on ruled foolscap paper, and sent it out. It did not even bring a rejection slip, was never returned.

Yet it was a good story. Almost unaltered, it made the first chapter of a novel later, and was praised. Its loss disappointed me at the time, but I soon forgot.

The early stages of the First World War caused relatively little stir in Ireland: this, although at that time Ireland was treated, for governmental purposes, as part of Britain. There was little or no open hostility, everyone on both sides of the Irish Sea taking the paradoxical position for granted.

The later-potent republican movement was not yet articulate. There were voices of rebellion—James Connolly's, Patrick Pearse's, Thomas McDonagh's, Maeve Kavanagh's, and others. But these were poets and philosophers in the main. Relatively few in Ireland heard them. The country was not yet a volcano. Only an incipient volcano.

For a healthy young man, intelligent and active but without any real interests, such as I was, Dublin at the time was a stimulating place. There was always *someone* to urge me on to—to various conflicting goals.

Too ignorant of Irish or any other politics to understand

much, too self-centred and implacably logical to be urged illogically, anywhere, nevertheless I liked the ferment, grew and throve in it.

Contented, I went to the opposite extreme from my early drifting, and was busy, doing nothing for the most part. Long since I had given up my few fleeting ideas of being a writer. But I could never see myself in the future as a blacksmith, nor as anything of the kind. Turned twenty, finely fit, and occupied, I read books, and made metal things for pleasure and thought of nothing at all.

An occasional shoulder-stretching of pride came when I made something beautiful or bizarre in metal, reminiscent of the things I had known only as designs in the Art-ironwork Class. Presently I was known for my wedding-presents. Whenever a friend was married, I made a wedding-present in metal, a set of fire-irons.

Some of them were top-rank work. All were made illegally, when I should have been concerned about the affairs of the Southern Railway. The manager of the department is long since dead. He endured much from me, in the way of long and flimsily explained absences and long hours of labour on illicit art-ironwork. I hope I did not hasten his demise.

The only other worthy objects I made in metal were a set of bronze ash-trays, repoussé, and a brooch in steel. The ash-trays really were lovely things, worth every stolen hour I had put into them. The bride to whom they were presented told a friend I had given her a pair of ash-trays from the sixpenny store.

A few years earlier I might have choked her for the remark. This time I only laughed.

The reception of the brooch was worse. The design had been lent me by a teacher at Dublin Technical School, and I truly had almost sweated blood and beauty into it together.

I gave it to an extremely attractive office-girl with whom I went around, although, since she was what we would nowadays call a dumb tottie, I was interested in her topography and average temperature and very little else. Probably she had expected some perfume or a box of chocolates. At any rate, she ridiculed the present.

For quite five minutes I hated her bitterly. But since she was really pretty, and knew all the things a dumb tottie should know, and since I had lost a good deal of my susceptibility to ridicule, I managed to laugh and make the correct Dublin speech for such an occasion. There were only two kinds. One kind used religious symbolism.

But I made no more pet-pieces in metal. I made nothing, not even a ballad, which was unusual for me.

Thus making nothing, and doing nothing, for more than a year I was merely a male. And I was very content with life.

CHAPTER XVI

> *"Boul' Bantly went rantin' the Lotts an' the Coombe.*
> *To polka big lowrie became his full bloom.*
> *For naira hair-baiter he'd lave pass him by,*
> *An' the Lott-wiggers called him big Jack Bung-yer-eye*
> *With a*
> Fol-*the-diddle-eye-doe*
> *Hangin' down to his knee."*

WHEN I was fourteen, my then busily prurient mind dissected the whole ballad in which the history of Bantly Gunnan is told, until I had run down all the myriad hidden obscenities. As a young man, normal now, and with an active, efficient mind, I found the Liberty-ballads even more interesting.

The change of my status, in the Liberty district, was startling. Since the commencement of my Inchicore life, I had never enjoyed a moment's intimacy with any of the people I had formerly known. The switch-over was immediate and absolute.

In the beginning, it may have been partly due to my discovery of new interests. But there was also the fact that ordinary people, worker or wealthy, did not fit into the Liberty scheme of things. The place was an Alsatia, on a large scale, and as such maintained its selectness.

When I passed through the streets, or in the crowded lanes, the most cordial acknowledgment of my presence was a casual nod. Often a blank stare took its place. This, from the men who, as young boys, had taught me to batter and fadge, from whom I had learnt a hundred details of the Liberty's festering under-surface life.

My glimpse at Seven Dials had sharpened my respect for the Coombe district. But over and above that, I was really bringing something other than a kinky curiosity, a morality-twisted ego, to bear on the people and their activities.

In the Liberty, I could feel, was a life unknown to the feature-man on the London *News,* unknown to H. G. Wells, undreamt of even by most of the people of Dublin. Years earlier, I had been part of that life. Now I was barely tolerated on the edge of it. But I knew my way along that edge.

The ballads had fascinated me, long before I had heard of the Liberty, back to the days when I played in the caves next door to our tumble-down slum.

Even then, when I was just over six, I had seized upon, and had been smacked for knowing, a ballad sung by Soodalem, then a famous Dublin character. The song told of a moon-struck young man who married a bride from the Coombe area, discovering to his surprise that her major and most pleasurable activity consisted of frequent and indiscriminate excretion throughout their new domicile.

Soodalem, needless to say, did not put it into any such Gentleman Whalen phrases, but into a combination of Joycean prosody and unmistakable monosyllables. That was why I was smacked.

For several years I had "followed" the life of the ballads, came to have favourite ballad-singers even before I knew the Liberty. When I grew up a little I studied many collections, found wealth in them, but found also, inevitably, that the best of the ballads were missing.

No reputable writer, or anthologist, could have hoped to get Scutchy Callaghan singing off-duty. Scutchy could never have given of his best, would be too busy stealing the writer's fountain-pen.

A rag-man by profession, occasionally a tramp for pure plea-sure, just as if he had been a romantic young bank-clerk, Scutchy always kept his "chanting" as a stand-by, when rag-picking failed him or when taking his ease in the pubs off Engine Alley.

In my ragamuffin days, Scutchy had liked me greatly, had respected and befriended me, had shown several times that under the filth and rags was something far superior to—the ego of many defunct humanitarian philosophers I could name. His comradeship with me was based on the fact that, as a scholar, Scutchy was lonely in the Liberty. I was a godsend.

Callaghan was barely literate, had been a rag-man and ballad chanter all his life. But it would be wrong to think that therefore I write patronisingly.

Not I. Scutchy taught me things about psychology, about ballads, about prosody, that are not in the books. Again, there is here no question of patronage—I mean, that the information *should be* in the books, but is not.

Why is it almost impossible to write the notation of a Spanish flamenco or an Irish flute-or-fiddle tune? Why does even the most sympathetic foreign singer always make an Irish ballad sound as if every word was an aliquot part of a ton or a mile or of two dollars fifty?

The books give no answer. It is supposed to be something vague called the genius of Spain or the genius of Ireland. That is not the explanation, though, and Scutchy Callaghan knew, for all his near-illiteracy.

Nowadays, when Cyril Clarke or any of the other music-adepts round Charing Cross Road finds a melody scribbled on a piece of paper, in which the time-signature is not 4/4, nor 6/8, nor any of the known fractions, but something like 35/67, he knows it is one of my "crazy ideas."

Really it is Scutchy Callaghan's wisdom. The facts justify him. Those ballads cannot be written or sung in any of the nice, convenient, regular, four-square fractions of a bar to which civilised people are accustomed.

They belong to a level of life, to a time and needs, alien to such immutably regular measurements. They belong to the Liberties of Paris or Barcelona, Dublin or Baghdad or elsewhere. *They belong to the places were the yard-stick, the pay-*

packet, and the printed form are alike unknown.

Perhaps it was not by accident that the Liberties were so named.

These were the things with which I was preoccupied, as I came along to be twenty-one. There was now little thought in my mind of being a writer; I was back to being interested because I was interested. The surface life of Dublin held nothing for me: I scratched below the surface.

Had I been more practical, or less inclined towards isolation, I might have made intellectual friends. I do not know. At the time I had not even one conventionally intelligent acquaintance.

Further, had I but known it, Dublin was even then bubbling under my feet, ready to erupt in the Republican rising of 1916. But I did not know.

Most of my acquaintances were ordinary middle-class people, shabby-genteel actors or working men. The only girl in whom I was interested held perhaps as much of my thoughts as I did of hers. Which was not much. We were a healthy pair not interested in thoughts.

She was very pretty but completely brainless, which last was no shortcoming as far as I was concerned. Her ideas never went far beyond presents, visits to a theatre, walks in the country lanes, and the drill-routine that passes for love with many. My own ideas marched with hers.

For the rest, we did all the things young lively people do, and knew calm, which was much, since neither of us knew nor laid claim to happiness. Once each month, on the last Saturday, she abjured impurity, and resolved to avoid wickedness (which meant me) for ever. Then on the following Monday we remembered the colour of one another's eyes again.

Many people in Dublin behaved thus each month. It did no harm to the Dubliners, but was a mind-murdering torment to those from outside. I myself did no abjuring of impurity. I had done all my share, and more, long since.

Moving about, I could see that we were as happy as most other couples. In fact, my girl was no more in love with me than I was with her, but we met and matched and proved our passion-time unwasted. Millions, I think, would have envied us.

In later years, from scores of intimate conversations, I learnt and was staggered to learn that large numbers of people, in many countries, regard things like my Dublin companionship as the *ne plus ultra* of love. For many, the things I felt and thought and did in the lanes and fields near Dublin, at that period, represent the highest level of love and courtship, one sometimes not in fact maintained after marriage.

Even when I was twenty-one, if anyone had suggested as much to me, I should have laughed—until I vomited. Scutchy Callaghan himself, and the alley-tarts of the Liberty, knew better.

Life is not like that. But the thought presents itself that perhaps the people do not really marry, have no drive of mind and body to do so. Perhaps they do not want to marry at all, only to fill in the printed forms, for the gendarme peeping round the corner.

At eighteen I had wanted to marry, not from a sense of doing correct things, but for reasons made obvious already. Now, although I knew little of love and marriage, I knew that the things which satisfied many, and which satisfied me for the time, were not the end of any story.

But even the slightest lift of mental companionship would have been priceless for me then. Such things were largely unknown in my Dublin—a very practical city. My drift was towards books, then to the things that went into books, and so fortunately back to the Coombe.

Thus I knew a wistfulness whenever I stayed to drink in one of the intimate Liberty-pubs, in the territory of the Lynches, and found myself barely tolerated. Gradually, on the strength of my early contacts, I managed to increase my leverage, was in time accepted by "the top Lynches" themselves. This was achievement.

The Lynches were a numerous family, three generations at least being alive at that time, all powerful personalities, all predatory and intolerant, brooking no interference, but almost always staying on the right side of the law.

The slum-people summed the matter briefly—the Lynches owned everything in the Liberty.

This was untrue, by several million pounds' worth of property. But wherever there was gain from a rookery of half-tinkers, a jumble of lodging-houses, a rake of reeking brothels, the Lynches were not far away.

They are all dead now, every one, three or four generations of a family that, dynastically, held most of the Irish Alsatia in fee, gone in a few years. Ragged, battered, old slum women, pagan or atheist at bottom, said piously that it was the judgment of God. In fact, the Lynches were never over-rapacious, were a free, careless, immeasurably generous family —as the slum women remembered when they had more civilised and law-abiding landlords.

Tom Lynch, a middle-aged man who had been a prize-fighter, took a strange liking to me. Strange because we were almost exactly opposites. I was a big, serious, very thoughtful person, with snobbish preconceptions and a grave intensity of manner. Tom was the extremely tough and dictatorial boss of the district.

It was probably a good thing for me that we never quarrelled.

All the Lynch men were big, swashbuckling, humorous people, completely amoral, and exacting a vast tribute from the Liberty-drifters, the gay-girls, the Dublin bookmakers— from all the habitués or migrants of Alsatia. Tom, Phil, Christy, young Tom, old Tom, and Larry strode the purlieus of the Coombe as if it were a manor and they were the lords.

In the whole of literature I know only one family to equal them—the Doones of Bagworthy. Elsewhere I have told some of their story. Here it is needful only to add my pleasure in having known them—they tided me over some pitfall years.

There is a risk of my being misunderstood. It is not merely that from the Lynches, and the other people of the Liberty, I got the material for a thousand more stories than I can ever write. There and from them I got something denied in these days to most men, something not read in the books nor learnt at the universities. I learnt life raw.

The familiarity with Kit Lynch, Tom Lynch, and the rest, gave me for awhile the entrée to the places where the ballad-singers laid aside their whinings and their misery, sang, as might virtuosos, for their intimate public and for their own kind. That sufficed me for a time.

All the chief "chanters" of the Liberty came my way, offstage. I count it one of the most valuable literary experiences I have known—and I have been luckier than most.

Salty Cheeke, one of the chiefs *circa* 1915, could make more use of a dramatic pause than many an opera singer. Rendering one of his favourites, he would arrest and almost freeze, with outstretched hand, popping eyes, and wide-open mouth from which no sound emerged, the whole startled pavement-populace of a street, before he exploded into his tense and telling climax-line. Salty always admitted it was a gift.

Charlie Slight had a bass voice that would have come near to challenging Paul Robeson. His name had a truly Chaucerian flavour, phonetically. I believe it was his legal name, but I have altered the second letter. Charlie specialised in tragic ballads. A particularly brutal murder, a constabulary clubbing of the 1913 period, a destructive fire accompanied by loss of life, were at any rate drink if not meat for Charlie. Sometimes he made his own ballads, sometimes he "bet-thered" those sold by the printer.

Another who made ballads, industriously, was Jem Scra. Brian Desmond Hurst tells a story of James Joyce walking for most of a morning with a friend, preoccupied and silent, later explaining that he had been searching for a word. The word was "the." Jem Scra would have loved that story.

He used to sit on a sack by the corner of Mulluckses Lane with a scrap of paper and a stub of pencil. Intimates, or casual Liberty-passers, would be consulted about ordinary words. But where Jem lacked what he called a "law-de-daw" word, he would accost the first respectable-looking citizen who came that way, and state his problem. He often got the word, too. Then, satisfied, he would dash away to the printer, and his falsetto would be piping the ballad outside the pub doors before night.

Most of all I personally liked Scutchy Callaghan's occasional lapses into chanting. Scutchy should have been a teacher really. Even when singing for "browns," he would stop suddenly to interpolate an explanatory note, in a quietly conversational tone, lest his hearers should miss the point.

Scutchy's favourite song was about Michael Dwyer, a rebel leader of the previous century. Dwyer was a genuine historical character, full of courage and resource, a combination of the English Robin Hood and what latter-day Europe would call a Resistance leader, and was of course dear to the rebel heart of Callaghan.

(Incidentally, the best mountain highway in Ireland, still called the Military Road, was constructed by the British Army in order to reach Dwyer in his mountain fastnesses.)

When Callaghan reached the lines telling how Dwyer had been trapped in a thatched cottage up a mountain, while the cottagers and their children shivered in fright and a company of soldiers surrounded the house, he never left anything to chance or misinterpretation.

> "Around the LIT-tle co-haw-att-tage
> They faw-aw-hormed in a ring-g-g,
> And called on MI-chael Dwy-high-eye-er
> To s'render to the King.

"And now, ye see, Michael couldn't have all them poor dacent people and their childher left there in the middle of the fightin', could he now? Sure, they'd be in the way for one thing.

> "We come—may-eh-hay-be—says Dwyer,
> We shall not keep ye long.
> But here be guil-l-ltless hill-folk

Have done the King no wrong.
Then let these guiltless people
Your ranks pass safely through,
And WHEN *they ha-a-ave departed*
I'll tell you what we'll do.

"Now ye see all the poor craychers comin' outa the cottage,
poor little childher an' all. NOW . . .

    "'Twas done. And then says Dwyer
    Your work you may begin. . . ."

The ballad went on to tell how the rebels were on the verge of defeat. Then one man, mortally wounded (Scutchy sometimes gave a brief laudatory sketch of his life) advises his friends to help him to his feet, open the door, and let him go out. The soldiers will fire and . . .

    "Their lead will only riddle
    My ALL-*read-head-ee dying clay,*
    And when their guns are empty . . .

"These was muskets, remember, not rifles; only one shot at
a time . . .

    "And when their guns are empty
    Dash THROUGH *them and away."*

Poor old Scutchy. I often wonder whether, after all, his methods differed so terribly from Homer's.

The Republican rising of 1916 jerked me sharply away from my Liberty-visits and my interest in old or new ballads. But the immediate effect on me was merely one of bemusement at first. Down at bottom I was too ignorant of Irish affairs, too narrow in my outlook, to see things clearly.

Rated by many as trivial and insignificant, seen by those like my father as a major military operation, the last and almost-certainly-won battle for Irish independence, the rising was in fact of the first importance. But few so appraised it at the time, or guessed at, let alone hoped for or knew, the resurgence that would follow its failure. Certainly I did not.

Almost immediately, Ireland at large and particularly Dublin began to stir, to seethe. Long before the first Republican prisoners were home, and on into 1917, the rebel organisations began to grow and continued growing. It was a time of sharp dividings, in Irish families and among Irish groups.

Many competent writers have told of this period in Irish history. For me the chief novel phenomenon was the way people practically lived in the streets, at the time when the Republican forces were taking shape.

Tom Wintringham, I think, has told how the people of the American cities during the War of Independence, and the citizens of Paris in the first French Revolution, clustered and clubbed in the streets, talking, perpetually talking, knowing the lift of liberty in the nearness of their fellows. Nowadays we still use the term in business, speak of keeping in touch with a man. Originally the thing must have been literal, factual. Dublin acted thus. People kept in touch.

My individual memories are of internal tumult at first, then of grave and serious decision, with of course the inevitable fantasies to follow. Externally, a filler-in of forms would have had to record that I went no more to the Liberty, that much or most of my reading was now markedly Irish-oriented; above all, that two of the ballads from the making of which I drew satisfaction had a rebel content.

Months drifted and nothing happened, to me or to Dublin. Chief memory of the period is that one day my brother Willie asked bluntly whether I was on the English side or the Irish.

With our family background, such a question was supposed to be unnecessary, was answered before we were born. Willie was already a member of the Irish Citizen Army, as were my two sisters. His question was routine, because as usual I seemed to be moping.

Actually I was a member of the I.C.A. at the time, but my inveterate secretiveness invited query. Some people boasted openly of being in one or other of the organisations. Some, like myself, carried secretiveness to a stage far worse than boasting. The sensible people did neither.

Later, and for awhile, it was in fact necessary for me to be discreet. There was a period when I was a member of the Secret Council of the Irish Citizen Army, was Willie's superior officer without his knowledge, could necessarily say nothing about it. But my make-up was such that I would have thriven on secrets, anyway.

More than once, in the early stages, I had met Archie Anderson, the Liverpool-Dublin sailor who collected small packages from the ends of the earth. Archie had shown rather plainly, in the beginning, that he regarded me as a slacker from the I.C.A.

Then, when he had somehow discovered my membership, he went to the other extreme, was often distressingly confiding. And once, in a burst of friendship, as a boy will pass another an apple, he dived a hand in his overcoat pocket and gave me a fistful of ·38 Smith & Wesson cartridges.

These were an important present at that time, as the particular size of ammunition was scarce in Dublin. Archie was always a strictly practical person.

Looking back, I think my major folly of the time was something none of my contemporaries would have rated as important. With all I knew of slum life, of real fierce factual living as opposed to the precise and sheltered and much-managed existence of respectability, I neglected the Liberty, let my cheap snobbishness carry me away again, as it had carried me before in a different direction.

The real story, the real life of Dublin, was there in the alley-ways. With a hundred opportunities denied to others, I did not avail myself of the chance to go in and live life instead of talking it. The other things, after all, for me were mostly words in books.

Generally I have dramatised myself at some stage or other in every important phase of my life. I cannot change that— but it is as well to know the tendency exists! During those Dublin days I was like an inexperienced producer trying to

lead a bad amateur actor through a play written by an im-
mature dramatist. And I was all three.

The Irish phrase for such a situation is the only one. I
"didn't know which end of me was up."

My drift-and-dream proclivities now operated in causing me
to be often absent, for a day or two at a time, from my work.
Such days I spent in the guard-room of the Citizen Army, or
gossiping with others, like myself, who felt the desire to keep
literally in touch.

The stone steps of Liberty Hall, which was then Citizen
Army headquarters, made venue for the gossiping. There were
always some of the boys who had not thought it worth while
to go to work that day. Round the fire in a big room upstairs,
or in the little guard-room, more intimate groups collected.
Jail reminiscences were exchanged, songs were sung, and once,
very proud of my powers, I "betthered," as Jem Scra might
have said, a long rebel ballad.

The short spell of enforced secrecy was of course a boon,
since it forced me to use a real guard on my tongue instead of
a dozen playboy pretences. But even then I was as evasive as
any fiction conspirator could desire.

Among the personnel of the Citizen Army I was, from the
very beginning and during all my short periods in Dublin,
something more than a favourite. Naturally it pleased me. It
pleases me now, to remember. Those I.C.A. men were
nobody's fools.

To be fair to myself, since it would be merely silly to let
cynicism loose, I think I was really a little above the Liberty
Hall average. Most of our members were working-men—
dockers, coal-heavers, sailormen, foundry labourers, and the
like. Of course, the book-lore and the intelligence and the
eternal questing mind of me counted.

Sometimes I felt slightly awkward, because many of the
men were, formally speaking, uneducated. But it mattered
little in fact. Keen and intelligent, doggedly courageous, most
of them had something much better than formal education.

Of course, there were always poets and authors, scientists

and intellectuals in the I.C.A., besides the labour ranks. Sean O'Casey and Liam O'Flaherty, Maeve Kavanagh, Doctor Kathleen Lynn, R. M. Fox, Maud Eden, Countess Markiewicz, and many others come to mind. But many of these were before or after the time of which I write; most of the boys were unhewn granite, straight off the Dublin waterfront or out of its factories and foundries.

With no sentiment at all, no axe to grind, and no interest beyond straightening the record of my own growth for this book, I remember the I.C.A. men as lovable and clean and fine, can think of no other small army to compare with them except that similar triple-tested force of Leonidas the Spartan.

Of course embarrassment came to me, then and later, because the soldiers of the Citizen Army rated me highly. As people everywhere have done, always, they trusted me fully, opened their lives wide for me to see.

It would be a travesty of impartiality, the ultima thule of mock-modest meandering, to pretend or suggest that I was unworthy of, or broached, the confidence often reposed in me. (As in my being made a member of the Secret Council, and in others ways.) But in cold fact everyone listed me far too high.

Perhaps it is general, instinctive. Perhaps people everywhere, even without knowing it, feel a sympathy with and an affection for a masterless dog, have similar feelings for that kind of man when they meet him. It may be an explanation.

Certainly Jim O'Neill or Dick McCormack, Joe Byrne or Martin King, Paddy Cullen or Peter Coates or any other of those with whom I was intimate, was worth a dozen or a score of me.

They rated me too highly. I rated myself too low. As things turned out, we were all wrong. That will do.

The reader may be ahead of me by this time, since I have been mentioning only men. If there had been any woman . . . Balancing the emotional and neural stresses of a politico-military environment against my curious involute make-up, the conclusion of that sentence seems easy. I did not myself feel it so for many years, but I can see it plainly now—if there had been even one girl in my Liberty Hall environment, perhaps my whole life would have been different.

But perhaps not.

At any rate, there existed no such girl. I knew Kathleen Lynn, the famous rebel girl-doctor, but she was several years older than I. Constance Markiewicz, the tragic and indomitable countess, I thought of as an old woman, although she was not. Maud Eden I respected, almost revered, but I did not think of her as a woman at all.

The other girls? My small cheap snobbery does not come into play here, nor need I admit even to having been over-fastidious. There was no girl in the Republican movement that met my mind, not one, except for those who mixed up politics and morals, the one of my father's brand, the other of my mother's. But I had passed that stage. And I was no ascetic. The emotion-thrust of me went elsewhere.

It was just as well. If I had intimately known an intellectual girl in the rebel movement, if I had loved and married one such, she or I would have broken, when she discovered sooner or later that I was a maker of foolish fantasies, who thought there was only one road in the world and wanted to peep at the end.

It was just as well. My Dublin girl was a beauty, without a single thought to the square yard, who believed all rebels were mad. So we talked no politics, and she knew nothing of my life. Thus there were two parts of Dublin to pull at me, and my value to either was little. Because I was really only a tramp.

No one at Liberty Hall thought that, and of course I was myself unaware of it. But some of the other young and coming writers who were there had like embarrassments, and they were more stable by far than I. Maybe writers are never very solid or practical, always a disappointment to their friends. The biographies, and some of the autobiographies, list such unhappiness again and again.

One result of my Citizen Army over-rating brought a thrill that satisfied even my personal conspirator-secretive mentality. One day, after a general parade, I was instructed, with four or five other men, to remain behind. This was the day on which I was appointed to the Secret Council.

It was fairly certain that a crisis in Irish-English affairs was approaching, that a large-scale clash was on the way. The members of the Army Council were of course theoretically anonymous. But the British Secret Service was efficient. When it was necessary, sooner or later, that Council would be unmasked.

So much Jim O'Neill, the Commandant, explained to us that day. Then the counter-plan. The presumably Secret Council was to be left intact, apparently functioning, a prize for the Secret Service people when they had quarried thus deeply. Behind was to be the real Council, unknown even to the members of the first. It was for this we were chosen.

Our instructions were given us, with general outline of the plan to be followed in certain events. Each man had specific duties, would be ready to drop into activity at need, while the enemy espionage was being directed against those superseded.

The need for discretion was impressed on us. In the Citizen Army that meant discretion. But it is thirty years ago, and there is no harm in referring to it now—the documents will be on file somewhere in the archives at Dublin.

At the end of our initiation, that we might be able to recognise appearance, voice, mannerisms, and other details, we were introduced to the key-person, from whom we would take all orders.

I gasped when confronted with a slim, low-sized, soft-spoken, and very timid-seeming girl of under thirty. This was Maud Eden, unmarried representative of an Irish aristocratic home whose tradition was the direct opposite of ours, a most efficient revolutionist with a steel-hard personality behind the façade.

Fortunately, there is a film-character to compare. A little slimmer and prettier, Maud in every other way was precisely like Miss Froy, the British Secret Service woman in *The Lady Vanishes*.

I wrote a spy story, with an Irish setting, that night. The

hero—a tall, handsome, dark-haired young man with a blood-stained bandage round his head—married the Irish espionage-girl at the end. Prior to his distinction as a Republican leader, the tall young man had been, among other things, a writer, an iron-worker, and a tramp.

Maybe Maud Eden will forgive me. I was only twenty-one, and I really knew little of ordinary life.

Several months passed, during which I was too busy for thought, too contented for introspection. Still my chief pleasure was in the gossipings of the guard-room at Liberty Hall, the avid interest in the jail-anecdotes of the returned prisoners, the perhaps hasty and perhaps justified emendation of many loosely made rebel songs.

The only practical sign of growth or interest was that I became very expert in the alteration and repair of small arms. Revolver-springs, I remember, were a speciality of mine—the work being done, illegally of course, at Inchicore.

Then a single short conversation brought me up with a round turn. My girl-friend wanted to get married. For the usual Dublin reasons. In our extremely brief and business-like talk I detected a certain complacency, because I was on the verge of completing my apprenticeship.

In a few months I would be a fully-fledged craftsman, highly paid, able to support a home in comfort. So my future was settled. Even a junior apprentice, because of his commit-ments, could not evade his amatory responsibilities. I, with my many years of servitude at stake, with my craft-majority only a few weeks off, was a fixture. Above all the apprentices at Inchi-core and elsewhere, I most certainly could not run away.

Oh—couldn't I? was my mental rejoinder, roughly eleven hours later. For a few minutes I felt angry, with myself and with Dublin and with my beautiful body-friend. Then I laughed, the thing was gone, as far as I was concerned, and I went on eating unripe sloes, for amusement, on the canal-bank at Rathangan.

Dublin and Toulon, Waterford and Liverpool, Carlow and London and the road from Arles, were already, at eleven hours' distance in time, telescoped and fore-shortened.

Of course I had known all along down inside me that I did not really belong to Dublin.

This time I took care that no one should take me for a tramp. I wore good clothes, although I was not well-dressed —I looked like a city workman in his Sunday best—and I had a few pounds. Consequently, I avoided cheap lodging-houses, and asked for no meals at the farms.

Tramping was a pleasantly colourful incident of my past. But it was of my past. In the towns I stayed at cheap, respectable digs, such as a fitup actor might use. The difference from a tramp-stall—in tariff—was often almost negligible.

At Kildare I came on the posters of a theatrical company, which had gone ahead the previous day, and of a circus which had just left. If I came on the fitup later, I decided, I would try if they could use me. That was as far as I went in planning.

Coming into Portarlington two days later, I encountered the John Duffy circus, just "setting up." In a quarter of an hour I was working, as a lumper, otherwise a performer of miracles twice daily, a man-of-all-work, with the emphasis equally divided between the last two words.

Duffy's was then, as now, the top-ranking circus of Ireland. (I think the property is at present in the hands of the fourth generation, same family.) Pay was good, food was excellent, conditions were thoroughly pleasant, and work was Titanic, unending.

It was a shock, after the complete democracy of Shaw's fitup and after the loosely organised life of the little scrub circus of my adolescence, to discover the caste-strictness of Duffy's. The average artiste simply did not know the average lumper was present.

For a young man who had already removed the bloodstained bandage from his fantasy-brow, replaced it in imagination by the head-fillet of the gifted and daring equestrian, leaped forward to thought-riots of passionate forgathering with glamorous ring-beauties—it was rather a shock to find I was just one more lumper.

In fourteen days, I helped to set up and pull down twenty-eight times, manhandled incredible weights for incredible hours, travelled two hundred and eighty miles by instalments, and had perhaps one quarter of a night's sleep.

At Athlone I burnt one hand badly with a paraffin lamp. That concluded my tour: a circus wasted no words and knew no formalities; bandaged lumpers were passengers.

I had no complaints to make. The situation did not call for sentiment on either side. Furthermore, old John Duffy had given me a week's pay, of which I had only earned one-sixth.

And besides, I needed a sleep.

CHAPTER XVII

When, strolling quietly from town to town, I found myself on the edge of Tipperary, there was no need to repeat the shamefaced slinking past of my earlier journey. Clean and "smart" looking, solvent, not in a hurry anywhere, I dropped in at the first remembered house.

Then for more than a week my progress resembled my former tramp-drifting, in that I never knew where I might eat or sleep. Except that here my chief task was to refuse food and drink. It was a lovely interlude. Tipperary had and has a fine tradition of hospitality.

Magnum opus of the week was something, to me, quite trivial. Several of my relatives owned little smithy-places, here and there in the villages. At one, a cousin of mine pessimistically regarded some job—a thresher-axle, I think—which was supposed to be incredibly difficult.

When I pulled off my coat and finished the thing in a couple of hours—an Inchicore smith would have given it perhaps half the time—my second reputation was made. I was not only a scholar: I was a master-craftsman.

Actually I had quite a shock of pleasure myself. I had not known I could do anything like that.

When I left the district, after seven or eight days of lazing, I had practically no money, although my friends were unaware of the fact. It is amusing to recall the thousand difficulties I had in sneaking off. For a person popular over a wide district, where everyone is helpfully anxious to send for taxis and look up trains, it is not easy to start away on foot!

Over at Carrigatoher, in the lee of the Keeper Mountain, I made friends with Dinny Rohan, a peasant who farmed on the edge of Camailte Bog. Rohan and I liked one another at once, and he did everything except hand over his farm on the first day. I spent several weeks at his place, most enjoyably, working a little, but mainly soaking myself in the atmosphere of the bogland.

Then gradually I felt the need to go on, and a chance road-side poster showed the way. La Comédie Irlandaise Company, fresh from its West End etcetera, would play seven nights at Nenagh, a nearby town. Since the company stayed a week, as against the usual "one-night stand," they sounded good.

Advertisement in the following morning's paper asked for a baggage-man, application to be made in person. Saying good-bye to Rohan in advance, I went along. There could hardly have been a large number of baggage-men on Camailte Bog that day, and I knew it was my job.

It was Sunday, at three in the afternoon, when I arrived. I finished work at one o'clock on Monday morning, had then to find digs in Nenagh. Fortunately, the matter arranged itself.

La Comédie Irlandaise, known in the profession as Lorry Dobell's crowd, was one of the biggest companies on the road at the time. Always travelling with at least twenty people, a full and ornate fitup, they had to take a good deal of money, could only play big towns, which meant that conditions for the personnel were good.

As in Colin Shaw's crowd, I took a single plunge into the pool of fitup life, and knew nothing more of time or place for long. This company was even happier than Shaw's; bigger and wealthier, hence with more attention to professional etiquette than was possible among seven or eight work-harassed people, they still kept all the freedom and freshness of the strolling player.

Lorry Dobell, the proprietor, then a very old man, still insisted on playing most of the juvenile leads. As a rule, when the half-intoxication of the game had hold of him, he did well, but occasionally he tired in a distressing way. Madge Merry-weather, his niece and the manager of the company, kept watch over old Lorry like a hen with a duckling, saw that he did not take too many chances.

Madge had been a trouper for years, had played "everything from Little Willie to the ghost in *Hamlet*," was now a plump little party of forty-odd, a good business woman, and a shrewd producer. Fred Wright, her brother, was stage-manager, and played character parts.

Crippled in both feet by an accident, Fred could only take a stride of some six inches. Yet, such was the suggestive power of his miming, no one ever noticed, even when he had to stride arrogantly across a bar-room floor or swashbuckle away defiantly.

Leo Strong, then playing character heavies, which means "second villain" colloquially, came to regular status and city theatres at ten times his fitup salary. He was worth it. Leo could, and often did, convince his wife or even himself that he was someone else, while studying a part.

Alphonse Heller, then a young comedy man, went to Hollywood years ago, is still there, still plays parts like those he did on the road in Ireland. Alphonse was so popular with girls in the Irish towns that Madge had to have him watched, each evening before curtain-up, to see that he was not being taken for country walks.

Stephen Hastings, pianist, served as orchestra, with the piano we travelled, in towns where the theatre orchestras did not function regularly. Ancient and of saintly appearance, with long white beard, mild blue eyes, and almost transparent skin, Stephen lived only for the half-hour after the show at night when, gossiping over coffee, stories were exchanged. He had probably the world's most extensive and variegated repertoire of filth.

The equipment for such an outfit as ours was large, called for miracles of packing and vast muscle-expenditure by the baggage crew. There were three baggage-men—none too many, although the number was quite large for fitups—and

Fred Wright generally joined in. Since he was tremendously strong in spite of his accident, he made much difference in time-tonnage.

Many of the shows we did were straight melodrama, often calling for "practical" scenery, which means appliances that will work, instead of mere pictures on canvas. Thus, in one show where Harry Boland, as a maniac, had a giant guillotine-like machine to shear off the beautiful heroine's head, Fred Wright made a most horrifying and very "practical" torture-engine in some six hours.

The limitations of stage space called for ingenuity in the use of "practicals" and an unerring judgment of time and distance. A haughty strut, if it is to convey character, needs good acting where the walk lasts for only three paces. The breakaway and capture of a delinquent, when concluded in less than twelve feet, demands high-order miming if it is to escape the ludicrous.

Nearly always the space-limits were conquered. Grizzled sea-dogs strode the decks of galleons, maniacs pursued innocent girls over mountain passes, crowds gathered at street corners—even a mass revolt of convicts came to a head, all in a rectangle eighteen feet by nine.

Only once or twice did the practicals prove insufficient, and each time the fault lay with a person, not with the things. One proof being that experienced actors joined from other companies, and played the practicals exactly as if they had never seen a Yorkshire moor, a stretch of the Sahara, or a highland glen, of more than five strides in extent.

The practical in a show called, I think, *Mother's Mind,* however, came once, unexpectedly, to be seen for itself. In the play, a Sir Jasperish villain pursued a Cornish fisher-maiden up the cliffs (four-and-a-half feet high) near her home. She dashed across a bridge over a ravine, then, when the villain still pursued her, swung a lever and dropped the bridge.

Whereupon the villain recoiled, gasping in horror, from the impassable chasm before him.

Peter Willard, the villain on the night in question, had met flocks of admirers, in Longford I think, before the show. Peter was most definitely not drunk—he had simply met many admirers. The slight list and twist in his gait were even appropriate to the Sir Jaspery part he was playing.

He lurched after Nellie Melbourne, the leading lady. Nellie skipped across the bridge, and when Peter still pressed his suit, pulled the lever and the bridge dropped out of sight. Peter gasped; recoiled; swayed.

No harm was done: it was all very effective. Then he swayed again, slightly forward this time, and did the only thing possible to avoid a fall. He advanced one foot—and crossed the yawning chasm in a stride, to stand beside the dumb-founded heroine.

But Nellie Melbourne, for all her youth, was a seasoned trouper, and "gagged" herself and Willard out of the mess. In small towns, after that, I always asked Fred at the railway, before unloading the baggage, "Bridge or gags for *Mother's Mind?*"

Gagging, the furnishing of impromptu lines, was almost a pre-emption of the fitup actors, since any heavy gagging is, strictly speaking, illegal and is not permitted in the big cities.

No gagging, however, could save the marvellously realistic sea-drama *Unknown* when its path unfortunately crossed with that of a Yankee flotilla at Buncrana. The U.S. Navy had then a base on Loch Swilly, and of course the boys from the flotilla, happening to be in, came along to the fitup each night, enjoying themselves hugely.

All went well until the presentation of *Unknown,* with practicals. This was a vast, fast melodrama of the sea, big scene in the last act being when the heroine (tied to the butt of a mast which, conveniently, ran through the cabin) and the hero (bound and gagged in a bunk) are abandoned by the villain to certain death, the conventional infernal machine ticking away their lives in full view of the audience.

Village crowds loved it. The big towns paid handsomely for it. Even Derry City and Galway stood it. (Otherwise Lorry

and Madge would have rubbed it from the repertoire at once.)
Then we played Buncrana.

Before a packed house, the drama rolled on, satisfactorily,
to its climax. Then the great moment arrived. The bound and
head-strapped hero rolled from his bunk, rolled across the
stage, and managed to struggle into place beside a wireless
instrument. There, heroically, he tapped out the S.O.S. with
his forehead.

Red lights flashed at the head of the machine, keeping time
with the bur-ur-ur—burr, burr, burr—bur-ur-ur of the radio
as it sent out its appealing signal. Lashed to the mast, the
heroine burst into song—"Nearer my God to Thee."

Then at last green lights flashed everywhere, the hero flung
aside his bonds (which had somehow come loose) and cast
away the earphones which the heroine had fixed in place with
her teeth, to announce, "They've heard us. We are saved.
Saved."

A mighty, rocking roar of merriment shook Buncrana. It
ceased, recurred, continued, increased, a gargantuan, howling,
shrieking, belly-splitting laughter that made dumb-show of
"Nearer my God to Thee," and amid which the falling of the
final curtain was hardly noticed.

Buncrana was the North Atlantic clearing-place for wireless
operators. Half of our audience were radio men. All the other
Yanks understood wireless technique. Instanter *Unknown* had
become a howling comedy.

Some of the boys explained later. Red lights do not show
where our electrician had put them. The heroic operator was
tapping out S.O.S., but the burr-burr sound occasionally said
O.S.O. Green lights do not appear at the time and place given.
Earphones were not worn with the type of machine under-
studied by our practical.

Otherwise the verisimilitude was perfect. Except that
in rolling across the cabin floor the hero had knocked the
infernal machine into the footlights and the ticking had
stopped.

Unknown came off the repertoire.

Some day, for my own pleasure, I shall write a book about the six or seven fitup companies I have known, and about nothing else. It will have to be a very big book, for every minute of fitup life is pulse-packed, and I can feel myself laughing already, for much of actor life on the roads is matter for laughter, however intensely tragic the person concerned.

Even after thirty years, the ghost of Flyblow comes up and insists on remembrance. Some actress in Lorry Dobell's crowd named him, neatly enough, summing him up on his first day at work.

Having rehearsed opposite Flyblow, wearily, repeating her cue-line again and again while he goggled and blawped, she said she didn't mind *flies* but . . . Also that it was a pity his mother died so long before he was born.

It was fair enough. Nothing nearer to a corpse ever ate bread or drew an actor's salary.

Flyblow joined La Comédie Irlandaise a week after my arrival. He was no baggage-man or bit-player or anything like that: he was an actor, he said. Madge Merryweather believed him. Flyblow had paid a premium to learn the profession.

There was no better dramatic school in the world than the old fitups, and people with money often paid a premium, although of course the majority of fitup actors were so born. Flyblow was a wealthy young man. If he had ever even seen a play or a stage, it was at school. But it was his own money.

Gaunt, gloomy, cadaverous, grave three decades beyond his years, Flyblow had a graveyard voice in which every speech, from a request for the butter to an assertion that someone was a liar, came in the same thick, adenoidal, grating monotone. He wanted to be an actor. Again, it was his own money.

His first part could not have been called onerous. Not Madge's worst enemy could have accused her of overworking Flyblow.

At the end of the second act in a melodrama, when the

blue-eyed, curly-haired hero is being falsely accused of cashing a forged cheque, the villain appears to be cornered when the clever heroine manœuvres her banker father, and all the other people involved, into one room. She has arranged for the clerk from the bank to be brought in without warning.

All is set. Hero and heroine are anticipating triumph. Then the bank-clerk, having been deceived by the villain's disguise, points to the blue-eyed hero and announces, "That's the man that cashed the cheque."

That was all the second act. In the third, the young man is of course disgraced, and of course makes good, and at the end of the third act all is well. The bank-clerk part was a tiny one, the kind of thing any baggage-man would play in the intervals of being the family doctor and the distinguished secret-service man. Flyblow was the bank-clerk.

He had precisely the seven words to speak. He studied his "Part," at his digs and in the streets, for five days. He rehearsed it—and kept the other people on-stage, fuming, while he rehearsed it—some eighteen times. It is one way of learning to be an actor.

"No, no, NO!" Madge Merryweather would scream. "Don't stand there like a sick sissy and say it as if you were saying the cemetery was full to-day. *Look* at the man. *See* him. Then tell it as if you could speak English. Again, please."

Whereupon Flyblow would repeat, in exactly the same small, thick, toneless voice, "That's-the-man-that-cashed-the-cheque," and another agonised scream of, "No, no, NO," would come from the prompt corner.

Twenty times Madge spoke the line for him, forcing him to say "CHEQUE," first, and then to add the other words, in the hope of adding something like rhythm and emphasis to the monotone. At last Flyblow achieved a remote resemblance to human speech, proudly announcing, "Tha sman a cashda CHEQUE." There was no doubting his happiness.

Came the night. The melodrama plugged its way, mechanically and satisfactorily, to the end of the second act. Then came the crowd scene, and Flyblow's début.

He had been mumbling his line to himself all day in the dressing-rooms, and everyone expected him to dry up. That was provided for. Any one of the three men on stage would be ready to gag if Flyblow went dumb.

He did not. Stepping forward a pace, straightening himself, Flyblow drew a long breath and glared at the blue-eyed hero. Then, minus the monotone for the first time in his life, he smote his chest and announced, loudly and clearly, "I'M the man that cashed the cheque."

There was no gagging *that*. Madge was barely restrained from murder. Flyblow was a baggage-man next day.

Life in the Comédie Irlandaise was comparable only to a perpetual lotus-dream. The towns of Ireland passed before us, each with its cluster of people intent on important affairs, hurrying to make or lose money, planning a future for others or straining towards their own. We hardly saw them.

Nenagh, Roscrea, Birr, Athlone, Ballinasloe, Loughrea, Galway, Sligo, Mullingar, Tullamore, Kildare, Cavan, Clones, Derry, Buncrana, Armagh, Enniskillen, Lisburn, Lurgan— there may have been a dozen, or twenty, or five other towns on that particular tour. After the first ten minutes they were all alike to me. Most of the company did not even concede the ten minutes.

Months passed, and I was still dream-drifting with Lorry Dobell's crowd. Only gradually I came to realise that almost without exception my fitup friends might have come out of Dublin Liberty. This, although none of them had ever even heard of it, most were middle-class folk, and two or three were young English people with money.

Essentially, they were Alsatians one and all. Riding by rail and carrying gear, they were nevertheless tramps telling the tale. Between Scutchy's didacticism, Jemmy Suttle's parson-thumping, and the earnest drama-presentation of Comédie Irlandaise, the difference was only one of degree.

They did not tell a brief story, many times over, for six-pences, in La Comédie. They told a longer tale, sometimes with practicals (like Suttle's wooden leg or his South African

medals, neither of which was more genuine than the bridge in
Mother's Mind) for a conglomerate of shillings and florins.

They would not work, regularly or sensibly, nor make anything, nor stay in one place. They did not know it, but they
were all tramps. Jack Callaghan, chanting his tales of Michael
Dwyer, was their comrade, had they but realised it. More, they
did realise it, instinctively and unmistakably, for there was
never mean patronage in their manner when our path crossed
with that of a strolling tumbler, a left-over clown from a
circus who made one-man show in the market-places, even an
itinerant conjurer, or a Punch-and-Judy man.

They were all tramps, although they did not so style themselves. Now I knew why I had dropped into fitups as if I had
been born there.

The economics of travel with a fitup would have emphasised
the connection with trampdom, even if nothing else had
pointed it. In every large town in Ireland there were actors'
digs. The charges were nearly enough at a flat rate, since the
companies continually came and went, the people met and
talked, and any overcharging would have been generally
anathematised at once—besides which, no fitup actor ever had
any money.

Between the clean, comfortable boarding-house where actors
stayed and the filthy holes which offered accommodation to
working men, the difference in charge was so small as almost
to shock. In many towns I had myself paid *more* at a "Good
Beds" place than I later paid as an acknowledged solid citizen,
an actor-gentleman.

Tramps' lodgings in Ireland had then, as now, three or four
prices. When I first walked the Irish roads, the stalls divided
into croker-pads, octokips, and deener-stalls, according to
the charge of fourpence, eightpence, or a shilling. At Cork
I had paid a shilling for one-sixth of a tramp-filled bedroom.

No fitup actor in Ireland at the time would have dreamt of
paying more than a shilling for one night's accommodation,
unless there were major compensatory advantages.

From the beginning I was amused at the ease with which the actor-people dropped straight into a new home at each town, each behaving as if he or she had been born in the house now seen for the first time. The married women, with catering to consider, and with the task of visiting the lodgings first (since their men would be busy fitting-up on arrival in each town)—the married women were miracles of adaptability and homecraft.

After a genial good-morning to the strange landlady, and an almost monosyllabic confirmation of tariffs, the actress-housewife would whip off her coat, don an apron, reach for pots and pans as if she had laid them down but one hour since, and make lunch ready for her husband, gossiping all the time as if she had been born in—"Er, by the way, Ma, what's the name of this place?"

With Irlandaise we never had any trouble about digs, since the company kept an advance-man on the road. Two towns ahead, booking halls, distributing publicity, arranging cartage of scenery, doing the hundred jobs of an advance-man, he always booked digs ahead, sent intimate brief postcards back along the road, with local hints.

I became friendly with Harry Boland, a character actor, and learnt much from him on- and off-stage. Harry had been "wearing make-up since he was two," but had never been out of fitups, although he was a really high-grade actor. Later he became known to variety-goers, in many countries, under his real name, Tom Williams. But I think his greatest histrionic feat was an impromptu, one night he and I strayed into a wedding at Carrickmacross.

We had not been invited, had only just come to the town on a Sunday, were opening at the Town Hall next day. Roaming about, having an occasional drink, Harry and I strayed into a large house where there was much merriment, with plenty of music and song of a kind.

We were made welcome, my companion being hailed as Dermot, were given several drinks, and had already pre-empted two attractive girls, when some elderly men commenced to discuss the neighbours and the family. They meant *our* neighbours and family. Apparently we were relatives—and it was not the type of gathering to welcome gate-crashers.

Boland gagged, industriously, for more than ten minutes, but without attaining any knowledge of who he was or what he was supposed to be. I supported as best I could. But most of my time went in noting that many of the male guests looked capably tough. The street door seemed a long way off.

"Hal roost yee," exclaimed Boland suddenly, and smote his interlocutor on the shoulder in exuberance. "Hal roost yee, bet Ay'd day fur yee. Craiste Goad, mon, Ah tell yee Ay'd day fur yee." He laughed, drunkenly, and leant towards my chair.

"I'm an Orange farmer from Lurgan," he whispered. "A bit of a scrapper and quarrelsome. Okay for character. But get us out of here sharp—*that's all the dialogue I know.*"

We sneaked out. Only a genius could have maintained the rôle so long. I myself did not understand one word of what Harry had been saying, in his character of tough Ulster small-farmer. But behind us, as we left, another hoarse bass voice used almost identical phrases in genial farewell. And Boland was an Englishman!

We criss-crossed among the large towns of Northern Ireland, then worked our way back to the Midlands before Christmas. Everything was quiet in Ireland at the time, and I knew I would have no commitments at Liberty Hall. I considered staying in fitups for ever, or at least as far as Cardiff. That was a long way ahead, perhaps five months—an eternity to a strolling player. Actually I left Irlandaise almost at once.

There was a small unpleasantness with one of the married men, very jealous of his wife, who thought I had been poaching. He was quite wrong, as a matter of fact, not because I was painfully moral, but because I was much more interested in one of the other girls. But of course, at such a time and to a person in such a state of mind, logic means nothing. One result of the squabble was that I got drunk.

Except for the last item, no harm would have been done. Madge did not tolerate anything of that kind. Again unfortunately, she and the stage-manager nagged at me, not knowing that even when drunk I was far from incapable. We were playing a costume piece—seventeenth century—and I had troubles enough about getting on my lace-and-ruffle outfit without being nagged at. The row flared up again before the middle of the second act.

Wearing a light-blue silk affair with frills on it, having tight white breeches and buckled shoes, also a wig with powder, I stood in the wings and argued with Fred Wright. He made what were—to me—quite meaningless threats, about fining me, resting me, and the like. My cue came while I was still snarling defiance.

The shortest way out was across the footlights and up through the audience to the main door.

That finished me. Drinking in a pub, still with my grease-paint and ruffles on, until the end of the show, I went back and changed in sulky silence. Madge passed me my money, correct to a penny, without a word. I was Ishmael again.

When the crowd had gone on, I went lazily down the road towards Carlow. It is amusing to remember that, although I had a few shillings, I walked. Harry Boland had automatically given me the name of the geographically nearest company, taking it for granted that I would be going to them. They were coming to Carlow. So I walked that way.

The town of Carlow bore many signs of the Roberto Lena theatrical company. Many large posters were on the walls of the approach-roads, lithographs and programmes were in the shop windows, the theatre was booked and billed. But the company was missing.

It was Christmas week, and they had decided not to open until December 26th. Three days to wait. At holiday-time. And my last few shillings had gone for lunch, drinks, and cigarettes.

Checking in at the biggest hotel—I knew no small one, and no actors' landlady would have an actor without a company and without money—I mentioned casually that I was joining the Lena company. That saved me from embarrassment, as I had no baggage except one small attaché-case.

Then I looked around for someone who might be a crypto-rebel, a Republican sympathiser—or even a friend of mine. Almost at once I picked the right man, owner of a drapery business, and an officer in the I.R.A. if ever I had seen one. I told him who I was, explained that I was not on business or anything like that, was merely waiting for a drama-company to come along, was broke. If I could have a couple of pounds . . .

He produced the money at once, and invited me to call at his home later for tea. On the way out, I turned back and asked him how he knew or thought I had told the truth.

"If you were a spy," he explained casually, "you'd have been mad to come here—four of the boys have had an eye on you since you came into town. If you were a crook you'd have told a better story. You wouldn't have come in here openly if you were a man on the run. A casual tapper wouldn't have risked being questioned. So you could only be one of the boys who was a bit hard-up. See?"

It was a valuable object-lesson, and increased my respect for the I.R.A.

After the holidays the Lena company arrived, a numerous cortège, with a fitup and scenery that to my already practised eye spoke of work. I hoped Roberto Lena did not want only a baggage-man.

As it happened, he did not want anyone, having just come from a stay in Dublin, where he had hand-picked his company for the rural towns. But—Lena was a trouper first and a manager second; I had a note from Harry Boland. I could be a baggage-man and play small parts.

We discussed salary, and I mentioned a figure slightly higher than I had been getting at Comédie Irlandaise. Lena agreed at once, and I could see I had made a mistake.

For several days in Carlow I had nothing to do, except be

footmen and doctors and clerks, since there was no baggage
to handle and two other men did the scenery. Then we moved
on to Newbridge, and on opening night the company was two
short. It was a "scarper."

The verb to scarper, used almost exclusively in theatrical
circles, has interested me for years. Almost anyone, offhand,
will call it rhyming slang, but there seems to be no clue. It
means (*a*) to decamp from digs without paying; (*b*) to pass the
barrier at a rail-station without a ticket; (*c*) to leave a dramatic
company suddenly and without notice. Two of our character-
actors had scarpered.

It was an annoyance for Lena, coming at the commencement
of the tour. All the plays in the repertoire had been rehearsed.
The parts left "adrift" were long and one of them was
difficult. There was no time to get a pair of actors from
Dublin.

One of the baggage-men, Lena explained, could vamp one
of the parts. But the other part was tougher. Did I think that
perhaps I could . . .?

Of course I said it would be easy, but Lena was dubious.
However, there was only a single day in which *someone* had
to study and get the feel of the part. We took a chance.

It was a character part, of a rather boastful and flamboyant
young man who talked a lot. Memorising it was an easy matter
for me. Also the rôle suited me.

Without a word except "good man," Lena increased my
pay by a pound at next salary call. This was the *ne plus
ultra* of praise from a fitup manager, and I swelled. I was
an actor.

Hamlet, I considered during the subsequent days, had never
been *really* played with complete understanding. Besides, Iago
was the true hero of *Othello,* and should be so played. Now I,
for instance . . .

I was off again on the non-stop fantasy express.

It was at Lena's that I had the finest example of shrewd
production I have ever known. Somewhere up in the Midlands
we were playing a melodrama in which I was cast as character

heavy. (I played character heavies now, every week, without discussion, did little else.) The character I played wore a revolver holster on a belt.

Now I knew how to carry a revolver holster, had learnt under Captain Dick McCormack, of the Irish Citizen Army, a hard master. There is only one right and safe way to carry a revolver on one's belt. It swings low, ready for the hand.

Lena took one glance at my make-up on the first night, frowned and said, "Good Lord, no, Jim. That thing looks like a horse's belly-girth down there." He took hold of the belt, moved it to an awkward and ridiculous position, said, "There. O.K.?"

I pointed out that such a place for the gun was fantastic and impossible. He heard me out, then sent me down in the middle seats while another man wore the belt both ways.

The wrong way was the right way—from the audience angle. The old fitup managers never saw any other. Many a modern producer (naming no names and quoting no titles) increases my respect for the Lenas and Merryweathers.

Life in this particular company was a thoroughly jolly business for everyone. For me it was more than that. I swotted and read and enjoyed myself continuously. I even wrote two plays! (In fitups an actor was lucky if he received three pounds for a play, luckier still if, after one month, he could recognise even one line of it.)

Val Vousden joined very shortly after Carlow, and stepped to the front at once. Val had been a gunner-major, I think, was just out of the army, had had little experience, but was an actor born. In the week of writing this I saw his name on the top of a big-theatre bill, read that he was still going strong, had a pleasant nostalgia for the fitup days.

Breffni O'Rourke was another who came my way at that time, who also "played them straight" on the road in England and Ireland. Nearly a quarter of a century in films and big-city theatres could not quite take the road-smile off Breffni's face. I think his last film was *Captain Boycott*.

Often doing three-night stands, which meant double work but double pleasure for me, we drifted up and down Ireland until our big moment came. We were going to play the capital, do a repertory season at the Queen's in Dublin. It is the Mecca of every fitup trouper in Ireland. Most of them never see it.

It might have been five days or thirty years since I left the city, for all I knew. I had never thought of Dublin since the day when—how long was it? What was the *date*?

Inevitably that started another kind of reckoning in months. I sent a letter to a friend, indicating my possible return to Dublin, leaving a few blanks for him to fill in. The reply was a wire—"Everything dealt with. Come on."

At least five positively ghoulish interpretations of the first phrase occurred to me that night.

We went on to Dublin, and I felt proud as a young captain with his first ship when I saw my name on the posters. Not one fitup-man in fifty ever played the Queen's. Here I was. Very well, then.

But rage and moral horror and righteous indignation cut across my self-congratulatory state when, on the second day, I saw my beautiful ex-girl-friend walking with an obvious clerk. A clerk! Here was a woman who . . . I choked with anger.

Briefly, she had known her Dublin as well as I. One variant of the Dublin populace-theme, the same beloved of "frank" Victorian novelists, was to advance the usual story. Without physiological grounds, so to speak. If the man hearkened and hastened to conform—good speed. If he did not—good riddance. No moralist in any of Lena's melodramas was ever so indignant as I when I thought of her baseness, remembered that I had been labelled good riddance. A clerk!

Twenty-five years later I met her, a widow now with two sons as big as myself, and we laughed over our mutual double-crossing. Almost I managed for a moment to regret my impetuous haste and my unprincipled cowardice when I remembered how lovely she had been.

243

It might have been well to have married and lived a placid-stream life, instead of battering myself against the world and tearing out heart-strings and walking the roads. It might have been better, the peaceful way.

But in that case she would have been *my* widow. I would not have liked that.

CHAPTER XVIII

DUBLIN was largely unchanged, after nearly a year, was still quiet. The armoured car and the searchlight, the curfew and the street-corner posse had not yet become part of metropolitan life. At Liberty Hall there was a feeling of readiness, but there was little activity.

At my mother's home opinions were divided about me. My father had died while I was away, and the rest of the family were not certain whether they wanted a sponger like myself in the place. Of course they were perfectly right—or rather they would have been perfectly right if they had been a little more stern. They were too easy-going.

My mother was uncertain whether, after all, an actor was not practically as good as a doctor or judge, almost certainly better than a smith. Could it be possible that I was being sensible at last, was going to be a gentleman and a genius in my own way—with of course, large quantities of money.

If she had only known the tiny sums negotiated at "salary call" in the Queen's!

One painful discovery, for my mother, my family and friends, was that I was no longer interested in Inchicore, had almost forgotten the name of the place. Always, no matter how long I had been away, however unexpectedly I had departed, I had gone straight back on my return. Now—of all times now—I made no move to go.

From the ordinary sensible point of view, it was unthinkable that a man should throw away his own or his family's money, throw away long years of apprenticeship without reaping the due reward.

I have always been logical. Twice I went over the matter at home. If they wished to suggest that I should cease to be an actor, go back to Inchicore and take the several pounds weekly which were now my due, I was prepared to discuss that. If, on the other hand, they thought I should remain an actor, but should produce sufficient money not to be a burden, I was prepared to discuss *that*. What did they want?

My mother at any rate did not know what she wanted. Or more precisely—she knew quite well, but was afraid to know she knew. Many people are like that, when discussing important matters. Facts are avoided as if they held plague.

My mother, naturally enough, could not bear to think of all that good money being thrown away. But also naturally the poor darling could not state it so. What she really wanted was that I should go back to Inchicore, take the fortune (in weekly instalments) that was to be mine, work as a smith all day, and then be an actor-gentleman, acquiring another fortune, in the Queen's Theatre at night.

It might and might not have helped the discussion if my relatives had known that I was only a promoted baggage-man, playing small parts, actually drawing my salary, such as it was, for practically nothing.

I went back to Inchicore. But it was for half a day, a quarter of a century later. As far as I know, a fledgling craftsman named Phelan is still on the books, absent without permission since the year 1918.

The stock season at the Queen's was a lovely time for me. With only minor parts, and with nothing else to do, I had all my days except for rehearsals, and most of my evenings, to spare. Many of the daytime hours went at Liberty Hall, but I met and talked with actors and writers, gradually began to feel my feet in the mind-world and among the obstacles around it.

Sean O'Casey was then a regular caller in the rebel circles of Dublin, particularly with the Citizen Army, of which he had been one of the first members. *Juno and the Paycock* was still away in the future, but even then O'Casey was busy feeling the lives of the waterfront and coalyard men, the working rank and file of the I.C.A., who remained with him, almost an obsession, for most of his life, until they forced their way out into the plays.

Apart from Liberty Hall, there was a large meeting-hall at Langrishe Place, the property of Delia Larkin, Jim's sister. Nominally a club for working men, the Langrishe Place centre was a venue for intellectuals, reformers, visiting writers of every kind, perhaps a few conspirators on the side.

But the clientèle in the mass were working men, of the Transport Union type, from Gloucester Lane and Townsend Street and the other poverty-stricken districts. They made history, as well as matter for drama, later.

Jim Larkin was away in America, and Delia, unobtrusively in the main, kept salon. People like Shaw Desmond or Wickham Steed, coming to Dublin, went straight to "Delia's" instead of along the more conventional well-trodden paths. A dozen young writers of the time owed chances to Delia Larkin.

Delia and my sister Maggie had married the brothers Colgan, two young Citizen Army men who later wore in fact the red brow-bandage I had only carried in fantasy. One measure of Delia Colgan's force and strength of character is that the hall habitués, the working men from Townsend Street, nevertheless continued to call her Miss Larkin.

Sean O'Casey was always an honoured caller, something far more than a friend of the family. He might almost have been described as an incipient Socialist hagiographer even then, for Jim Larkin was the nearest he knew to a deity, and the satellite saints were the labourers of Townsend Street and similar districts.

Not a bad choice, either. Jim Larkin needs no praise from me or from any man. The labouring people of Dublin made miracle daily, in the War of Independence, and before, and after. Sean seized them as the chief characters in any story of

Dublin. Townsend Street is his Mecca. And there are the plays, and the films, to prove his craft-mastery.

But I still think that the real pulse of a city is not in the poverty-stripped homes of nearly destitute labourers. I still think that as and when the drifting riffraff of a city's Alsatia moves, so and thus can one know whither that city will move.

Labouring people, in the nature of things, know small opportunity to be mentally alert. Long hours of work, little experience of people, worry and poverty and a restricted life, do not sharpen the intelligence. It is the lean, keen, Alsatian who marks a city's tempo.

It came to me suddenly one day that the work-folk are like the wheels of a clock, but the drifter-people are the hands that tell the time. British troops were arriving, a long convoy of lorries, and a few big guns behind a far-stretching column of infantry.

The citizens, the working people, needless to say the Citizen Army men, were sullenly impassive. Rookery rats, tramps, chanters, gay-girls, and the whole flotsam of the Liberties were wild with delight, screamed their exultation and cheered till their throats cracked. The Liberty is always on the winning side and might is right around Mulluckses Lane.

"When those people are on our side," I said to Captain McCormack, "we've won." He thought I was mad.

Less than three years later, quite near the same spot on the waterfront, a prostitute smashed a bottle on the head of a man with whom she had been commercially engaged. While an ambulance removed him, she screamed abuse and outraged indignation.

Fantastically, she had the sympathy of the bystanders, as she seemed to expect. All, at any rate, understood her horror on discovering that the man in civilian clothes was a Black-and-Tan—i.e. one of those the Liberty had so deliriously welcomed.

That is what I mean by saying that a city's movements are pointed by those of its Liberty, if it has one. Villon knew. Gorki knew. But few writers since have ever even walked the highways, let alone known the alleys. It is so much easier to copy from Harrison Ainsworth or . . . (To complete that line wild horses will be required.)

The poorly-paid workers of Townsend Street did the work of Dublin, fought its battles, bought with their blood the things it desired. The riffraff did nothing. But they were the recording instruments, the delicate pointers. They had to be. The workman had the flimsy security of a job and a pay-packet; the drifter had nothing except a nose to smell out a meal and a stall—which same are not obtained from the loser.

Fortunately, it is easy to clarify here. An English tramp would dispose of the matter in fewer than twenty words. The slinkers of Mulluckses Lane were tramps. Townsend Street people were young mugs.

Having walked up Watling Street, I have nothing to add. That day in Dublin I tried to explain all these things to Dick McCormack. He thought I was mad. I went home to write a play about the Liberty.

The first two acts of the play took a fortnight to write and, at the end of the time, bursting with importance, I showed them to Bob Lena. He read the script carefully, since he had a higher opinion of my powers than I had myself at that time. Then he handed the sheets back, with the most devastating eight-word criticism I have ever heard, "That's not a play; it's a bloody lecture."

I have never forgotten that criticism either.

In the few weeks of the stock season at the Queen's I grew and changed fast. Also I worked hard, at things no sensible person would call work. My views about Dublin—it would be called a political commentary nowadays—went into some eighty very bad verses.

At the same time I tried to re-write the two acts of the play, could already see Lena producing it at the Queen's, with some *really* good actor, who *really* knew the characters, in the lead-ing rôle! But I had only explanations of things, not utterances of people. It was no good.

At the same time I re-wrote the Joe Jarrett story and sent it out. Again it did not bring even a rejection slip. Then a journalist friend, my divorce-story man of ten years earlier, warned me of what happened to pen-scribbled manuscripts.

This was a jolt. I had little money to pay a typist, and could not use a machine myself. Finally, Archie Anderson "lent" me five pounds, after some particularly satisfactory small-firearms trade, and I was able to get the Jarrett story typed. I sent it with a story about the bogland around Denny Rohan's at Carrigatoher to my man at the *Daily News,* oblivious of the fact that the paper had changed and that they did no short stories.

In those weeks, too, I worked hard at the novel of the Dublin Liberty. In my mind I called it "the" novel, although it would perhaps have been two thousand pages in length if I had had my way. Later it became *Muchmaker,* one of my best books, I think, died stillborn, the author at the time being in a place where no publishers call.

When our Dublin run was within four weeks of its end, the first small clash of my two half-lives came. At Liberty Hall no one took much notice of the fact that I had changed my occupation from smith to actor. At the Queen's no one knew nor cared about my membership of the I.C.A. Then Constance Markiewicz came home.

The Countess Markiewicz had been released from prison in England, was returning to Dublin. Naturally there was a turn-out of the I.C.A. to welcome her, since she was one of ours. We were to march through the city, mass outside Liberty Hall, generally demonstrate our affection and loyalty.

The mobiliser notified me in the ordinary way. Excuses for absence were not, as a rule, currency in the Citizen Army; at the same time, in my own case explanation would have been easy. But I wanted to parade. That engagement was for 7.45 p.m. Curtain up at the Queen's was at 8.

Some of the boys laughed and pulled my leg when I arrived on parade. Ironical questions were asked about my multitude of admirers in the Queen's gallery, whom I had failed. Of course the boys did not know I had again committed the final crime of theatre-land. I had scarpered.

Next morning Roberto Lena gave me my money and called me many kinds of a fool. I was vastly more sorry than he about it, but what could I do? I liked the Countess.

After a few days I told my family and friends that I was going to work at Ford's new place in Cork. Already I knew well that it was easier to give silly reasons for going anywhere than to say one was going.

This time I did not walk, but rode a passenger train to Cork. However, I did not have the opportunity to scarper that. The ticket-man had my name and address, but the Southern Railway has not yet sent in the bill—perhaps they found out that I was theoretically a railwayman!

Clean, cheerful actor-digs in Cork cost sixpence per night more than my first tramp-stall.

Mooning around in Cork, after a few days I realised that my money would be gone in another week or two, began to think of fitup advertisements and of borrowing a typewriter. At the same time I observed that I was being followed in my aimless meanderings around the city.

At first I thought that some detective or secret-service man was selecting me for attention. Then I decided that Cork I.R.A. would have doubts about wandering strangers of no known occupation.

This was rather awkward. I knew no one, had no credentials to speak of, was not on any political or other business, was not going anywhere or doing anything.

All that was quite normal—for me; but I knew how thin such a story would sound to Cork I.R.A. if, as I feared, the same was mainly composed of respectable people.

The bane of my existence has been the baseless, grossly unfair, and fantastic assumption that a person must always have an occupation, a residence, and fixed interests. Everyone takes such things for granted. To be doing nothing and going nowhere is universally regarded as wrong.

Consider Mr. J. Smith, of independent means, on a walking

tour, resident at the Dorchester, London, or the Waldorf, New York. Consider even John Smith, of Number One, High Street, Wigan, or Number Two, Main Street, Poughkeepsie. Here are citizens, with status, description, and legal existence.

Then consider one calling himself Smith, of no occupation and no fixed residence, who . . . The man is practically a criminal already!

It is not written in any modern code, but people are supposed to stay in one place and do one thing and have one set of interests. I could feel in my bones that Cork would be no exception to that rule.

At a hall like the Langrishe Place venue, I tackled the likeliest person and, taking care to ask no questions and giving him little opportunity for any, I had a short talk. Telling my name, I mentioned casually that I belonged to the I.C.A., casually showed a membership card, indicated that I might be staying around for awhile.

There was a silent pause. I stated further that anyone interested—and eligible to make such enquiries—could find out all about me from the Commandant in Dublin. Meanwhile, if anyone had put a man to follow me, perhaps he could be taken off, as he was getting on my nerves.

Then I turned to go. That, I thought, was fair enough. But of course I had forgotten that I was in a civilised place. I was interviewed by three other men, one of them Taig Barry, the famous Cork republican. Long before the first few dozen questions had been asked, I knew it was no use.

Why had I come to Cork? Why had I called to see *them*? Why, if I was in the I.C.A., did I not stay in Dublin? Was I looking for work? Or on some special job? Or was I on the run? Was I coming to reside in Cork? How long should I be staying?

What could I say? In the syllabus of Cork civic life there was no neat ruled space for such an entry as "Drifting, unfocused, incipient writer."

The men's attitude changed towards the end, especially

Taig Barry's. If I did not want work and was not on the run
and had not come to live in Cork or to volunteer for the Cork
brigade, if I had no business and no status, then I could only
be a spy or an imbecile. Fortunately, they seemed to decide
that the latter alternative was the correct one.

Then I was invited to stay for the night with the man to
whom I had first spoken.

My actor digs were comfortable and very cheap. Two old
commercial travellers who stayed there had a fund of stories.
The daughter of the house was intelligent, pretty, and un-
attached. Her father had hundreds of books. No one minded
what time I got up or went to bed. But I accepted the invitation and went home with the Cork man.

This was Con Collins, then a leading figure in Republican
circles, afterwards Member of Parliament for Cork in the first
Irish Legislature. He took an instant liking to me personally.
But I knew how much difference *that* would make if I came
under suspicion.

Collins and his wife were a cultured and likeable pair,
genuinely attempting to make me feel at home. But—it was
plain that I was merely being inspected while enquiries were
being made about me in Dublin. The whole business was very
boring; but I knew that for security reasons the Cork men had
no choice. That is, taking for granted their preconceptions
about people and jobs and permanent domiciles.

Thus I was afraid to walk away, lest it be taken as evidence
that I was—the kind of person who walked away.

After a fortnight, weary of being followed everywhere and
of continual small trappy questions, I said I was hard up and
wanted to find myself a job. That too was dealt with. I was
sent to Haulbowline Dockyard, the British Government's
depot on Spike Island. More, I was given a note for a man,
told he would employ me. My respect for the organisation of
which I was such an insignificant member increased still
further.

On the train from Cork, a large, ingenuous young man
travelled in the same coach with me. By a series of strange

coincidences, he too was a smith, he too came from Dublin, he too was going to Haulbowline. This was going a little too far —I nearly asked him if his name happened to be Jim Phelan.

At the dockyard, where my companion presented himself side by side with me, the man explained that he had that week received orders to employ only people demobilised from the Navy. My friend and I went back to Cork, where he vanished down a side street.

The Spike Island visit furnished me with one bright idea. Why, I wondered, if these Cork chaps were so clever, didn't they have a whole procession of men joining the Navy or Marines? Then, when each had got hold of a rifle and ammunition, and went on leave . . .

It was what might have been called a political variation of the listin-leg! A few discreet enquiries showed that the I.R.A. had been doing such things, on a bigger and better scale, for some years, that their forerunners had done it in a really big way—in 1866. My inspiration was rather anachronistic, and my admiration increased still more.

Life became very tedious and uncomfortable. The Collins couple were thoroughly friendly and nice, but they were, after all, merely people detailed to house a suspect. They could not even go out together, risk leaving me alone in the house.

It is easy to laugh now. But I might quite easily have got myself shot. No doubt *that* would have taught me the desirability of keeping to one address and one job! In the end I moved to another lodging, where Taig Barry stayed.

Barry was openly hostile most of the time, but I liked him much. Entirely without reservation or subtlety of any kind himself, he naturally suspected one like me from whom unconventionality oozed. A great scholar, he forgot his hostility when arguing or expounding, which suited me. But neither he nor the others ever relaxed for long.

Then I thought of something. There was a typewriter at our lodgings, and I had written a short story. When I found that the pages were being read, almost as they came from the machine, I typed a long letter, and left *that* to be discussed.

Writing to my Company Commandant in Dublin, I explained the position in some detail, asked him to send me instructions if I was required in Dublin, otherwise to send the O.K. about me to Cork. Of course the letter was discussed. Of course Barry knew it was a trick. It was plain that they believed I had only written the letter and left it around to be read, as a kind of spurious credential.

Then, when I had sealed it carelessly, I asked Barry if he could get it through to Dublin for me. The social barometer went up several degrees next day. The yarning and gossiping, that night, reminded me of the guard-room at Liberty Hall. I was accepted.

Next morning, disgusted, I left, after a short explanation with Barry and after leaving a note for the others. What kind of a spy did they think I was—a half-wit or something? What secret agent, paid even ten or twelve pounds a week, would not have known how to write precisely such a letter. *Shot off!*

I found a job at a coachworks a few miles from Cork, but was a failure. (The owner stood over me, grunting, all the first day. Not even a *failed* genius could work under such conditions; on the second morning, when he recommenced the grunting, I smote him and hurried away.) Then I spent five days with a poverty-stricken little fitup, playing only the tiniest villages, and left in disgust without my pay. Presently I worked as a timber-feller, about thirty or forty miles from Cork.

Although I had never even seen a tree felled, unless my infant experience at Chapelizod was to count, none of the people took me for a novice. *Tout au contraire*—I had charge of one small gang on the second day.

After the etiolation of Dublin and Cork, the late nights and indoor life of the fitups, forestry swiftly proved marvellous. I became big and straight and strong again, the long-handled axe and the two-man saw wakened the muscles that had gone to sleep. I throve.

Some form of niggling, nagging squabble grew up among the other men, five in number. It happens often, where groups of men live together and one of them does not measure to average sample. The real reasons are never stated. The people simply niggle and nag.

The greying, bent, cadaverous man, fiftyish, who coughed, did not say that he wanted me to be bent and grey, cadaverous, with a cough. He made small mean difficulties, coming a dozen times near to a sock on the jaw. The little weedy fellow who hated women, and prayed, did not say he wanted me to be like him. He said—to no one—that the Dublin jackeens were all workhouse brats, and he lost the saws or blunted the axes. To fell him would of course have been unprovoked.

Many people, everywhere, live in that way, all the time. It is very foolish. Time and life and happiness are wasted by it. But I think the important thing is that the people must themselves believe their silly lies. Whoever heard of a negro being lynched because he was rather more virile than those who condemned and slew him? Of course such things are never said. People make the cheap little nagging unpleasantnesses, without cessation.

Every intelligent person knows how erosive such an environment can become. But there are only two things to do. As a rule, if I wanted to stay in a place, I picked the biggest man and administered a little carefully calculated physical violence. Then, while the others mumbled—*sotto voce, entendu*—about savagery and unfairness, one got a little peace for a few weeks. But I did not often wish to remain in one place. Generally I walked away from the niggling.

"Giving" my job as charge-hand to a village poacher I liked, I walked away across the mountains towards Dungarvan. The blue Atlantic, and two small, black, circular islands, white-ringed, soon deleted the mental picture of my "workmates." The road went in sickles, upward ahead of me, then over the top and down a corkscrewing steepness into Dungarvan. My world was a good place again.

In Dungarvan a motherly woman at a boarding-house immediately set about making a favourite of me. There were three prices for everything in Dungarvan—for strangers, townsfolk, and favourites, descending sharply. I came in the last category, for no reason I could define.

There was a typewriter at the digs, and I wrote two stories, both about slum-life in Dublin. (Not young-mug slum; drifter slum; there is a vast difference.) Mally, my Dublin journalist friend, had told me one did nothing with short stories except through an agent. The two stories went to an agent, and were not even acknowledged. They cannot have been very good.

At Waterford I dropped into my former waterfront prowl for the first day. Also I called at Messrs. Murphy's to pay my respects to the secretary, but she was not there; the people told me she was married. An advertisement asked for blacksmiths, to join the Tank Corps of the British Army, and I had a recurrence of my listin-leg ideas, with other even less practical fantasies. Next day I passed through London, on my way to a place with the fiction-sounding name of Wool.

Amusingly, all my former experiences repeated themselves here. People told me their secret hopes and fears, everyone liked me, I was promoted twice in the first few weeks, and swiftly discovered that I could do almost as I liked. I liked prowling the tank park.

This was a vast, heather-purple moor, the place of which Thomas Hardy has written as Egdon Heath. In those days there were whole stretches where the heather could not be seen, because rows of fighter-tanks were lined up, side by side, thousands of them, thrown out on the Heath, unwanted and almost forgotten.

After the First World War, countless motor-vehicles were thrown out into dumps, left to rot because the war was over and no one was interested. These tanks went into a similar category. It is doubtful if anyone even knew how many there were.

If I had been an efficient conspirator, and if the I.R.A. had *wanted* tanks, a company of men could have driven away a machine each, across that heath, and in all probability no one would have noticed.

The heath itself was of great extent, without any large road, and was in the loneliest part of Dorsetshire. It was the kind of place where anything might happen. But no one, except a lonely prowler, or a very occasional soldier with a girl, went beyond the fringe. If there was another prowler besides myself, I never saw him.

Long afterwards I heard that Pat Keating had been doing, efficiently, the job I was bungling amateurishly, and that I often unwittingly embarrassed and obstructed him. But I knew nothing of that in the days of which I write.

Often, in the late evening, I thought the rows of tanks, black against the light-lifting heath, looked like ranks of giant graves. The few bare dunes looked ghostly at night, and the solitary eminence had the significant name of Gallows Hill. I found it an eerie place, and the general feeling must have been similar, for hardly anyone crossed at night.

By day there was no one either, since there were no villages on the heath and the military camp was below its edge. In the late afternoon, or very early evening, a strolling soldier might open a tank door, but only to take a girl in for a quiet talk. For the rest, one lonely and distant sentry, with an unloaded rifle, kept watch and ward.

I had no girl in that part of Dorset, but I often opened a door, as was my right and privilege if I so wished, since I was a blacksmith, a trusted man, and a great favourite. Captain Dick McCormack would have swooned with delight if given my opportunities.

Every tank had one quick-firer gun, and sometimes two, mostly removable. More, and most interesting—that is, if my background be remembered—there were almost always a few loose rounds of ammunition, often many. Besides which, a large proportion of the two-pounders had been left with a live shell "up the spout."

McCormack and the Liberty Hall boys would have stripped that heath like a harvested field. Unfortunately—or otherwise —I was no McCormack.

When any decent, industrious, reliable person would have been relaying that ammunition to Dick Mannering in Bristol or Archie Anderson in Liverpool, or to any of those who knew such commerce, I was much more likely to be playing chess, or moping around the tiny moor villages, picking up the landmarks of Thomas Hardy's novels.

Tess of the D'Urbervilles interested me particularly at that time, most of the places named being adjacent, especially Egdon Heath. The village of Bere Regis, called Kingsbere in the novel, was about three miles from the tank park. For a time it was almost my home.

Dorset folk are canny and standoffish. Further, the people of the district had no love for the Irish, some local men having been killed in Dublin. But I remember that Bere has four small streets, perhaps two hundred houses, and that I have slept at almost every house in the village. *That* is popularity!

Much of the chess I played, in the intervals of wasting my time around the tank park, was with a curious, overstrung, distant person who might have been Irish but had never been in Ireland. Acting-Lance-Corporal Shaw was on (some of) his correspondence. I never had time to find out if he was really Lawrence of Arabia. Everyone in camp said so, as a dead secret reminiscent of the Dublin *Sporting Echo*. Except those who said he was the rightful King of England, with similar theories.

When I got a long leave and went to Dublin, I was even more depressed than in my tormented days. I was doing nothing, going nowhere—and it was not even my own choice of nowhere. Some of the boys at Liberty Hall were hostile, others took it for granted that I was on a special job. My fantasy of staging a great raid on the Heath never emerged from the chrysalis stage.

For some time Dora O'Brien and I had intended to marry "when a chance came," and we decided that this was a chance. After my marriage I felt disinclined to return to Wool. But I caught the mail-boat, with a day to spare, nevertheless.

In London on my way through I went to see William O'Brien, who had been at school with me and then worked in Fleet Street. Although we had very little time, O'Brien introduced me to two editors and—more important as it turned out—to a reputable agent. Getting into the train at Waterloo, I began to feel like a writer again. The incongruity of the last word did not even strike me as funny.

Nowadays, needless to say, I take it as evidence of my tenacity, my prescience, and unshakable confidence in myself!

Back at Wool I dropped into a narrow groove, a circumscribed repetitive drift more erosive than any padding-blankness. I did nothing, and even my chess was poor. The opportunities for good efficient malefaction, in the tank park, were entirely wasted on me.

That, however, did not save me from trouble. Someone, somewhere, saw fit to send a letter to Wool, in which I was depicted as—as an efficient, sensible, and determined conspirator not addicted to fantasies might have been.

Fortunately, I was on exceptionally good terms with everyone in the place, had chances to come and go, almost *ad lib.*, had many friends. I got to know about the letter in time. A woman, I think, only semi-literate, and from Dublin.

It was my own fault.

A leave was due to me, and a cock-and-bull story hastened it. With precisely eleven pounds in the world, and with about six hours to spare, I left Wool in a hurry. There would be questions. Thousands of them, all eminently fair and logical and just. What was the use of staying, to attempt the answering of questions?

If Colonel Hudson be alive, he will, I know, forgive me for the way I deceived him. It was unavoidable.

On the way out I did not delay in London, but kept going to Holyhead and crossed to Dublin that night. As far as I was aware, only Dora noted my arrival. I did not want to talk, nor to see anyone, and I did not like Dublin now, much.

My discharge was not due for nearly four months. In my mind, it was a race between two competing teams of form-fillers. "My" form-fillers, the time-expiry team, won. Colonel Hudson was always a good fellow. If he had been a snooty bureaucrat, I should have been form-filled as absent, just in time to make me a good deal of trouble. Fortunately, he was not like that.

Dora had no illusions about me, and had mercifully not visualised herself as a placid middle-class wife or a craftsman's bride, with me cast in the rôle of gold purveyor. She knew me. When, after less than a month, I said I was going to Galway, she merely enquired if I should need one shirt or two.

Of course I had only said Galway because it was the name of a place. I wanted to go somewhere because I wanted to go somewhere.

One could not say things like that to Dora. She and I were in love with one another, as much as or more than most other married couples. But one could not say things like that to her, to any normal, respectable, well-bred girl.

Nor did I yet know that there were in the world any girls to whom one could say such things, and be comprehended. That first night out from Dublin I slept at the paddincan of Kinnegad.

CHAPTER XIX

KINNEGAD is a large country town, at an important junction of roads from all points of the compass, near the centre of Ireland. It is a busy place, with numerous strangers continually arriving or leaving. As late as 1945, in the hotel-guide of the Irish Tourist Agency, not one hotel was listed for Kinnegad.

First thought of the stranger is to dismiss the place as tiny and unimportant. That is incorrect: Kinnegad is bigger than many towns for which seven or eight hotels are listed. Next thought is that even if big it must be a dull town, with nothing to be seen.

Actually it is a caravanserai, a swarming-place for the myriad floating people who even to-day throng the roads of Ireland. Twenty-five years ago it was even more crowded.

Half the tramps and tinkers, ballad singers and thimble riggers, wandering puppet men and the riffraff of road shows, from all over Ireland, seemed to be coming and going in Kinnegad. Such, however, do not patronise hotels. I stayed at the paddincan.

The centre of the town was an open space, with a few trees shading a bumpy pavement to one side. The main street, part of a main county road, passed at one end. Four smaller streets led away into the open country.

At the busiest street corner, two brown-faced women with babies flitted back and forth, begging. Across the road, outside a pub door, a man for all the world like Scutchy Callaghan bawled a ballad. Needless to say, it was a patriotic, a Republican ballad. Alsatia is always on the winning side, and the

Irish Republicans had practically won their war. Slowly, down one of the by-streets, eyeing the houses in caution, came a file of unbridled small horses.

A battered brown wagon, behind, held a jumble of babies, and a white-haired man leant to one side from the driving-seat to watch the line of horses ahead. Four small carts, donkey drawn, at the tail of the cortège, drew into the square and halted. An ancient woman limped from shop to shop, offering diminutive bunches of lavender for sale.

At the quietest corner of the square a group of men stood around a tiny green-baize table, whereon three cards flipped loosely to and fro, while the owner told of wealth to be gained by the sharp-eyed. Ragged and poor-looking, his manner exuded opulence and security, his every phrase bespoke careless acquaintance with riches.

Occasionally he glanced up in annoyance, when a man who played the flute in a gutter nearby went up to a shriller note, interrupting the flow of the card-patter. But in the main the cardman was all good humour, and in an hour his gains were some three shillings.

Covered with dust, striding awkwardly, a tall, powerful man came into the town from one of the side streets. A bundle under one arm might have held a suit of clothes, and a newspaper packet stuck up from his coat, the paper torn, the end of a bread-hunk emerging. The man cringed past while a policeman glared at him, then he turned the corner and went on up the main road out of the town.

Two tramps came down the same narrow street, each carrying a thin stick, each wearing a battered mackintosh although the weather was warm. Both were bearded, but upright, and they carried no visible bundles. Without hesitation they brushed past me, nodding, into the doorway of the paddincan.

A tramp woman, with a bandage over one eye, leant to say something to a lady who had halted her car. Two small children hovered near, watching the policeman at the corner.

Besides these, several townspeople passed in the streets, going about their business.

In anecdote and casual gossip, I had heard about Kinnegad a hundred times, had built myself a mind-picture of the place, composite of my own experience-fractions and the stories of Maxim Gorki. I had imagined a kind of Irish but smaller Nijni Novgorod. This was better.

There was a drowsy peace for me, there in the strong sun of the summer evening, watching the drifters come into their town, meet and pass, talk and traffic, and go on. As a good Catholic turned to Rome, a good Moslem to Mecca, the drifters turned to Kinnegad. It was a Liberty town. It was my town, and I belonged to it.

What was the use of talking, of making silly pretences and rushing away every while, saying now I knew what I wanted to be. I wanted to be nothing. I had never been anything and I never should be. I was no smith nor writer, no soldier nor revolutionary, no poet nor actor, and not even a ballad chanter. For nothing at all, anywhere, was I of any use.

Perhaps, though, I could *be* a ballad chanter! Impartially, I listened to the singer outside the pub. No—he had not quite the genuine twist to the end of a line, nor quite the reliable vowel-stretching on the second bar, had none of the little touches that made a Scutchy Callaghan. I could do better than that.

Most I would like to walk along, stall at the paddincan wherever there was one, and tell a story instead of singing a ballad, in every town. That would be better than chanting.

But there I was again, off at random, pretending I was a writer and wanting to do things. Why? For what? Why do things?

Wealth and fame and the love of women, the old Austrian fellow had said, wealth and fame and the love of women were the needs that drove a man. Maybe if he was thwarted he made Cellini's things or built Milan Cathedral. And that way he came to wealth and fame and the love of women after all.

That lifted no pulse in me, and my breathing quickened nothing at all for the thinking. For wealth—I had four pounds: it would get me to Guatemala if I wanted to go there, or farther. Also I had an attractive wife in Dublin if I wanted to be respectable and reliable and steady. Further, two years', or even one year's, hard work would make a known actor or writer of me. The twist in either direction was there, if I did not want other things.

Well, I did not want anything. If the old Austrian fellow was right—and it could be—then if a man did not want wealth or fame or the love of women, there must be something wrong with him.

But there was nothing wrong with me. I could work or fight or make love or talk or think as well as anyone I knew, better than some. Now it could hardly be that everyone else was wrong. Only a crazy fear-fumbler would think things like that. But I really was nothing and never would be anything and did not want . . .

What was the use of being top in logic at school if a man couldn't pile a sorites to the end, topping it off with the last syllogism to peak the pyramid? Very well, then.

Of course I had been stating baseless negations, saying I wanted nothing when I wanted much. What was it but that old trick of mine of refusing to niggle and nag about shares? What else?

When Jim Maher had given my sister two half-crowns for us to buy sweets, my share had been a florin. Of course I had thrown the florin away. It was, I thought, the most natural thing in the world. I did not want a florin. I wanted half a crown.

Now I was twenty-six, not seven, but all my life I had done that. Many times I had gone without a smoke, but I had never smoked a bad, cheap cigarette. Even the stop-gap girls I had known were the physical pick of Dublin or elsewhere.

Very well, then. What was the use of saying I wanted nothing? I wanted everything.

Even that was vague, and a cheap cheating, a fear to put a tail on the last syllogism. So—I wanted a thousand pounds every year, and that would be enough for a tramp on the roads. Because I wanted to stay and walk along the roads as well.

Now you cannot batter and fadge a thousand pounds in a year on any road.

So—I wanted a girl, as lovely as Dora, and with a mind that would meet me. This love-girl I would want to be near all the time. Else I would not want her at all.

But a girl did not go padding the roads. Not the image-girl. Not even the secretary-girl out of Murphy's in Waterford. She would think a man was mad if he asked her to pad the macadam.

So—I wanted the people to like me and know I was Jim Phelan, and be glad when I came. As people did, whenever I stayed for long, and talked.

But adrift between towns there is nothing for fame, and people would only know of a tramp that he chanted a ballad or told a story at the cross-roads. That would not be much.

Now I had it. Instead of nothing, I wanted more than my share. Not that either—but I wanted more than was to be got in a world where my many needs were all contradictory, cancelling one another out.

So I wanted nothing. And I was going to be nothing, as I had been. I was just a drifter and this was my town.

A great peace came to me, that evening in Kinnegad. The assessment, and self-searching, had been long overdue. But as will have been seen, it was unusual and complex, its logical thread over-difficult to hold at the end. Now I knew that because I could not have my half-crown I did not want life's florin. I wanted nothing.

The Kinnegad paddincan was whitewashed outside, with a thatched roof. The kitchen was large, and in a vast fireplace the fire was on the ground. A long table occupied one side of the room, forms and a rough bench and a few broken chairs being scattered about. By the fire, in the evening, seven men besides myself, and five women prepared supper.

A stout man, with one eye slashed into an unsightly whiteness, gave instant decision when any squabble arose about priority with the pots and pans. There were few squabbles, since each of the women cooked for a man, and one of the others, like myself, took only tea.

The stout man, identified in talk as Jem Butler, spoke and acted as if he had lived long in the paddincan, was its recognised ruler. Only after supper, from his questions to the other people, did it emerge that he had not been in Kinnegad for a year.

Supper done, everyone sat around the fire, some huddling close, although it was a warm night. All the talk was technical.

Since I was well-dressed and had a packet of cigarettes, everyone in the kitchen, without exception, had tried to beg from me. The correct reply of snarl and curse, followed by a good-humoured grin and the lying statement that I had no cigarettes, sufficed to establish me.

Everyone in the kitchen, without exception, had then run an appraising and predatory glance over my clothes and shoes. I mentioned Barrel Bane's, a notorious lodging-house in Dublin Liberty, and they left me alone, getting on with the business of the evening.

Jem Butler asked if old Dunnie, at the Lodge, was still all right. Someone said that was spoilt, was a washout now, and Butler swore. One of the women said the lodging at Enfield had shut up. This raised much talk, as apparently there was only one lodging-house in the place named.

One of the tramps who had passed me as he came in, earlier, told with some complacency that Admiral Waller was at home. A younger man, making prompt query, was told to have a Navy discharge, or be able to talk one, and always to salute Waller with his stick under his arm. Half a crown Waller was. Five bob if you got him in the evening after dinner, but getting him then wasn't so easy.

A red-bearded man enquired if you could come the double on Major Ferriss now. Immediately two others burst into laughing stories of having collected florins from the Major, not twice, but three times in the same day, only trivial changes of appearance being necessary, because the poor old devil was as good as gold and as blind as a bat, and half the time he guessed you were having him on, but he was just born right. Everyone liked those stories.

An elderly woman, with a mild, placid, beautiful face, said they were working on Roundwood Reservoir, that there were over a thousand navvies in the camp. Lip-licking queries followed, to be damped when she said there was no lodging of any kind for miles, except for a girl on the game, but there were twenty navvies in each hut, and the bastards like tigers.

She spoke throughout in a musical and lovely voice, looked like a nun as she told of the hardships of a whore in the mountain villages.

Everyone hung on the words of a woman who had four half-crowns. With a hundred details, and answering a hundred questions, she told of a new discovery. I listened, eager as the rest.

The Black-and-Tans had burnt the town of Balbriggan some time earlier. Coming just before the truce between the I.R.A. and the British, the Balbriggan burning had been one of the last major incidents of the war, had stood out. Many working people had been left homeless. It had not been a very great military victory.

The narrator had "tried the Balbriggan fanny" in various fields, without success. Then she had had an inspiration, had gone to the very last people from whom she, a putative victim of the Balbriggan burning, might have expected sympathy. Four half-crowns.

Capably, she gave instruction to the others. Women were better than men. You were green, lost like, making your way to friends in wherever it was. You picked only law-de-daw garrison people, the worst bastards you could find.

Now you said your house had been burnt accidental like. A whole lot of houses in Balbriggan had been burnt accidental like, see? So you were broke, and kind of lost, not knowing the roads and making your way to your friends. The more law-de-daw they were, the better they came.

This was something more than shrewdness. The destruction

at Balbriggan had naturally been glossed over in the British Press, and in such Irish papers as favoured the British. But everyone knew the truth.

Naturally anyone who had gone to the I.R.A. with a story of his or her sufferings at Balbriggan would have met with sympathy—and questions. On the other hand, appeals to the ordinary populace of Ireland would not require, and would not be helped by, any such elaborate story. But the law-de-daw people!

The tramp woman meant the wealthy Irish families whose culture and sympathies were English. Such people would, naturally enough, be feeling a little shamefaced because "their" Government had employed such a force as the Black-and-Tans. At the same time wild horses would not have drawn them to admit that the heroic defenders of British liberty in Ireland could or would have burnt out a lot of innocent people at Balbriggan.

In between these two conflicting streams of thought comes the decent, humble working-class woman whose home at Balbriggan (doubtless treasured and sacred) had been burnt accidental like. Just when a lot of other houses in the town had been burnt accidental like.

Half-crowns! Only the really top-rate propagandists, in the service of the various Governments during wartime, learn the ultimate secret of delivering to a populace a wholly unexpected story which—down at bottom—that populace wants to believe. Half-crowns!

Smoking and listening, I sat up with a jerk. This was not a paddincan kitchen. This was the rehearsal-room of a fitup company, and there was Madge Merryweather, producing, with stern injunctions about the delivery of lines, the timing of entrances, the approach to an audience—only the law-de-daw people.

Then it was late and we went to bed. The thirteen of us slept in the same large room. Twelve sighs came, before the in-bed smoking and gossiping, when my friends saw that I knew how to strap all my clothes in my belt and loop the belt

over my arm, having first lifted the legs at the head of my bed
and put a shoe under each.

With my apparel, as a subject for general interest, deleted
from the agenda, we gossiped until late, one of the younger
tramps, while the rest of us talked, savagely beating his wife.

In the morning, after breakfast, I was amused and slightly
self-contemptuous to find that I was reluctant to leave. I wanted
still to sit about and watch the people and listen to the talking.
But everyone was preoccupied and busy. The evening was for
study and rehearsal; the day for presentation of the play.

No one in the paddincan took any notice of me, and I was
last to leave. With the exception of myself, everyone who had
lodged there on the previous night was a seasoned professional
tramp. As I went down the road towards Athlone, I wondered
how a person I mentally called Lilyfingers, a writer of alleged
tramp articles in two London papers, would have fared in
Kinnegad.

He would never until his dying day, I thought, have been
able to say the people had not made him welcome. They would
have loved him. His clothing and small property, down to his
last dirty handkerchief, would have furnished at least two
days' communal income. Not even a tramp navvy, probably the
toughest type walking the roads, could emerge from a paddincan possessing anything whatever.

Yet, among the people themselves, not a spoonful of sugar
had been stolen.

It was not honesty, nor even elementary comradeship, but
convention. The convention happened to differ from the
normal, that was all. Dog does not eat dog, but it is unnecessary
to postulate altruistic motivation in such a case. There are other
more pleasant—and more easily acquired—things to eat. So
too moved the people of the paddincan.

And these were the people of whom Harrison Ainsworth,
George Borrow, Robert Service, even Alexander Dumas, and
a dozen others had *dared* to write, without one scrap of knowledge! Why, it was as bad as that fellow writing the slop-
sweetness about barrack-rooms, not even knowing the smell

of one. Or what-name writing about firemen in stokeholds, never having gasped even once to a lungful of sulphur.

They ought to be . . . Why couldn't . . . ? Surely people who read books ought to . . . *If only I had a typewriter*.

I felt very virtuous and pleased with myself, mainly because I had known when to remember Barrel Bane's place, as I went down the road to Athlone. Almost I felt like the apostle of a new religion, whose temple was to be the paddincan. People would like that word.

The term seems to be very ancient, and I have never been able to discover its derivation with certainty. Charles Reade's description of a lodging-house in *The Cloister and the Hearth* seems to have been genuinely documented, was possibly built round some early authentic story of a real paddincan. The word may mean padding ken, a place for tramps only. Even to-day the last two words hold good.

There was one paddincan at Athlone, packed because the fair of Ballinasloe was close at hand. Tramps on foot by the score, tinkers and didicai in hundreds of covered wagons, come into Ballinasloe from all quarters at such a time.

Any stranger, any person without preconceptions, would assert, after a single glance at Ballinasloe Fair Green, that the event was a hosting of drifters. But people are accustomed to civilised habits of thought; in the official lists, and the newspapers, the great gathering is described as a sale of cattle and horses. Only the police of the district know the description to be incorrect.

Several times I have written of Ballinasloe and similar vagrant gatherings. But in those early days I had no desires beyond seeing and feeling the life of the places, and knowing, albeit uncomfortably, that I belonged to them.

Down along the Shannon I went into Portumna, and across into North Tipperary, passing the Keeper Mountain and Dinny Rohan's without announcing myself. Then over into Carlow, with my last few shillings jingling forlornly, with the weather turning cold, but still too clean and well-dressed to be convincing as a tramp requiring only food and a barn-corner.

Still heading on up Carlow, fairly fast, although I was bound nowhere, I thought of turning back, going down into Waterford to look for a ship. But ships only brought one to places where one was still, and would be, nothing. It was easy to be nothing, without ships.

During all one afternoon I thought of going to Dublin, to look for Dora. But it would mean unhappiness for her and misery for me. Although she never urged nor even suggested, I knew she wanted me to settle, to live like other people, to have a home and a status, to be something. While I was nothing. Not Dublin.

A sign-post at a crossroads pointed to Sally Gap, out over the top of the Wicklow Mountains. Country people told me not to go over, as the road was snow-bound and dangerous. But I had a mind to cross those hills, and after all, the walking was only hard work, without danger, although I did not see a person in thirteen miles of climb.

Then, on the other side, among frozen bogs and black hills covered with early snow at the tops, with the silence of the ice-bound mountain lands all around, I saw men swarming like ants, in a valley. Blocking the valley from side to side, half a mile across, a neat and regular embankment was rising slowly, coming up towards the level of the valley rim.

This was Roundwood Reservoir in the making. All the hundred knots of men seemed to be frantically busy, doing nothing, scramble and heave and haul appearing futile as aimless play. But the embankment grew.

Crazy-looking old-fashioned locomotives puffed their way through from distant fields, struggled up to and along the top of the bank, where long lines of wagons were tipped. Giant steam-excavators clawed and ripped at hills, tearing out their entrails to be loaded in the wagons and hurried away to be part of the dam. Everywhere the ant-men swarmed.

A little earlier I had read Pat McGill's *Dead End* and *Moleskin Joe,* had known instinctively that the ring of them was true, but had never seen a navvy camp before. In half an hour I was interviewing a shrewd, hard-eyed engineer.

He knew I was no navvy, that was plain. Further, it was plain that he was not the type of person to tolerate tramps on his dam. But I did not look or speak like a tramp.

While he hesitated, I mentioned—sketchily—my railway experience, said I was "not too bad" as a smith, knew a good deal about locomotives. In the distance I could hear a steam-hammer thumping, and I promptly added that I was accustomed to work with steam-hammers.

I think the last line got me my job. Below his consciousness, experience was trying to tell him I was a tramp, a liability. But no tramp would have been such a fool as to talk about steam-hammers.

He asked if I would act as a stand-by, for the place where the locomotive repairs and smith-work were done. Five pounds a week—a farm-labourer *might* have got ten shillings a week at the time. Meanwhile, until he required me, was I game to work as a navvy? Next morning I was part of the swarm out on the dam.

Most of the men lodged at the small peasant farms on the hills around, the remainder in big wooden huts down at Roundwood. Many of the hill peasants, formerly poverty-stricken, were at work on the dam, lured by the Klondyke-figure of five pounds a week. Meanwhile, their women at home charged the navvies to the limit for lodging. The tramp woman had been right—there was no alternative accommodation.

For weeks I was fascinated by the navvy men, by the strange way in which they came true to type, a fine, virile, indomitable type, loyalty and courage seeming to be bred in the bone of them. Sharply contrasting were the peasants from the hills, lured in by the miracle of big money for merely *working,* their Sancho Panza cunning and counting brought up more strongly by the elemental strength and directness of the true navvies.

In all, I only spent a few weeks at Roundwood, but I think the place gave me some of my best stories. Elsewhere in this book the subject of literary origins has come up. Here again—the peasant and navvy stories, like *Happy Ending, The Bell*

Wethers, and *Johnny the Rag,* belong to my days on the Roundwood dam.

Then the snow was deep, and in any case, I was going. For of course I was not a navvy and had only wanted to see Roundwood. Besides, the snow *was* deep.

Men always left, in numbers and on the flimsiest pretext, at such times, and the harassed engineer had only a cynical grin when some ten of us went for our "time." I went the snowy road down to the nearest town, thirteen miles, and took a train to Dublin.

Dora and I did not exchange a dozen words about my wandering. But we were happy for awhile, and left talking alone. Each of us would have liked to be as the other, but neither could, and we did not niggle or nag. Days drifted, and I did little, even thought little.

At Beresford Place, outside Liberty Hall, I came alert one day and for awhile. A huge crowd of poor-looking men listened to an orator who spoke of the things Dublin's vast numbers of workless people knew instead of life. At the end I went to talk with two of the speakers.

The movement which was then growing up, in Dublin and elsewhere, had its real prototype in "Kelly's Army," the hosting of tramps who had swept across America some years earlier to Washington or near it, Jack London and Bart Kennedy two of the number. In one of the books Wells had told me to read, Jack London had written a humorous account of his membership of the Kelly force. But few or none of the Dublin men, I thought, knew about their American forerunners, except the orator who had lifted the crowd into a "gude conceit o' themsel's," one well known to the world later, Liam O'Flaherty.

O'Flaherty was a magnificent speaker, with an ineradicable twist of mischief in his makeup. This organising of a beggars' legion, comparable to the host of the beggar-syndicate described by Dumas in *Twenty Years After,* obviously appealed to him. It did to me too.

The thing was done in the grand manner, and made much

stir, even became news in many countries for a time. One of the things I remember—I was an officer of some kind; I have forgotten what—was the issue of our manifesto. Doubtless the thing is in the archives at Dublin, since it became part of recent Irish history.

Its language has not, I think, been approached since the days of the American War of Independence and the first French Revolution. Nowadays manifestos tend to be stuffed with statistics, brimful of contingencies, hesitant of purpose, phrased in mean, cheap, stodgy official English.

Not ours. Liam O'Flaherty "drafted" it. The drafting meant that Liam wrote the manifesto, it was discussed by the central committee, passed with hardly a monosyllable altered. No single document of the Second World War came anywhere near it for sheer literary power. Posted all over the city, it alone practically convinced the citizens, even without the army of the hunger-prodded behind it, that Dublin owed a living to Townsend Street.

All our people were working men, only one minor crook turning up as a member. There were *no* drifters in our ranks —except myself. The Liberty people avoided us. I think they were afraid that if the workless army had its way, employment would be found for all the people. And then what would become of the Liberty!

The unemployed army made news for awhile, then the stir died away. Discontent was on my shoulders again.

After a short—and lively—trip to Cork, with Liam O'Flaherty and some other friends, I returned to Dublin alone. A week later I was gossiping with Archie Anderson as the Dublin steamer came up to the pier-head at Liverpool.

There was a quiet, unhurried feel about Liverpool that I liked. From the first day I was at home, nearer to peace than I had been for months.

The vast line of docks inevitably drew me, and much of my time went in learning the names of ports as strange-sounding as Tyre and Sidon. I got a guinea for an article about the vast lodging-house where I had stayed on my previous visit to

Liverpool, and promptly I wrote one about the paddincan of Kinnegad.

Genial and progressive, liking me a great deal personally, the man to whom I showed it nevertheless told me bluntly that it was "phoney." There were no such places, nor people. In England or Ireland eight men and five women did not go to bed in the same room. There was nothing to be said. I made some rather attractive iron gates that week, for six pounds. *They* were "phoney," cheap copies of ancient art-ironwork, the designs remembered since my days at school in Dublin. They were quite phoney, but no one knew.

Only that week I discovered that there really were people who preferred margarine to butter and canned salmon to fresh. And I was nearly twenty-eight.

My job at the ironworks was well paid, but I was often absent. Very often the work I did was memory-copy of my school experiments, but no one seemed to mind. I sent for Dora, and life was calm for long.

For Dora, I think those months represented something like happiness, because I was at last a citizen and a husband, a person with a home and an income. I do not know. It may be. In less than a year I was not a citizen any more, and Dora was dead. A tiny cut, neglected because insignificant, made septicæmia, and gave her three days of life. But those things were ahead, and for the time we were happy.

One of the most enlivening experiences of those days was that I met Joe Jarrett twice, in the intervals of his sea-going. He too had become a big, broad-shouldered fellow, was very certain of himself, and we behaved like two schoolboys when we met. To my surprise, he thought and spoke of himself as a writer, although nine-tenths of his time was spent in stoke-holds. Some of his stories were published, and one or two long poems—we drank the money down Bootle dock road.

Then the Civil War came in Ireland, and the Irish Republican movement was rent from top to bottom. There was fighting in Ireland again, not with the Black-and-Tans this time, but between the two halves of the formerly united and victorious rebel organisation. In Liverpool-Irish circles the break had its counterpart, although most of the Liverpool men took the republican side.

For me, the awakening to the fact of the final and murderous rupture was slow. I had no really clear grasp of the situation, was too much of a dreamer to be practical and alert. Gradually, as bits of news profoundly important came through, from week to week, I came up into partial awareness.

Dick McCormack was dead, killed in Dublin by his former comrades in arms. The I.C.A. men, almost without exception, had fought on the republican side. Con Collins, my host from Cork, was a Member of Parliament in the anti-Republican Government. My brother Willie was in prison, captured after an early action in Dublin. Liberty Hall had been fired by the former republicans, now the Free State Government.

Immediately all the former furtive small traffickings, on dock and waterfront, of the men who could handle illicit packages of arms began again. It had seemed for awhile that the whispering and smuggling were over. Now the Mannerings and the Andersons and all the scores like them were busy again, taking a profit often, taking deadly risks for nothing more often still. Under the surface Liverpool seethed. The English authorities knew or guessed much about the minor conspiracies and the trafficking, but could do little, were not unduly concerned in any case. Fantastically, the bigger risks were from the Irish side of the sea.

My own share in the furtive political activity of the time was slight. But inevitably, because of my secretiveness and my play-acting propensities, some even of the initiates set me down as efficient and busy. Also inevitably, the Liverpool police, like everyone else in my life, rated me too highly.

I had rather a shock one morning, down at the pier-head, when Detective-Inspector Moore (himself an Irishman, I think, since he deliberately addressed me in Gaelic to begin with) stopped for a quiet chat. In the course of his casual remarks, all in the most friendly manner, he advised me to keep myself out of trouble. His meaning was plain. It was more plain a second later, when I had said laughingly that I was a black-smith, and he had immediately riposted with a few details of my dock-wandering.

It was my old curse of the fixed place, the fixed habits, the fixed unchanging existence—which I never had. If I was a blacksmith, what was I doing prowling around docks? There was no answer.

With the Liverpool-Irish Republicans I seldom crossed paths. That is, openly. But again, one or two of them set me down as a capable and active conspirator, when in reality I was doing very little. Much of the time, indeed, I was doing nothing whatever, not even writing except for two or three political articles. These last, I think, would go to confirm the beliefs of Inspector Moore and his friends.

Moore and the others were in a peculiar position at the time. A year or two earlier they had had to deal with Irish revolutionaries as such, as open enemies of the British Government. Now the position was changed, the Irish were "only fighting among themselves," minor arms traffickings were no longer a nightmare. Wherefore the Moore warning was friendly. But it was a warning.

Liam O'Flaherty came in one day unexpectedly. He had been in the fighting in Dublin, had escaped. One of his pieces of news was that the war on the republican side would now become a guerrilla, carried on, firstly, in the Wicklow Mountains. That had seemed inevitable, as soon as the big guns began to sound in Dublin, but I had not expected it so soon.

Although he was supposed to be on his way to America, O'Flaherty had decided that he wanted to be in the continuation of the fight, in the mountains. He urged me to go with him, advanced arguments with both a political and a personal pull. Walking the dock-line, calling in at an occasional pub, we discussed it for most of the day. In the end he went and I stayed. His name is on the roll of honour in R. M. Fox's book of the period.

There were a thousand things I could not tell him or anyone. Yet, had I but known, he was one of the few people in the world who could have comprehended. Not knowing, how could I tell him I felt nothing and hoped nothing, that I knew no loyalties to tear at me, had no convictions to drive me, wanted everything from the world but expected nothing and would take nothing. People thought such things, uttered, were mad. I left them unsaid.

Then I was busy with small things, and forgot to analyse or brood. Besides, I realised that I was being watched even more closely than I had been at Cork, but I registered little except passing annoyance.

Once, on Liverpool landing-stage, I was hustled into a room by detectives, searched, questioned. But I had only been seeing a friend off the Dublin boat. Once an obvious detective came to make friends with me at the place where I worked. And once, while I was out, a large and friendly man called on my land-lady—to collect the parcel for the Dublin steamer, he said.

It is laughable to think that my most illegal activity of that particular period was to send a few revolvers, per Archie, to a friend from Liberty Hall.

The Liverpool police had really very little choice in the matter, by and large regarding the whole business as a bore. The Irish were fighting among themselves. It was no business of anyone else. Of course, there were laws about illegal posses-sion of firearms and illicit transhipment and the like. But such was routine. However, the legal Government in Ireland—the former rebels—were now *persona grata,* were the friends of Britain.

XYZ, formerly a rebel, could now write, confidentially and on equal terms, to police headquarters. Willie Horan, the Liver-pool Commandant, whose opinions had not changed, had five years' penal servitude. Thus it went—some were up and some down. The game of politics is like that.

I being mainly busy with fantasies, none of that would have mattered to me. Except for my overrating.

At that time the I.R.A. chief in Britain was of the utmost importance to the republican movement. Naturally he was feared, and his destruction was desired, by the anti-republican body, at that time the legal Government of Ireland. Naturally the British police would "play ball" with a lawful Government, as compared with a lot of rebels. The "O.C., Britain" was suspected to be in Liverpool. The Liverpool police did not know who he was. But they thought I was he.

Of course I was not, nor was I one-tenth as good a man as the officer in question, who was well known to me at the time.

There is a difficulty about writing in sequence of the many seemingly disconnected events of that period. Many of the people concerned are alive, and it is not my purpose here to write any story but my own. Yet it is difficult to avoid laughter, so fantastic were some of the elements.

One morning I talked in a pub with Joe Jarrett, during his second visit home. In the next bay of the pub, behind the partition, a man listened eagerly to every word, now and then making a furtive note, glancing guiltily sideways at the mirror in which I watched him. Joe was talking about Hawaii, from which place he had just returned, wishing he could get me and Liam O'Flaherty, for whom he had a great affection, to go there. The man noted it all. That, I thought, was worse than Cork.

Such incidents were laughable, but I swiftly had reason to do other than laugh. The fault was my own, and even if I felt inclined to whine, there would be no opportunity. From first to last the Lancashire police were rather bored than otherwise with Irish people and incidents. It was an incident, pure routine, when one evening I was charged with shooting at a man.

It was quite true. The man stood in court, and swore that I had fired at him in the street, that he had seen the bullet coming like, had dodged it, then that I had fired at him again. He was publicly congratulated on his escape and for his courage by the magistrate.

It was quite true. All except the dodging of the bullet, naturally—I probably missed that part. But there I was, in

Dale Street police headquarters, with a charge of using firearms to meet.

This was not very exhilarating. But next day the charge was altered to one of murder. I thought it was a joke, then that it was a crude blunder. The man could not have died—I had deliberately fired over his head, had seen him in court, fit and well, on the previous day, when he swore that he dodged the bullet. They were mad. That was it.

Deliberately I have put the record here, as it came to me, the chain of events as they occurred in my experience. Some six hours afterwards I realised that this was another affair. It was another man who was dead. But how on earth could I have shot him if I was busy shooting the bullet-dodger? Were they mad?

The whole business was very straightforward and simple really, and the people were neither mad nor vindictive. Simply, they knew some things I did not know. The court records and the newspaper reports can tell the next section of the story better than I can. It is a brief section. As was but fitting.

A mail-clerk had been shot in a raid on a post-office. The affair had no connection with Irish politics, was an armed robbery (of four pounds, I believe). The prosecuting barrister stated, and the judge emphasised, the fact that the prisoner, one Jim Phelan, had not shot the man in question.

Nevertheless, I had been there or within easy reach of the place. Also I was armed. The dead man had been killed by a ·38 Smith and Wesson bullet. My gun was an automatic of much smaller calibre.

But in English law I was guilty, nevertheless. Because I had been present or in close proximity, had participated in the raid, was armed, was demonstrably willing to use firearms, in English law I was guilty.

Fair enough. Without that law, almost any clever lawyer could put up a watertight defence to almost any murder charge. Without that law, unscrupulous people could plan murders, scheme others into committing them and paying the penalty, go scot free themselves. I was always top in logic at school. Fair enough.

The judge asked if I had anything to say before sentence of death was passed on me. I had nothing to say.

Once more and for the last time—what was the use of saying anything?

CHAPTER XX

Name: Phelan, James Leo. Age: 28. Height: 5—11.
Weight: 186 lb. Occupation: Nil. Next of kin: Nil.
Religion: Nil. Property: Nil. Previous convictions: Nil.
Marks and scars: Nil.

THE printed form, that talisman of modern civilisation, is really only a very empty myth, an infantile substitute for knowledge, a nursery play at the listing of information. The entries above represent the best that a printed form could offer as a synopsis of this book.

What more and what less can I say than that it is nonsense.

The entries above represent, as records go, the man who sat in Manchester Prison and waited for death. Neither my friends nor my enemies will call me arrogant for naming such record a mockery.

Even in the condemned cell I laughed as the busy, serious, and quite impartial people went earnestly about their task of tabulating statistics. They were getting the record right, putting Jim Phelan on paper.

Then I lost the laugh when I realised that the only vitally important entry was the 186 pounds of my weight. They would have to get that right. For the hangman.

Hangmen, too, I soon deduced, had printed forms to rule their activities. One paper would have as its subject-matter the praxis of slaying by rope. The rope would be tried with a sack of sand equalling the to-be-dead man's weight.

No person in all the world knew why. Some long-dead

bureaucrat had written it, that was all. But the printed words are sacred, especially for a legal slaying. So—Phelan, James Leo; 186 lb.

Quite half the writers of the world have preoccupied themselves at one time or another with the thoughts and feelings of a man condemned to die. It is comprehensible enough. Few other situations or environments make for such a removal of thought-trammellings.

The problem of time, of the river without estuary or source, has intrigued the minds of men for as long as we know. The whence and whither of things has always been first and last question for the thinking.

The questions about life and death come second, naturally enough, for those who cogitate, philosophise, and propound. Until, on a death-bed it may be, the thought comes suddenly that the two questions may be one.

But few have time for philosophy or theorising on a death-bed. No known record exists, of any worth-while pronouncement made at such a time on such a matter. Death, as a rule, does not wait examination and analysis.

A healthy man, on the other hand, will seldom know the irrepressible urge, the intellectual passion-prod, to turn and drive his full mental force against such problems. Why should he? The feat is almost beyond human power. Life does not really admit the existence of death.

Often in Ireland I had stood on a long bog road, looking forward into mist and back into mist, the road running between like a narrow endless bridge. Now I was on such a bridge, hurrying forward towards the mist at one end.

But unlike the majority of men, I had time to think about it, because the mist had appeared while I was at my mental zenith, not when I was on my death-bed. Further, I was able to think clearly, with a keen, alert brain, because although dying, I was not sick.

Above all, I had nothing to distract me, no luring thoughts or plans or hopes, had no future to plot and not even a signpost to read. I had nothing to think of, in the world, any more.

Wherefore I could peer into the mist, and consider it, without fear of external influence and without need for self-deception.

It is a time of great testing, the time when a man is to die without being ill. Mean small hypocrisies and puny facile deceits of self are thrown away, count as nothing, and a man, if he has an active healthy mind, may look at himself and his world without blinkers or blinds.

This, I think, is the reason so many writers, from Hugo and Moore to Zola and Oscar Wilde and a hundred others, have come again and again to the thoughts of the healthy dead man.

From talk with many warders, who had seen some eighty men hanged, I was able to form a picture of the eighty minds, compare them with my own, and thus appraise the efforts of the writers.

Only Oscar Wilde, of them all, came even remotely near to grasping the concomitants of that glance at the mist. True, in *The Ballad of Reading Gaol,* he made ghastly and ridiculous blunders, but in the main he could feel his way along that road. A mighty achievement, for one who was but socially executed, not physically strangled with a rope.

My first feeling was one of great sorrow. Almost anyone will understand, since the feeling is a matter of general experience. Men everywhere know, can recapture with wistful effort, the sorrow that comes when a child has forgotten a song.

That was the sorrow I felt in the first hour. They had locked me in, with two warders to watch me, and I was sad.

Almost at once, and for hardly a fifth of a second, came a feeling of panic. I wanted to go away. I had always gone away from unpleasantness. Now . . .

Now I asked an ancient warder, very quietly, whether I could have any books. The actor deep inside me came to the surface, took charge, produced and directed and scanned my lines. Panic was not in my part. Panic brought nothing.

That last thought was the beginning of realisation that my position was peculiar. I was out of the world, away from the pull of things, but still alive. A man in hurry or worry, sick or overworked, in love or in anger, would not be able to get away, would not have time or opportunity to weigh the worth of things, would not know the vast number of things that brought nothing.

In the following days I learnt that many pulls, strong as steel cables to haul at the heart and mind of a man in the world, were like panic and brought nothing. I knew panic no more, ever.

A Church of England clergyman came to see me, although I had named no creed as mine. He was sheepish and not over-cultured, apologetic and ill at ease. His relief when I talked about chess was delightful to know.

At the end, as if it were a talisman, he laid a tract on my bed. It was plain that he was no hypocrite, but it was painfully clear that he had not been top of his school at logic. For most certainly he could not have believed that possession of a small printed form could alter the end of the road that ran into the mist.

But I had forgotten. He could. Since he still was alive in the world of men, pulled this way and that by the weak small hopes and fears, he could believe such things. More, he could not and dare not know that tracts brought nothing.

One feature of life, or perhaps I should say of death, in that place was the constant, unexpected, and always prosaic re-minder that one's business in the house was to wait, until a certain day and hour, for a man with a rope.

In the beginning such things irritated me, but after a while I was glad of them, since they often cut into a compound of varying thoughts, acted as catalysts, clarifying, precipitating. They often saved time by the reminder that some tempting mind-way was a dead end.

Thus, one day I had been yarning with a young warder who was a keen horticulturist. He had smuggled in some plums from his garden for me, was holding forth about an apple tree he had grafted himself, boasting about the beauties of fruit it bore.

When I smacked my lips in anticipation and winked at him, he blurted out, "Oh, Christ, but they won't be ready until

September." An instant later he looked horrified, nearly bit his tongue out, spluttered like a drunken man.

I was to be hanged on the 15th of August.

Again, I had been reading Cervantes, of whose works there was a splendid edition in the prison library. I wanted the *Novelas Ejemplares,* but the young librarian warder told me I could not have it. Someone had it on loan, in a part of the prison where books were only changed on Wednesdays. The hangman was coming on Tuesday.

Little things like that came continuously, a series of tiny jolts, far from unpleasant after the first few, a kind of serial *memento mori* that most efficiently banished any drift towards self-deceit.

This last I considered quite seriously as a palliative. Men had been victimised by it in every age. Would it not, perhaps, be possible to make use of it as a tool for a change, to use it as a kind of insulation against fact?

Since I had some acquaintance with psychology, knew the tricks that the deep-drifts of a man's mind may play on him, and some few of the tricks that can be played on them in turn, I considered a euthanasia of deliberately-induced self-deception.

After all, one would be a fool to have even a minor operation without an anæsthetic, if one were available. The tricking of one half a man's mind by the other half happens millions of times daily, but only to weak people or those hard-pressed by the world. In the case of an intelligent person, the mind-tricking would have to be deliberate.

Some of the devices were known to me, from auto-hypnosis and dream-inducement to a technique of sense-coupling with which I had myself been playing. To efface the condemned cell and the rope would be easy.

O. Henry, another writer who was drawn by the theme of the dead-man-alive, has a story of a man in a condemned cell. One day, suddenly, while waiting for death, he is released, joins his wife and friends, is happy, walking up the garden of his old home. At that point the men came to fetch him for execution.

O. Henry left the story unfinished. Significantly, it was his last, written on his death-bed. It is an artist's analysis of involuntary self-deception.

The author argues, between the lines, that a mean, shallow, sadistic moron can quite successfully pretend *to himself* that he is a genial, logical, cultured, and Christian citizen. Millions do, daily. Therefore a similar deception, on the part of a rather decent person under great strain, would be almost inevitable.

Thus far O. Henry. Of course he could not finish the story.

My own problem was slightly different. I would have to do the thing myself. But I thought I knew everything necessary. Besides, I was in the one place in the world where there was nothing to fear if the experiment failed.

Since I could retire at any time I liked, I went to bed early that afternoon, while the sun was still shining, and "put myself out" as I had often done before. The only difference was that this time I threw away the usual safeguards.

The sun was still shining, and I was naked, on a narrow beach at the foot of a low, jagged cliff. Out at sea an island was barely visible, and farther away was a patch that might have been another island.

Most of the time I was too busy to look out to sea. There were eight of us men, with seven women, all naked or nearly so. We made nothing and did nothing, only picked up colya from the stony little beach.

Colya was a flat shellfish, rather like a clam. They were scarce, and hid below the sand, but I could spot a hiding-place by the two little holes he left when he went down. If I found one I shouted. So did the others. The only word used was colya.

A simple shout meant that one had been found. The same word meant question as to whether my woman had found any. Piped, the same word meant that I had a big one. Yelled, it meant I had found two or three together. Snivelled, it meant my woman had been mistaken, had got an empty shell. Repeated quickly, it called us all to where a woman had found a big circle of the little holes. Growled, it told a fat man to seek the things away, somewhere not beside my woman.

That was all our talk. The fat man was brown-faced and strong, with one slashed eye all white. I could see his eye, and I knew it was all white, but I could only say colya. Then we all slept together, huddled on the sand in the sun at the foot of the cliff.

I could see us huddled in the sand, and I could see the top of the cliff and the small island beyond the big one. Also I could see the bits of colya left lying on the beach.

Twice I passed, and watched us huddling together. But the bits of colya were too near the huddle of bodies, and I flew away. On the small island I fed, and found my mate who had been eating small fish, then flew back, slowly curving to meet the wind and drifting down to the small stony beach. But the huddle and the colya were gone.

Later I flew to the cliff-top and slept. Below, the sea came up, many times nearly to reach me, but I slept again.

The place I was on moved outward, slowly at first, then faster so that the branches and twigs made noise in the wind. Then all swept rushing, and my da-twine was gone, in the crash and break of the green. Then I was gone. Afterwards I stood to shout on a grassy bank, and sang. But I had forgotten my song.

When I jumped from the green I came sneaking because a black dog had eyes in its breast, but I looked down through the stones at my father asleep in his convict clothes while the warder watched and whispered.

When I got up from bed a wardman looked at me, and I got back in the bed for sleep. Then I rolled out on the other side. My girl said I was getting out on the wrong side of the bed. We laughed, because that was a joke in Ireland, to mean a man was in a bad humour.

But it was not a bed. My girl and I were both dressed, and the bank where we had slept was bracken. We went on, and she walked the road with me until I stopped to cry because I had forgotten my song and the men would fell me and take my da-twine and cut the white wings of me so that I would never fly over the colya beach again.

But she looked in my eyes and said my words in a soft love-voice. I was to look in her eyes, keep to looking in her eyes that were tawny, and listen to the love-voice of my girl that walked the roads, and I was to cry no more. Tawny-eyed soothing to sleep, and I knew I would remember my song.

While we walked over to the towns, by Guatemala and Colya Beach and down to the bogs of Camailte, I had always the tawny eyes and the love-voice, to make sleep with no black things.

And there was my son.

A tall, straight child, and strong, he was grave, but had no fear in him, because neither his mother nor I had ever torn him with the rackings of a mutilation-morality. When he wept, it was because he loved, or that he had somehow forgotten the way of a song he had known.

He did not cringe or look on the ground when I came, but greeted me with grave and certain eyes. Neither did he call me daddy, nor pater, nor any of the names, but Jim. So that when we talked he was a man or I was a boy as we needed.

He was saying, "No, Jim," again and again to something I thought about clipped wings. "No, Jim," he told me more loudly. "It is not for me, not for Gentleman, not for you. Not for you."

Then I closed my fist to fell him, but he continued to say it. "Not for you. Silliness for silly, Jim. It will not be for you. Now the shrivelled warder is coming over. Not the silliness, the shrivelled warder."

My son went away, and I sat up as the shrivelled old warder, who had tried most earnestly and most ludicrously to bring me "under the blood" as he called it, leant over my bed and peered.

I sat up and said hello, but he only mumbled something and went to write in his occurrence book.

It would not do. There was something lacking, or something added, which put the facile self-trickery of daily life beyond my reach. All the double-twisting had been worked out of my mind, in torture and torment, years ago, and now I could only see things as I saw things.

But it had been very interesting, even if unsuccessful. Nevertheless, it was plain that I had only been trance-drifting, my mind turned in on itself, with the tiny hard brain-core I called Jim Phelan waiting patiently to assert that the silliness was not for me.

Some years earlier I had learnt a small detail of psychological practice which will be familiar to many. Big and healthy, if I lived too much alone I had sex-dreams. Presently I learnt to superimpose a small safeguard at such times.

So that when the ravishing houri normal on such occasions turned up in my dreams, it was usual for her, at a certain stage in our conversation, to jerk my arm sharply and say, "Wake up, Jim. You're going to—oh, come on. Wake up."

It was amusing to have had my trance-born son using the old familiar technique on me.

Everything else, in a very few minutes' examination, showed as coming from inside. My white-eye-slash man, I could see, bore strong resemblance to a tramp from Kinnegad. The tree-crashing business seemed to mean that I had somehow identified myself, when a baby, with the tree itself.

The seabird episode puzzled me for a little at first. Then I laughed at myself. Straight totemism, I believed. My real name is Ua Faolain, of which the English form is Phelan. The Gaelic word means seagull.[1]

I had been looking forward to the man on the bollard at Toulon, and feeling a little beyond, looking back at the boy on the bollard in Dublin, and feeling a little beyond. That was all.

But I should like to have known the history of the word colya.

From the gossiping and the dropped words of the warders, I gathered that I had slept for many hours, without moving.

[1] To avoid embarrassment on either side, it is necessary to state that the Irish author, Sean O'Faolain, and I are not related to one another.—J. P.

They had considered sending for the doctor, but had postponed it from hour to hour. Then I had wakened. I tried the experiment no more.

All the time I had been maintaining a mask of complete imperturbability. It was a mask, for of course I was afraid, and I did not want to die. But it would bring no profit to allow other perhaps inferior people to know such things.

The mask was convincing. One young warder, a talkative and genial young fellow, told one evening of a joke he had made. People near his home, who knew the duty he was doing, had asked, as people will at such times, how the man was "taking it." The young fellow had said he was not certain whether the sonofabitch was fined half a crown or sentenced to death.

Most talk of this nature was propaganda, a kind of life-insurance, as it were, a brand of confidence trick which had as its object the avoidance of "trouble." But the youngster was different from the breed, and I believed him.

I had better proof that my imperturbability was accepted. The warders on duty with me were compelled to keep an occurrence book, in which every detail of every moment of my life was entered. Naturally the last person in the world to be allowed sight of such a book would be the subject-person.

When a priest or parson came to see me, the warders stood dutifully outside the door, ready to rush in if necessary, but meanwhile, as by law required, allowing the condemned man to pray with his spiritual adviser. On such occasions I always sat at the warders' table, chatting away about whatever came to mind—and reading the duty-book.

It pleased me that there was not one word indicating the slightest wavering or weakness. If I had even whimpered once in my sleep, or sighed heavily, it would have been "wrote down." Everything was "wrote down," God knows why.

The warders had all come to know me well, and I knew most of them better than they knew themselves. Many smuggled small things for me, some few showed open physical fear, some continually whined that they were only doing their duty, apropos of nothing whatever.

Two or three displayed something like superstitious awe, others showed the opposition-hostility which means the same thing. One, the horticulturist, would, I think, have started to dig a way out through the wall for me if I had said the word.

But he was only a jailer temporarily and by accident.

He had been an A.B. in coastwise sailing-ships, read much, although he was not educated, yarned continually. One evening I mystified him and gained his admiration by showing him card tricks. A curious thing followed.

Having been puzzled four or five times in succession, he grabbed the pack of cards half-angrily to change the game. He then made the impossible conditions that he himself should shuffle the pack, that I should not touch the cards nor approach him, and that he should draw the card I was to name.

The very conditions indicated the state of his mind.

He drew a card and I named it. Another card and I named it. Then, putting both hands together, palms outward, before his eyes, he bowed very low, in a curiously ceremonial way, as perhaps an Indian child might do.

They were two flukes, but he did not know. Neither did he know, when I questioned him, why he had made the strange bowing-motion, had never done or heard of it before.

There were other small things of the same kind, many of them. The psychic atmosphere of the place was tense.

I liked the young ex-sailorman, and, although I did not link myself to any sentimentality, I thought it would be a great pity for him to be killed. He was a clean-thinking, intelligent youngster, not long married, had been half-starved in the employment slump, had taken the jail-job temporarily, well knowing what it was, despising it and himself, but making no wretched pretences about "duty."

I knew it a pity that, if he came for duty on the last morning to see that the man walked to the noose, there would be an ending. Also there was a middle-aged man, the nearest of all the warders to conscious thought and self-knowledge, whom I liked. This would be a pity if he too came for duty on the last morning.

The others? They were tradesmen. If a red-hot iron burns the blacksmith, if a whale smashes a whale-boat, or if a bull kills a butcher—those are the risks of the trade.

Almost continuously, from the very first day, the older warders had been making crude, disingenuous propaganda in their gossiping. All of it led in the same direction—to the axiom that good men, brave men who were not afraid to die, went quietly to the scaffold.

They were terrified, those old men, and why should they not have been? Already I knew well, and would have known even without the tongue-slipped words and the angry chance-phrases, that some few men here and there did not go passively to the rope. The very abject, or those deluded into hoping for mercy even while the hangman earned his money, yes. But of course no healthy man so went.

The whining apologetics about only doing their duty had a basis. They knew the things they had to do, those old men, when one declined to be led.

But my imperturbability mask was convincing, and naturally the old men hoped. The propaganda was concerned with the first few yards only of the last journey, that was all. They only had to get the man three feet outside his door, and *then* he could be as brave as he liked! But I was not supposed to know those things.

It all ended peacefully. It was over in a second. You never felt it. A good man just laughed. There was no hurt. You never knew. Ten thousand such phrases went into the wretched footling attempts at propaganda. Faugh! . . . Its folly nauseated.

The whole point was that there would be only two men in the cell at first. Then the hangman. Outside the door might be twelve men, all with clubs and some with firearms. That rope was not to be wasted. Two hundred other men were within reach if needed. Not even with Dick McCormack beside me, and with four revolvers, could I have passed.

That much I knew. Also that I did not hope to pass. But also that I could not walk to put my head in a noose. In Dublin I had seen cattle slaughtered, noosed with a rope and slain with an axe, and not even they would walk to the rope. Naturally I could not.

The most I could hope for was a fight. They would club me or shoot me or stupefy me with drugs, and then hang me after all. But they would have to do those things. Empty propaganda phrases would not suffice as an alternative.

But everything turned on the first few seconds. After those seconds there was no chance for even a fight. But during them, while there were momentarily only the usual two warders, making their last hour of "duty," a powerful and agile man, with courage and with a weapon of some kind, could front an army, make them show and use their force.

The printed forms dealt with the removal of everything that might be used as a weapon. The warders' chairs, their table, my own table and chair—all would be sneaked away during the last night, to leave only an iron bedstead, fastened to the ground.

Nevertheless, I would have a weapon. Nothing much—nothing more than would fit in a man's sleeve, the kind of thing I had often used in Dublin during the Constabulary attacks. Nothing much, but enough to serve me for those first few seconds, make the brute-force behind the nice phrases show itself.

Wherefore I was glad my young ex-sailorman would not be on duty that last morning, and that it seemed likely the grizzled chap would be absent. Jim Phelan was going down—but he was taking the hangman with him if possible. Thus were my thoughts.

One amusing side-light on the situation was that in two books which had reference to such things the passages were torn out! This, although I knew one of the books almost by heart. Truly the people had child-minds. They were mean and vicious, capable too when in strength, commendably implacable it might be, but with the minds of children for all that. Unnecessarily so, for it is a simple matter to kill a man. But the little printed papers had them in thrall, and they had to do it in a certain way, at risk of mutilation or death, proving themselves bestial and whining about "doing their duty." The funny little child-minds.

As the time came near when I should be leaving the world, I gave a day to running over all the possible philosophies, religions, codes, and customs which men have made and upheld and in some cases reaffirmed on the threshold of death. Maybe, somewhere, there was one such code which I had lightly overlooked.

But at the end of the day I knew that I still knew nothing, that as far as I was aware no one else knew anything either. Only that there was mist at the end of the road. But I knew that better than most.

Towards the end I wrote to H. G. Wells, an ordinary letter with no mention of the place in which I was. He had written me twice in Ireland, and I wrote as if replying. Wells had a theory about superior people, and had once written about the facing of death. I wanted him to have the letter, afterwards, as a commentary.

Also I wrote to Upton Sinclair, telling him about the trance-session, since I knew he was interested in psychic phenomena. There were no other letters that mattered.

At the last week-end a most amusing incident made me want to write a postscript to Upton Sinclair. On the Saturday morning a warder looked in my cell and asked if I wanted to go to church.

I did not attend church, but they came each Sunday as by the forms bidden, to enquire. It was Sunday, not Saturday. I had lost a calendar-day by the trance, had not known of the time-passage when I woke.

So *that* was the best self-deception could do!

On the Monday I smuggled out all the cigarettes I could reach, hid them in many places on a row of lavatories which were used by the prisoners in my absence. Then for an hour I knew the sorrow of the lost song again.

Instead I made another, a sonnet to serve as my epitaph.

"Last Chapter

"The story ends. The final theme is set.
One lonely chapter now remains to write
Before I close my book and bid good night
To all who, in its narrow compass, met.

"Perhaps some pages I would fain forget,
Some blotted leaves, some words not spelt aright,
But, all in all, each busy chapter's flight
Has given, and gives me, little of regret.

"The story is but brief. I had proposed
A somewhat longer volume to inscribe.
But now when, all so hurriedly, 'tis closed,
I pen the end, disdaining whine or gibe.

"And to the tale, though of a book but half,
Write 'Finis' with a flourish, and a laugh."

And that was all I could do about it. Now I would have one small fight on the last morning and that was all. I had no wisdom to leave behind written for anyone, none for myself. All my philosophy would not have needed fifty words.

I knew nothing about the beginning or end of the world. Nevertheless, I did not approve of civilisation. People should not inflict their morality on others, especially children. Not three people in ten millions are capable of sustained, conscious, logical thought. Vast numbers of people are unhappy because we pretend this is untrue. The pretence is profitable to some. But the profit is very little, is not worth while.

That was not much wisdom for a man to leave at the end of his life.

At midnight on the Monday the Governor—brought from bed to meet the London messenger—came in my cell and read a long paper to me. I was respited, would go to penal servitude for life.

Next morning I went to a cell with an iron-bar gate. This was the kind of place in which I was to stay, in whatever prison, for life. Now I could not go away from the unpleasant things any more. To lose a song would be easy, in a place like that.

And where was my son?

The window was small, and the light was dirty, a chequered thin light of the closed spaces. But now I was finished with walking the roads. There is not much room to walk, in a cell twelve feet by seven.